Trafford College

KT-168-159

Boys, literacies and schooling

WITHDRAWN

- 8 NOV

1 3 DEC 2010

- 2 MAR 2011

1 0 NOV 2011

- 8 DEC 2011

2 9 MAY 2012

EDUCATING BOYS, LEARNING GENDER

Series editors: Debbie Epstein and Máirtín Mac an Ghaill

This timely series provides a well articulated response to the current concerns about boys in schools. Drawing upon a wide range of contemporary theorizing, the series authors debate questions of masculinities and highlight the changing nature of gender and sexual interactions in educational institutions. The aim throughout is to offer teachers and other practitioners grounded support and new insights into the changing demands of teaching boys and girls.

Current and forthcoming titles:

Madeleine Arnot: *Boy's Work: Teacher Initiatives on Masculinity and Gender Equality*

Christine Skelton: *Schooling the Boys: Masculinities and Primary Education*

Martin Mills: *Challenging Violence in Schools: An Issue of Masculinities*

Leonie Rowan *et al.*: *Boys, Literacies and Schooling: The Dangerous Territories of Gender-based Literacy Reform*

Boys, literacies and schooling

The dangerous territories of
gender-based literacy reform

Leonie Rowan, Michele Knobel, Chris Bigum and Colin Lankshear

Open University Press
Buckingham • Philadelphia

Trafford College
Library

Acc.
No. 38732

Order
No. 24777 BQ

Date 11 12.09

370 · 19345 ROW

Open University Press
Celtic Court
22 Ballmoor
Buckingham
MK18 1XW

email: enquiries@openup.co.uk
world wide web: www.openup.co.uk

and

325 Chestnut Street
Philadelphia, PA 19106, USA

First Published 2002

Copyright © Leonie Rowan, Michele Knobel, Chris Bigum and
Colin Lankshear 2002

All rights reserved. Except for the quotation of short passages for the purpose
of criticism and review, no part of this publication may be reproduced, stored
in a retrieval system, or transmitted, in any form or by any means, electronic,
mechanical, photocopying, recording or otherwise, without the prior written
permission of the publisher or a licence from the Copyright Licensing Agency
Limited. Details of such licences (for reprographic reproduction) may be
obtained from the Copyright Licensing Agency Ltd of 90
Tottenham Court Road, London, W1P 0LP.

A catalogue record of this book is available from the British Library

ISBN 0 335 20756 1 (pb)   0 335 20757 X (hb)

Library of Congress Cataloging-in-Publication Data
Boys, literacies, and schooling: the dangerous territories of gender-based literacy
reform/Leonie Rowan . . . [et al.].
    p.   cm. – (Educating boys, learning gender)
    Includes bibliographical references and index.
    ISBN 0-335-20757-X (hard) – ISBN 0-335-20756-1 (pbk.)
    1. Boys–Education–Social aspects.   2. Masculinity.   3. Sex differences in
    education–Social aspects.   4. Gender identity.   5. Language arts.   I. Rowan,
    Leonie, 1966-   II. Series.
LC1390 .B69 2001
371.823–dc21   2001021593

Typeset in 10/12pt Sabon by Graphicraft Limited, Hong Kong
Printed in Great Britain by Biddles Limited, Guildford and Kings Lynn

This book is dedicated to all those people who help kids to read, to think, to explore their world and their opportunities, to take chances and to confront both the strange and the familiar with equal courage,

and particularly to

Darcey James Rowan
(1928–1998)

who read, and made it seem natural.

You know matey, you have to stand on top of a mountain for a really, really long time, before a roast duck will fly into your mouth . . .

DJR

Contents

Series editors' introduction   ix
Acknowledgements   xiii

Introduction – Dangerous places: debates about boys, girls,
schooling and gender-based literacy reform   1

1 What about the boys? The rhetoric and realities of the new
   gender crisis   10

2 How, who, where, when, why and what way? Mindsets on
   gender reform in schools   27

3 Some really useful theoretical company for transforming and
   transformative literacy education   57

4 Mindsets matter: an overview of major literacy worldviews   77

5 Making it not so: transformative literacy practices for girls
   and boys   99

6 Exorcizing digital demons: information technology, new
   literacies and the de/reconstruction of gendered subjectivities   125

7 From Pacman to Pokemon: cross-generational perspectives
   on gender and reform in a 'post-feminist' age   162

   Conclusion   198

Bibliography   212
Index   231

Series editors' introduction

Educating boys is currently seen – both globally and locally – to be in crisis. In fact, there is a long history to the question: what about the boys? However, it was not until the 1990s that the question of boys' education became a matter of public and political concern in a large number of countries around the world, most notably the UK, the USA and Australia.

There are a number of different approaches to troubling questions about boys in schools to be found in the literature. The questions concern the behaviours and identities of boys in schools, covering areas such as school violence and bullying, homophobia, sexism and racism, through to those about boy's perceived underachievement. In *Failing Boys? Issues in Gender and Achievement*, Epstein and her colleagues (1988) identify three specific discourses that are called upon in popular and political discussions of the schooling of boys: 'poor boys'; 'failing schools, failing boys'; and 'boys will be boys'. They suggest that it might be more useful to draw, instead, on feminist and profeminist insights in order to understand what is going on in terms of gender relations between boys and girls and amongst boys. Important questions, they suggest, are: what kind of masculinities are being produced in schools, in what ways, and how do they impact upon the education of boys? In other words, there is an urgent need to place boys' educational experiences within the wider gender relations within the institution and beyond.

Despite the plethora of rather simplistic and often counter-productive 'solutions' (such as making classrooms more 'boy-friendly' in macho ways) that are coming from governments in different part of the English-speaking world and from some of the more populist writers in the area (e.g. Steve Biddulph), there is a real necessity for a more thoughtful approach to the issues raised by what are quite long-standing problems in the schooling of boys. Approaches for advice to researchers in the field of 'boys' underachievement' by policy makers and by teachers and principals responsible for staff development in their schools are an almost daily event, and many have already tried the more simplistic approaches and found them wanting. There is, therefore, an urgent demand for more along the lines suggested here.

This is not a series of 'how to do it' handbooks for working with boys. Rather, the series draws upon a wide range of contemporary theorizing that is rethinking gender relations. While, as editors, we would argue strongly that the issues under discussion here require theorizing, it is equally important that books in the area address the real needs of practitioners as they struggle with day-to-day life in schools and other places where professional meet and must deal with the varied, often troubling, masculinities of boys. Teachers, youth workers and policy makers (not to mention parents of boys – and girls!) are challenged by questions of masculinity. While many, perhaps most, boys are not particularly happy inhabiting the space of the boy who is rough, tough and dangerous to know, the bullying of boys who present themselves as more thoughtful and gentle can be problematic in the extreme. We see a need, then, for a series of books located within institutions, such as education, the family and training/workplace and grounded in practitioners' everyday experiences. There will be explored from new perspectives that encourage a more reflexive approach to teaching and learning with references to boys and girls.

We aim, in this series, to bring together the best work in the area of masculinity and education from a range of countries. There are obvious differences in education systems and forms of available masculinity, even between English-speaking countries, as well as significant commonalties. We can learn from both of these, not in the sense of saying 'oh, they do that in Australia, so let's do it in the UK' (or vice versa), but rather by comparing and contrasting in order to develop deeper understandings both of the masculinities of boys and of the ways adults, especially professionals, can work with boys and girls in order to reduce those ways of 'doing boy' which seem problematic, and to encourage those that are more sustainable (by the boys themselves now and in later life). Thus books in the series address a number of key questions: How can we make sense of the identities and behaviours of those boys who achieve popularity and dominance by behaving in violent ways in school, and who are likely to find themselves in trouble when they are young men out on the streets? How can we address key practitioner concerns how to teach these boys? What do we need to understand about the experiences of girls as well as boys in order to intervene effectively and in ways which do not put boys down or lead them to reject our approaches to their education? What do we need to understand about gender relations in order to teach both boys and girls more effectively? How can we make sense of masculinities in schools through multi-dimensional explanations, which take into account the overlapping social and cultural differences (of, for example, class, ethnicity, dis/ability and sexuality), as well as those of gender? What are the impacts of larger changes to patterns of employment and globalization on the lives of teachers and students in particular schools and locations? The series, as a whole, aims to provide practitioners with new insights into the changing demands of teaching boys and girls in response to these questions.

Literacy (or a lack of it) has been at the heart of much of the recent public and political concern about boys' school-based achievement and there have been many interventions into this debate – some useful, others not. We are, therefore, delighted to be able to publish this outstanding contribution to thinking about *Boys, Literacies and Schooling*. Leonie Rowan, Michele Knobel, Chris Bigum and Colin Lankshear do not offer easy answers in what they describe as the 'dangerous territories of gender-based literacy reform'. Indeed, rightly in our view, they counsel against approaches which give 'off the shelf' (apparent) solutions to the alienation that many boys feel in relation to schooling in general and literacy practices in particular. Rather, they take the reader down an intellectually and pedagogically invigorating path towards understanding the dynamics of gender, literacy and other 'differences that make a difference' (like socio-economic status, ethnicity, sexuality, indigeneity).

Using accessible language, which is nonetheless theoretically nuanced, they have achieved that rare thing – a book which is at once academically rigorous *and* practically useful. There are no lesson plans or specific exercises here, but rather accounts of real initiatives, in real schools and a clear analysis of how they did or did not work. These are set within the context of a clear exposition of different 'mindsets' with which gender and literacy can be and are approached and an analysis of the likely outcomes from these different approaches. They demand of educationists something more difficult, yet more energizing and more likely to be successful, than the 'back to basics' strategies adopted by so many policy makers or the essentialism underpinning tying literacy education to some notion of what (undifferentiated and homogenized) 'boys' will like.

The flaw in these approaches is perfectly illustrated by a scene from a school in London researched by the series editors. The children in a Year Five (age 9–10) class were using the only time now available to children in English primary schools to sit and read a book of their own choice – the five or ten minutes during which the teacher took the register. During this time, the researcher (Debbie Epstein) noted one of the boys as being totally absorbed in his book (a novel). At the end of roll call, the teacher said, 'Now kids, put your books away. It's time for literacy hour.' The boy walked, as slowly as he could manage, still reading, from his desk to his drawer to put his book away. Desperate to finish the chapter, he delayed as long as he dared before returning to his desk to spend an hour, divided into short bursts, on the tools of literacy – spelling, 'comprehension', phonics.

The authors of *Boys, Literacies and Schooling* argue convincingly that we need to move away from such (often counter-productive) 'easy answers'. They offer educators a different, more challenging, but ultimately more successful set of strategies. These involve: developing deep knowledge of the *particular* kids and what they bring to *particular* classrooms and contexts; starting where the kids (and teachers) are, but moving beyond that through making and enabling connections; being brave enough to experiment with learning processes; and rigorous enough to assess the outcomes realistically. Literacy education is, as they say, 'always accountable to producing demonstrably better outcomes' that '*work* for people in the world' (p. 210). And, as they continue, 'they will always involve much more than literacy basics and, indeed, literacy outcomes alone'. What this book provides for educators are the tools with which to develop such outcomes, using their highly developed professional skills of analysis and pedagogy, in real classrooms and different contexts. We are proud to have it in this series.

Debbie Epstein
Máirtín Mac an Ghaill

Acknowledgements

There are a great many people who have helped us to bring this book to completion and we are grateful to all of them.

Our sincere thanks go to Jenny McDougall and Teresa Moore, both of whom have provided invaluable research assistance for this project as well as substantial amounts of moral support. Jenny has also played a significant role in the editing of the manuscript and we are extremely appreciative of both her tact and her honesty! Thank you.

We would like to thank Debbie Epstein for her timely and encouraging feedback on the proposal and the manuscript; and also Máirtín Mac an Ghaill for providing us with the impetus to finish the conclusion before Christmas! We thank them both for this opportunity.

Anita West and Shona Mullen from Open University Press have both provided excellent support and we are indebted to them for making the whole process so stress-free.

The book is based on the stories of a great many boys and girls in schools, and we are grateful for the openness and understanding displayed by all the students we have been lucky enough to work with.

All the authors have benefited from support provided by Central Queensland University, and particularly from the Faculty of Education and Creative Arts. We must acknowledge particularly the Research Advancement Award scheme at CQU for providing Leonie with some extra time to work on the project. We acknowledge also the contribution made by Language Australia to the *Confronting Disadvantage in Literacy Education* research project which informed sections of the book.

There are innumerable friends and colleagues who have had a positive impact upon this manuscript, either through their direct contributions or as a result of their general supportiveness and interest. In fact, there are too many people for us to name, but we need to thank particularly Pat Moran,

Anne Musso, Lindsay Fitzclarence, Jane Kenway, Cecily Knight, Bernadette Walker-Gibbs, Grant Webb and Christine Woodrow, who (whether they knew it or not) all listened, nodded and smiled at *really* crucial times.

We also wish to express our appreciation of the support provided by Lynn Smith, who worked on one of the school-based research projects that inform the book; Jeanette Ferguson who transcribed hours of tapes and Judith Wright for, well, most things!

We must acknowledge also the invaluable support and intellectual stimulation provided by all the members the Feminist Reading Group in the Faculty of Education and Creative Arts at CQU. The energy, insight, wit and good humour of this group has been a true source of inspiration: thanks to you all.

A particular debt of gratitude is owed to all the students and staff who contributed to the subject Gender as a Social Justice Issue: their insight, their humour and their willingness to push some boundaries was, and remains, an inspiration.

Finally, we must thank our families especially our mums for their support and their interest, and also for understanding when we weren't available to visit, chat, play Nintendo or cook interesting food. Our most particular thanks go to Luke, Adam, Cassandra and Stephanie Bigum who were patient but never perfect: and who gave us lots of good advice. C'mon, let's go to the beach!

Introduction – Dangerous places: debates about boys, girls, schooling and gender-based literacy reform

An opening story

During the five years 1996–2000 two of the present authors taught in a core subject called 'Gender as a Social Justice Issue' taken by students enrolled in primary and secondary teacher preparation projects within an Australian teacher education programme. The subject provided students with opportunities to explore theoretical perspectives relating to gender; to engage with contemporary debates relating to the production and regulation of 'masculinity' and 'femininity'; and to make explicit the impact that gendered norms have on various dimensions of schooling practice. Conscious of the resistance students in this particular rural and rather conservative university bring to this kind of subject matter – and sensitive to the need of spending a lot of time reassuring students that the subject will *not* be an exercise in male bashing – the teaching team gave students the opportunity in their first tutorial to identify their hopes and fears about the subject.

In the second half of 2000 students seemed particularly willing to take up the invitation to express their opinions about what a gender-based subject might offer. They were clear and direct in articulating what they hoped the subject would explore, and what they hoped it would leave alone. Their desires were neither simple nor homogeneous. They were, however, rather loudly and passionately expressed. Some argued, for example, that they needed to learn more about boys – and masculinity – in order to teach boys more effectively (a real concern because, as everyone knows, boys just aren't doing well). This group hoped that this tutorial series would help them understand more about natural masculinity. Others felt that they needed to learn more about boys in order to help boys to be *less* masculine, and they expressed a desire for strategies that would help them to disrupt boys' commitment to traditional masculinity.

Still others claimed that focusing on boys would only remind them – boys that is – of their marginal status, and that what we needed to do in tutorials like this was learn how to focus on students as *individuals*. A different group expressed the opinion that the whole boys debate was nothing more than the kind of male whinging that women had gotten used to, and that we shouldn't dignify it with our attention. For these students, girls were living through just another backlash and subjects like this at university should be designed to help teachers negotiate these and other anti-women sentiments. Someone offered the fascinating piece of information that girls could say tongue twisters faster if they were menstruating, and another person replied that anyone making that kind of claim needed to rethink their career path. A noisy group argued that all that gender stuff had been sorted out way back in the seventies and couldn't we just get on with learning how to teach, and another offered the rather bored-sounding suggestion that we all needed to chill out and keep a sense of humour.

As they had done in previous years, the tutors worked hard to assure the students that the subject was neither anti-male nor anti-feminist. The tutors spoke openly about the nervousness they always felt before entering tutorials, because of the stereotypes people often held about 'gender studies' and those who work in the field. Some students acknowledged that they had been concerned about being 'forced' to work with left-wing-lunatic-wouldn't-touch-em-with-a-barge-pole-seventies feminists. Others acknowledged that they would have been more worried if they hadn't previously met some of the teaching staff and discovered that they were, in fact, just 'normal women'. One male student captured this attitude well when he said 'I was a bit anxious before I came – I mean having to work with – and I don't mean to be rude, but you know, *feminists* and all that – but the tutor, well, she's *nice* and, we're even allowed to talk about guys; so I reckon it should, hopefully, be okay.'

Along with all the other perceptions students have expressed about the subject both before and after studying it, this rather startled concession that perhaps a person could be simultaneously a feminist *and* interested in boys' education and *nice* illustrates a point we have long been aware of: discussing boys' education is difficult. Teaching gender studies is hard work. Opening up debate about the educational needs of boys *and* girls is time consuming. And going into any of these areas can lead into dangerous territories.

The focus of the book

This leads us to the focus for this book: a focus that is at once simple and complex. We are interested in boys in school. More specifically we are interested in tracing some of the links between boys' diverse educational and social experiences and their varied and varying literacy levels. This necessarily involves us in exploring the ways in which boys are increasingly represented as the 'new losers' in contemporary educational settings and the multiple solutions that have been put forward to meet this 'new' gender equity challenge.

While these goals may seem simple enough there are challenges to be overcome and risks to be taken if we are to achieve any of them.

Three challenges are worth mentioning here. First, as is already apparent, discussions focusing on boys, schooling and literacy take us into emotionally charged territories. It would be difficult to find a teacher in Britain, Australasia and North America who has not heard during recent years the plaintive cry, 'what about the boys?' It would be similarly difficult to find a teacher who had not heard (or made) the arguments that 'feminism has gone too far'; that schools are 'over feminized' and 'anti-male' and that what we need to do for boys is return to a world where their unique male qualities are recognized and valued. Regardless of whether one takes up or rejects this 'anti-feminist' and 'pro-boy' attitude (and the opposition between feminists/women and boys which it works to construct), the fact remains that there is controversial and highly charged terrain that needs to be negotiated whenever one moves into the boys/school/literacy debate.

Second, debates surrounding boys, schooling and literacy involve a wide range of people. While early gender and schooling projects have largely been initiated and implemented by women (often feminists), concerns about boys' educational needs have been expressed by a diverse group of people. These include not only those with a background in gender equity but also others – parents, friends, media commentators and an increasing number of men – who are new to the whole area (including some who glimpse an opportunity to air longstanding anti-feminist prejudices).

A third challenge arises from the fact that many of the people who are now involved with the boys' education debate hold preconceived ideas about the motivations and agendas of other participants in this field. Many who are 'new' to the area look suspiciously at those who have a history of working on school-based gender reform projects. If all these 'newcomers' have heard about the work of 'gender equity experts' is that they have created school environments that discriminate against boys, it is not surprising if they look suspiciously at such 'experts'. On the other hand, many people with experience of working on gender reform projects have spent years negotiating the indifference or hostility of others. Not surprisingly, they are sceptical when some of these same people (or others who seem to be like them) move into debates focused on boys: is this another backlash? Are girls now meant to suffer?

To complicate things further, all the key terms at the heart of this debate – boys, gender, literacy and reform – are defined in multiple ways. There are many ways to think about literacy. There are many ways to conceptualize gender-based reform. There are many variations to the category 'boy'. It is far from being the homogeneous term it is often represented to be. Issues of race, socio-economic status, location and sexuality intersect with gender to impact on the kinds of schooling and literacy experiences boys (and girls) are likely to have.

It is possibly because of these complexities that discussions around boys, schooling and literacy so regularly become heated and passionate arguments. While there is nothing inherently wrong with either heat or passion, we are well aware how easily an impassioned discussion can degenerate into a heated argument that soon loses sight of the issues at the heart of the debate. More specifically, we are aware of how easily genuine concerns about boys and their educational experiences can get lost in complex and emotionally charged debates that often result when the topic is raised. This is part of the reason for the sub-title of this book: *The Dangerous Territories of Gender-based Literacy Reform*. To open up debate around boys, girls, schooling, gender reform and literacy is to enter into a dangerous space where debate can descend into brawling, and where it is difficult indeed to articulate clearly one's concerns. Moreover, even the most focused and dispassionate exploration of boys and their literacy experiences is challenged to negotiate and engage with the sheer volume and scope of material relevant to the issue. This involves diverse opinions about the nature and origin of the problem, as well as diverse opinions about possible solutions.

Because of this diversity, and the confusion, frustration and anger it readily evokes, one of our primary goals for this book is to provide a detailed map of the various fields that relate to discussions of boys, schooling, gender reform and literacy. We aim also to interpret and identify pathways within these fields that we think have the best chance of promoting the development, implementation and success of literacy programmes that respond to the real needs of boys *without* generating new problems for girls. This is an important point. Like all who enter the boys/literacy/school debate we have our own beliefs about the 'real' problems facing boys, and the 'best' ways we can respond. We discuss these beliefs in more detail through the following chapters. It is important, however, that we make our starting point explicit at the outset.

First, we acknowledge that there are significant challenges associated with boys' education that need to be addressed, and that many of these are longstanding and deeply entrenched in education systems.

Second, we believe these challenges are directly related to the ways schools specifically, and other cultural institutions more generally, circulate understandings about what it means to be a 'boy' and a 'man'. We begin, then, with the belief that narrow and restrictive understandings of normative masculinity have consequences for boys, and that these consequences include the construction of boys who are regularly alienated from literacy classrooms and literacy experiences.

Third, we are convinced of the need for educationally based programmes that work to contest narrow and limiting understandings of what it means to be a boy and that contribute to improving boys' access to and enjoyment of literacy lessons. At the same time, however, we accept that this work cannot be seen as separate to work concerned with the educational needs of girls. Boys' education is fundamentally connected to girls' education. Hence, educators need to develop an understanding of the ways *gender* reform in schools and literacy contexts can meet the needs of girls *and* boys alike. We are, then, committed to providing a framework for thinking about gender reform, literacy and the educational experiences of boys and girls that result in effective, sustainable and *transformative* schooling practices. We are not at all interested in maintaining traditional frameworks for making sense of boys and their educational and social needs. As a result, this book examines issues to do with the education of girls and boys, and proceeds from the understanding that we cannot focus on issues of masculinity without attending, also, to issues of femininity.

Fourth, we believe that in order to construct such a transformative framework – and for it to be implemented in any sustainable or effective fashion – we need to bring together people, places and ideas that are commonly, if not routinely, kept apart. This involves drawing upon and responding to the diverse groups of people who have discussed explicitly boys' educational needs. But it also involves making connections with people, ideas and resources that have not figured prominently within the boys' education debate.

Fifth, notwithstanding the fact that pursuing debates around boys, girls, schooling and literacy can lead us into dangerous – or hostile – terrain, we believe it is important for educators to develop skills to negotiate it. Furthermore, we believe that learning to navigate tricky (and often foreign) spaces has the potential to lead us (and by us we are talking about ourselves as the authors of the book) beyond the immediate danger posed by the unknown, towards futures that become possible only when we take some risks.

Whence, *Dangerous Territories*. While we have personally experienced gender equity debates as danger zones within which discussion can quickly become argument and good ideas are easily rejected, this isn't the only meaning that can be assigned to 'danger'. In the safety-conscious decade of the 1990s it became common for us to warn ourselves and, more particularly, our children about dangerous things, dangerous places, dangerous people. Kids in schools know all about the danger posed by strangers, drugs, poisons, the sun, the rain, traffic, bullies and sitting too close to the TV. Marketing and corporate discourses have also introduced us to the dangers of standing still: of failing to innovate, failing to move, failing to change with the times.

Within different discourses – or ways of communicating that are associated with particular contexts and beliefs – therefore, danger is associated with both the new and the old. There is nothing inherently dangerous about where we are or, indeed, anything inherently risky about other locations. Following an unknown and dangerous pathway doesn't always bring disaster: it can lead to new and better locations, new and better lives. And staying where we are isn't always bad: it can give us time to marshal our resources and reflect upon what to do next. The trick, it seems, is to know which choices are going to lead us to where we ultimately want to go.

In using the term 'danger' throughout this book we want to signal much more than just the risks of following some pathways. We want also to indicate the productive value of taking risks, exploring the unknown and letting go of the familiar and the 'safe'. This involves embracing 'dangerous possibilities' and seeing these not so much as risky but, rather, as risqué: that is to say, as lively, animated, spirited and capable of moving us beyond immediate dangers into new ways of thinking about and 'doing' gender reform in literacy contexts.

We have a definite agenda here. The old, familiar and comforting models around literacy, schooling and gender have not taken us where we want to go. Schools and literacy classrooms have produced and reproduced narrow and limiting understandings about what it means to be a boy and what it means to be a girl. This has had real – and *really* dangerous – consequences for our kids, our societies, ourselves.

In this context we can choose to stay within familiar and 'safe' territories or we can try other paths – or, more accurately, a network of paths – that take us beyond the limitations of culturally bounded, institutional governed, dominant discourses, towards new, and as yet ungoverned, cultural spaces. Audre Lorde (1990: 286) makes a passionate statement about the political importance of new ways of thinking, new ways of acting. She identifies a need for

> new definitions of power and new patterns of relating across difference. The old definitions have not served us, nor the earth that supports us. The old patterns, no matter how cleverly rearranged to imitate progress, still condemn us to cosmetically altered repetitions of the same old exchanges, the same old guilt, hatred, recriminations, lamentations, and suspicion.

In this book we take up the challenge of finding a productive and effective way to speak about the complex and emotional issues surrounding boys, literacy and schooling. To achieve this goal we seek to explore ideas, practices and ways of knowing that are unfamiliar to many people. We are committed to letting go of familiar and known responses in favour of the unknown and the risky. We will make connections between people and practices that are commonly kept apart. We will move beyond the limitations commonly associated with stereotypical notions of boys, girls, schooling and literacy. And we will use whatever theoretical resources support us in this undertaking. In this way, we are positioning ourselves as what Rosi Braidotti (1994a: 23) has described as 'intellectual nomads': people interested in crossing boundaries, and committed to 'the act of going'.

With all this in mind we have structured the book in a way we believe will allow us to navigate successfully the complex terrain while working towards a transformative model for thinking about and going towards new ways of dealing with literacy in schools.

In Chapter 1 we distinguish between what can loosely be described as the rhetoric and the realities surrounding the current 'what about the boys?' debate. We identify risks associated with overly emotional or inflammatory discussions around the needs/rights of boys (and girls) and the 'real' challenges that educators concerned with the literacy experiences of boys and girls now face. In naming our desire to distinguish between what might loosely be termed 'rhetoric' and 'reality', two further challenges immediately become apparent. First, we have learned over the past twenty years that there are few genuinely homogeneous categories in the world. To speak of 'boys', 'schools' and 'literacy' as though they are unified and unproblematic categories is therefore a dangerous and, indeed, meaningless gesture. In working to map the experiences of boys within schools generally and literacy classrooms more explicitly, therefore, we are aware of the need to provide multiple maps which are able to identify and acknowledge the existence of many, many different boys, who are located differently within many, many different schools and who experience many, many different versions of literacy.

Consequently, we cannot, in fact, identify the 'real' experiences of boys in literacy classrooms. Any such attempt is doomed before it begins. We *will* attempt, however, to map common and recurring patterns of experience. In Chapter 2 our overarching goal is to identify the context to be negotiated by any attempt to conceptualize gender-based literacy reform. To respond to this context and the 'real' challenges it poses, educators need a range of conceptual and practical resources. To this end, Chapter 2 reviews the strengths and limitations of various 'solutions' advanced in answer to the boys/literacy crisis. We align ourselves with those resources that can be seen as transformative in intent and possibility. We discuss the characteristics of this transformative mindset and make explicit the ways in which the theoretical resources that have helped to produce it can assist in making sense of various approaches to gender reform and various perspectives on literacy.

In Chapters 3 and 4 we explore the articulation between these theoretical perspectives and various literacy mindsets.

Chapter 5 builds on the theoretical resources relating to literacy and gender reform explored in the earlier chapters to tell two different stories about possible responses relating to boys and their literacy needs. The chapter compares and contrasts essentialist and anti-essentialist perspectives on gender-based literacy reform and highlights some of the dangers and possibilities associated with each.

Building on this distinction, Chapters 6 and 7 explore in more detail the risks and potential associated with two common strategies used to shape transformative literacy practice: the use of technology and the attempt to respond to generationally specific interests. In reviewing both the potential and the limitations of technologically mediated or generationally targeted literacy practice we will highlight the difference between those implementations which contribute to the critique and transformation of limiting gender norms, and those which work to reinforce and reinscribe these same traditions. These chapters also explore challenges associated with implementing and sustaining any kind of gender reform project in what is often described as a 'post-feminist' age.

In the concluding chapter we acknowledge the very real challenges associated with attempting systematic gender-based literacy reform and offer some final images for helping to conceptualize and sustain this work.

Our aim throughout is to examine ways in which various mindsets relating to gender, masculinity, gender reform, literacy, technology and popular culture can either open up or close down new conceptualizations of what it means to be a boy, and what it means to be literate. We will identify those mindsets that appear to us to have most to offer diverse groups of people concerned with the educational needs, experiences and outcomes of the boys and girls in contemporary schools. These include parents, teachers, students, media personalities, community members, those who are new to gender debates and those who have worked in the field for years.

Our data come from a range of places. We draw on various research projects we have conducted since 1997. We employ vignettes taken from our collective experiences in education over the past ten years. We use 'imaginary conversations' and anecdotes put together to capture the tenor of particular school-based literacy or gender reform projects. We also extract from a wide range of materials collected at schools and school forums over the past ten years.

It is important to note that throughout the book we explore practices associated predominantly with school-based literacies: that is, the kinds of literacies most commonly measured, benchmarked and assessed within western schooling systems. We also identify, however, a range of non-school literacy performances and highlight the importance of links between everyday literacies and classroom practices.

Our commitment to making new connections, and taking risks, relates not only to practices inside schools, or to conversations among academics. One of our fundamental goals, indeed, is to make connections between the ideas, beliefs and practices of academics, teachers, parents, kids and community members. For this reason we have tried to make the book as accessible as possible, while trying to stay close to traditions of academic writing. This is a dangerous move that risks satisfying no one at all! It is, however, something that is important to try to do. Rather than trying to have the proverbial foot in both camps, we are interested in the possibility of doing away with rigid distinctions that would construct camps as distinct, oppositional and fundamentally different from each other in the first place. We are not claiming that we have left behind all academic discourse. Nor, indeed, do we believe this is necessary. Despite common stereotypes, teachers are not anti-theory, and teacher educators are not inherently out of touch. We have tried to make the relevance of various theoretical concepts as explicit as possible and hope to demonstrate that there is nothing as practical as a good theory. In this way we hope to help to strengthen connections between those who are positioned by their involvement in close and personal relationships with boys, girls, schools and school-based literacy practices, and those who are positioned by working in universities.

Two final points are important. We will argue that any attempt to engage with the literacy needs or experiences of boys must attend to the multiplicity of the category 'boys' and to the diverse ways masculinity is experienced and negotiated within any school. Consequently, it is not possible to advance one-size-fits-all strategies for reform. There is no single literacy worksheet that can meet the needs of every classroom. There is, in short, no quick fix. Nevertheless, we believe there *are* ways to move forward. Throughout the book we present stories of gender-based literacy reform that emphasize possibilities for change and that celebrate alternative, multiple and *literate* performances of school-based masculinity.

Each such story relates to specific cultural, historical and social circumstances. Hence, we do not conceptualize this book as any kind of 'final word' or 'real story' on boys, schooling and literacy. The book is intended to function as a starting point, not an ending. We hope the book will provide those new to the debate with an orientation to a complex terrain, while also indicating some new and challenging pathways for those who have negotiated the space for a longer time. Out of respect for both these groups we have tried to avoid, in the various chapters, lengthy recitations of statistics or data reported elsewhere, and have included, instead, summaries of key material and indications of useful sources for those wishing to pursue a particular issue or idea in more depth.

Finally, our decisions about what to include and leave out, and about what to highlight and downplay, were influenced first and foremost by knowing that it is the boys and girls at the heart of our discussion who will live with the consequences of our ability (or inability) to have productive conversations, make new connections and negotiate risky and dangerous places in our attempts to respond to their individual and collective needs. They are worth the risk.

chapter one

What about the boys?
The rhetoric and realities
of the new gender crisis

Debates associated with boys, literacy and gender reform draw us into complex and disputed territories. Accordingly, our goal in this chapter is to provide a detailed map of the complex terrain associated with boys and their educational and literacy experiences. 'Complex' is a key word here. The wide range of emotions that are attached to debates around boys, literacy and schooling make it difficult to progress the discussion beyond the emotional level towards a space where action and intervention are possible. Yet because there is so much at stake we need to get better at having these debates. As a step in this direction our main goal in this chapter is to distinguish between what might be called the rhetoric and the realities of this new gender crisis, to put us in a better position to determine where action needs to be taken, and what this action might look like.

While it is probably impossible (and not even desirable) to isolate the debate from emotions surrounding it, we will try to disentangle some of the individual strands of argument that have become closely entwined. We aim to identify some of the data that have fuelled the debate, and to highlight different and conflicting political positions used to make sense of this material. The challenge here will be to steer a course between oversimplifying complex arguments, on the one hand, and alienating readers with unnecessarily detailed accounts of particular issues or ideological positions, on the other. Consequently, we will not attempt to provide an exhaustive account of all that has been said or written about boys and their educational outcomes or, indeed, about girls and *their* educational outcomes. We *will*, however, try to provide an overview of the kinds of claims regularly made about the experiences of boys and girls in schooling contexts, and to use this as a basis for identifying the risks associated with the various positions attached to these claims. We aim to identify patterns associated with the ways boys and girls and their various educational experiences are discussed and critiqued.

The chapter is organized in two sections. The first discusses the emergence of the boys/literacy crisis as an identified area of public concern, identifies the emotions that have been associated with the debate and considers the risks associated with the production of boys as the 'new losers' in contemporary school contexts. The second identifies what 'we' think we *know* about the performance of boys in schools generally and in literacy contexts more specifically. Here again we are looking for recurring patterns that can be taken as indicators of significant and widespread problems, rather than trying to address an exhaustive database.

'It's life, Jim, but not as we know it': masculinity in crisis and the failure of boys at school

During 1999–2000 the authors collectively participated in twelve forums focused on boys and their educational needs. A plethora of school-based activities concerned with boys, literacy and masculinity have helped to generate a sense that boys have somehow slipped off the schooling agenda, and that we need to redress the neglect that they have endured for so long. Publicly articulated concerns about boys' educational outcomes have become very common over the past ten years. It would be a mistake, however, to begin here by assuming that no one had previously looked seriously at boys' education. On the contrary, people have been exploring various issues associated with the relationship between boys and schooling for a very long time. According to Elaine Millard (1997), differences in boys' and girls' educational achievements were discussed as early as 1867 in a Schools' Inquiry Commission in the United Kingdom. Debates about the kinds of education most suitable for girls and boys continued on and off for the next hundred years, until in 1987 questions associated with the education of boys were raised by feminist Madeleine Arnot when she asked explicitly, 'how are we to educate our sons?' And for more than twenty years a great many feminists (and pro-feminist men) have also expressed concern about the need for us to attend not just to the quest for educational equity for girls, but also to positive educational experiences for boys. Bob Connell has drawn attention to a minor panic within the USA in the 1960s about the way schools were 'destroying "boy's culture" and thereby denying them their "reading rights"' (Connell 1996: 115). In this context, Lingard and Douglas observe that 'it is not new news to those who have been involved in schooling for a lengthy period of time that boys are slower to read than girls and require more remedial intervention' (Lingard and Douglas 1999: 115).

Even so, it is only during the past ten years that relatively well known data about boys' literacy levels have been taken up in any sustained way by public and institutional discourses. Much of the early writing focused on the common roles assigned to, or taken up by, boys in various school contexts. It explored the various versions of masculinity performed within schools, and the effect these had on boys, but primarily on teachers and girls. In this literature, attention was drawn to the ways in which schools are involved in producing particular understandings of 'masculinity' where masculinity was in turn understood not as a natural phenomenon, but as 'a social construction about what it means to be male in certain times and certain places' (Kenway, 1995: 61). Much of the early literature here was closely allied to work focused on school-based gender reforms aimed at girls. There was an emphasis on the ways girls were disadvantaged by school-based celebrations of various forms of masculinity. The concern was for the ways in which particular versions of masculinity – particular ways of being a male – as well as fundamentally patriarchal perspectives were privileged within school structures, curriculum, pedagogical and assessment practices.

The audience for the considerable volume of work on how schools participate in constructing and celebrating various forms of masculinity was often confined to people working in girls' educational reform projects. For this audience, understanding the construction of masculinity was recognized as a necessary stage in working to effect the kind of cultural transformation necessary to enable the valuing of girls within and by their schooling systems. Although this was seen as something that would have positive outcomes for men, the catalyst was, for the most part, concerns about girls. As Jane Kenway argued in 1994:

> to put it simply most feminists want boys and men to change so that they cause less problems for girls and women and themselves, so that the sexes can live alongside each other in a safe, secure, stable, respectful, harmonious way and in relationships of mutual life-enhancing respect.
> (Cited in Mills and Lingard 1997b: 51)

Within a similar framework, many teachers and policy makers interested in gender equity provided opportunities for girls *and* boys to reflect upon the social construction of gender, and made use of the kinds of gender-neutral and gender-inclusive teaching strategies intended to improve educational and life opportunities for both sexes. In the broader context of school culture, however, understandings about the ways in which schools help to produce particular versions of masculinity and femininity were seen to make few demands on boys. While boys were expected to 'accommodate' the new and emerging type of girl, they were seldom asked – in any *institutionally* supported fashion – to reflect upon on issues to do with their own 'boyness', their own masculinity. Boys, in a sense, were just part of the backdrop against which girls were encouraged to improve their own educational experiences and educational outcomes.

In more recent times, however, data associated with *boys* and *their* schooling outcomes have received considerable press. Many people in diverse countries have responded to the plaintive cry 'what about the boys?' and the angry riposte 'what *about* the boys?' Both sides of the argument have helped to generate a very real sense that 'we' – all caring and concerned citizens – are now facing an educational crisis for which 'we' – particularly interfering feminists who have privileged girls and those who have let them get away with this – are largely responsible. As one commentator claims, 'To say boys are toxic and are failing is all a bit glib. Boys are not failing. It is we who are failing them' (Bantick 2000: 79).

Within this crisis discourse, media commentary, 'folk' wisdom, government reports and academic research in the UK, the USA, Canada and Australia (among other countries) have been used to fuel public claims that boys are the 'new losers' in our schooling systems. Is there a teacher, a parent, an academic in the over-developed world who hasn't heard about the existence of 'facts' to prove how 'our' boys are now 'failing at school' (*Economist* 1996: 24). We are assured that there is ample evidence to demonstrate the 'plight of boys' (Willis 1999: 1). And we have been told that the past two decades have witnessed an 'alarming decline in boys' attainment and participation at school, noted in almost all industrial countries' (Biddulph 1995b: 1).

Commissioned research projects argue that 'the tables have turned. Boys have become the new disadvantaged' (Teese *et al.* 1995: v); political figures identify the existence of a 'culture of defeat' (Wells 1999); and widely quoted articles and books even suggest that we are witnessing a 'war on boys' (Summers 2000). In the quest to lay blame, people have identified many favourite 'whipping girls' (Faludi 1999: 7), and the war against boys has been widely seen as the initiative of 'misguided feminists' (Summers 2000) or 'meddling gender equity experts' (Buttrose 2000) and associated with the 'anti-male attitude so prevalent in schools' (Buttrose 2000: 78). Underpinning much of this crisis rhetoric is the belief – both implicitly and explicitly communicated – that if boys are now losing at school then girls must clearly be winning. This kind of sentiment sees claims that girls are 'out-performing' boys, leaving boys behind, 'beating boys' and so on.

The intertwining of discourses of crisis and competition that characterizes many discussions about boys, girls and schooling has two immediate effects. It generates a sense that boys and girls must now compete for a finite set of positive schooling outcomes: some will win, and some will lose. Second, it attaches an air of urgency to the discussion by implying, as it does, that if the situation has gotten so bad for boys so quickly, and if girls are so clearly on a 'winning streak', then something must be done to stem the tide as soon as possible. There are strong resonances here with the Monday morning analysis that takes place around weekend sport results. While boys might have been the premiership team for most of the 1900s, latest results appear to indicate that they have fallen off their game and allowed an unexpected and underrated contender to sweep them off the podium. Clearly, we need to sack our (feminist!) coach and rethink our match strategy.

This sense that we have been witnessing a hard fought contest between boys and girls is reflected in the title of a recent research project focused on the outcomes of boys and girls in Australian secondary education: *Who Wins at School?* (Teese *et al.* 1995). This problematic title – acknowledged as such by the authors – highlights the extent to which debates about boys, girls and schooling play on our emotions, inviting us to pick a winner, and put our time, our energies and our resources into seeing that winner home.

Christine Hoff Sommers's book *The War on Boys* (2000a) provides an especially stark illustration of the ways boys and girls are set up as competitors for various markers of social success. It includes the following observation of the differences between American girls' and boys' current sense of themselves:

> It's a bad time to be a boy in America. The triumphant victory of the US women's soccer team at the World Cup last summer has come to symbolize the spirit of American girls. The shooting at Columbine High last spring might be said to symbolize the spirit of American boys.
>
> (Sommers 2000b: 1)

It is difficult to sympathize with any point of view that links women's success at soccer to mass killings at a high school in such a way as to suggest some causal relationship between the two. Indeed, it is precisely this kind of inflammatory comment that works to make productive discussion around boys and schooling such a challenge.

We may rightly be critical of the terms in which the debate is often couched, and alarmed at some of the strategies employed by people who wish to draw attention to the 'plight' of boys. At the same time, it is important to acknowledge that there certainly *are* some boys who are experiencing school in very negative ways, and that the crisis rhetoric *has* played some part in getting these issues on a public agenda. The point we want to emphasize here, however, is that the public debate that has grown up around boys and school is tied as closely to a perception that things are *different* as it is to any hard data that things are *worse*. This makes debates around boys and literacy particularly challenging. It requires us to distinguish between politically motivated scare mongering aimed at reinstating boys to their 'naturally' superior position on the one hand, and genuine and sensitive concerns for boys and girls that seek to extend work dealing with the construction and reconstruction of gender norms for girls to the lives of boys on the other.

Of course, it is tricky to distinguish between those who 'really' care and those who are in the debate for their own purposes. Even to say that we are more interested in pro-feminist positions is to invite the question highlighted by Bob Lingard and Peter Douglas: 'what feminism are we pro?' (Lingard and Douglas 1999). We will employ here the definition of pro-feminism advanced by Lingard and Douglas.

> Pro-feminism sees the need to change men and masculinities, as well as masculinist social structures, while recognizing the hidden injuries of gender for many men and boys. Pro-feminists also support feminist reform agendas in education and more broadly, and at the same time recognize the structural inequalities of the current societal gender order, and of the gender regime within educational systems.
>
> (Lingard and Douglas 1999: 4)

Our position will highlight the relationship between pro-feminist and feminist agendas relating to literacy and educational practice. We begin by recognizing the need always to move beyond the surface of any boys' education debate in order to develop an understanding of the politics attached to the various ways of speaking and writing about boys and their school lives. More specifically, we recognize the existence of different and competing positions concerning the relationship between boys' education and girls' education. As we have seen, in dominant discourses associated with the 'crisis' in boys' education, girls and boys – and men and women – are regularly positioned in opposition to each other. This reflects what has been described as the kind of 'backlash' politics that has increasingly been used to try to undo some of the hard won reforms of the various waves of feminism.

In this context, it is important to acknowledge that discussions around the ways boys are currently positioned by and performing within mainstream schooling structures are closely tied to social and cultural concerns about the roles to be taken up by men and women respectively in the present and future. For example, a famous article in the *New Economist* that examined changing employment patterns for men was called 'Tomorrow's second sex'. The article was accompanied by a picture of several young anxious-looking boys peering out from behind the bars of what might be anything from a communal jail cell to a school security screen. A similarly emotive picture is provided by the cover of an edition of *North and South*. The headline reads 'Man alone'. It features silhouettes of young boys sitting on the top of a small hill, looking across the rooftops of a distant town. Another newspaper article reviewing the controversial film *The Company of Men* implies that there are only two subject positions open for contemporary men: 'Misogynist predator or feminist victim' (Slattery 1998). This is a familiar and repeated pattern in countries like our own. We have witnessed a barrage of newspaper and magazine features, journal articles, books and TV programmes with titles like 'The trouble with boys' (Bantick 2000), *Stiffed: The Betrayal of the Modern Man* (Faludi 1999), 'The crisis of manliness' (Newell 1998) and so on. Steve Biddulph's *Manhood*, Robert Bly's *Iron John*, Warren Farrell's *The Myth of Male Power* and Daniel Kindlon and Michael Thompson's *Raising Cain: Protecting the Emotional Life of Boys* are four well known and influential books belonging to what we call the protest masculinity framework. Such works share a tendency to argue that something fundamentally 'masculine' – the real 'manliness' of men – has been problematized, criticized and carelessly thrown aside by an overly zealous commitment to advancing the cause of women. These texts – and *many* others – help to lend credibility to and naturalize discussions around boys/school/literacy that emphasize crisis and seek to assign blame. Although there has been a significant increase in the number of texts celebrating the emergence of new figurations of masculinity, these are heavily outweighed – in number, emotion and press coverage – by works that portray men as lost, abandoned or betrayed. It is important here to recognize the risks associated with dwelling too long in the middle of such dramatically structured debates.

Discussions of men as 'lost' or 'betrayed' reinforce the idea that men and women are of necessity on different sides of the fence when it comes to debates associated with gender generally, and boys' education more specifically. Different dimensions of the 'what about the boys?' discussion position men and women in opposition to each other – as competing victims – and, in the process, generate stereotypes about the 'nature' of the men and the women, the boys and the girls, who are at the centre of the discussion. As noted above, men are regularly represented as 'feminist victims' or 'misogynist predators', while women are commonly assigned the role of 'meddling gender experts' or 'misguided feminists'. Such name-calling discourses discourage the kinds of collaboration among men and women that could benefit boys. They also position those with experience in gender equity in a problematic relationship with those who are new to the field. Many people who have recently begun to explore the relationship between gender and educational performance have thus been encouraged to look suspiciously on those with histories of working on issues to do with gender equity and schooling, and regularly assign at least some of the blame for boys' current problems to them. There is, then, a real risk that the experience and knowledge of those who have worked for years to improve the educational experiences of girls *and* boys will be ignored (at best) and actively devalued (at worst). This in turn means that many gender reform projects designed to respond to the needs of boys do not manifest an understanding of what has been learned during 20 years of work focused on improving the education of designated groups.

The chance that ill-informed interventions will be designed and implemented is increased by the air of urgency that characterizes claims that boys are now in crisis. It is certainly difficult to resist the imperative to action when confronted with claims that 'we' are failing boys and that their health, their welfare, indeed their very survival are dependent upon our abilities to respond to this with due haste. But rushing into reform without understanding the strengths and weaknesses of various reform strategies only increases the chances of failure. This has in turn the potential to widen further the rift between 'new' and 'old' gender workers.

A related risk is that those who *do* have an understanding of the history of gender reform will become alienated from the debate. This could result either from consistent claims that the current situation for boys is somehow their fault, or from realizing that, as an area of concern, boys' educational needs have in a few short years acquired a much higher public profile than girls' educational needs ever did. This risk cannot be taken lightly. Many people who have worked tirelessly to improve the educational experiences of and outcomes for girls have done so from fairly marginal positions. In de Certeau's terms, many attempts to address girls' educational needs have functioned as 'tactics' of subversion: subversive moments that worked to disrupt dominant conceptions of 'education' without being able to depend upon the support of the discourses that were most powerful in these contexts (de Certeau 1988: xix).

Those involved in early and ongoing efforts at gender reform in school illustrate Audre Lorde's point when she writes that traditionally 'it is the members of oppressed, objectified groups who are expected to stretch out and bridge the gap between the actualities of our lives and the consciousness of our oppressor' (Lorde 1990: 281). This was certainly the case with girls in schools. Women had to identify it as an area of concern, and argue for its legitimacy. They had then to seek funds and other resources to support reform efforts, and argue about their legitimacy. They had then to implement, evaluate and modify initiatives, and argue about *their* legitimacy, while regularly negotiating hostile and resistant contexts which saw little to be concerned with in the first place.

The dramatic rise of popular and institutional interest in boys' education has been very different. Within the crisis discourse explored earlier there are few calls for those concerned with boys' 'failure' to justify their claims. There are few demands that the data be examined to prove which boys are failing and where this is happening. Likewise, there is little sense that the problem is relevant for and of interest to men only. Instead, there is an underlying assumption that boys are the responsibility of women *and* men. In particular, they are the responsibility of those women who have messed up schools in the first place.

The emotional nature of the 'what about the boys?' discourse can, then, lead to polarized responses and hasty reaction, and/or a kind of stubborn inaction where teachers – often women – object to the discourses which construct schools as overly feminized and anti-male.

A real consequence here is that lessons learned about the importance of defining carefully the nature of any gender-related problem will not inform the development of programmes directed at boys. In Chapter 2 we address at length several points related to this. Meanwhile, it is important here to note the danger that boys and girls will, respectively, be conceptualized homogeneously and in opposition. For example, boys may be construed as uniformly failing at school, in the same ways, and for the same reasons. Girls, in contrast, may be seen uniformly as 'winning' at school, and for the same reasons. This, however, is obviously not the case. Twenty years of gender work has established that any attempt to address the needs of girls or boys must always ask, as an opening move, 'which girls, which boys?' (Collins *et al.* 2000).

The complex set of discourses associated with boys and the crisis associated with their social standing and their education can take boys' education debates in many directions. Some of these are more dangerous than others. Discourses of crisis do not automatically lead to effective and transformative practices. They can also leave the situation relatively unchallenged, and may actually reinscribe the initial disadvantage.

Jean Baudrillard provides a useful perspective here via his discussion of the Watergate scandal in the USA. According to Baudrillard, the construction of – and response to – a designated, clearly identifiable, high priority crisis is a key strategy for powerful, mainstream organizations, institutions and discourses. He claims that 'the denunciation of scandal always pays homage to the law' (Baudrillard 1983: 27). In the process of identifying and responding to social, political or 'moral' crises (for example, those highlighted by feminist educators with regard to issues of access and equity), institutions have a remarkable capacity to turn 'scandal to regenerative ends', They can create the illusion of 'purification' and, from this basis, move happily into the (same old) future (Baudrillard 1983: 27).

Maurice Blanchot offers a similarly cautious and analytically useful discussion of the political significance of discourses of disaster. He argues that 'the disaster ruins everything, all the while leaving everything intact' (Blanchot 1986: 1). In other words, it is possible to argue that despite popular rhetoric, the phoenix does not always arise from the ashes of its cremation. Sometimes all that we end up with are the charred remains of a large, dead bird.

In negotiating the 'what about the boys?' rhetoric, then, it is important to be aware of its fundamentally political nature. Those who participate in this debate do so from various complex (and often contradictory) positions. This, of course, is always the case, since there is no 'neutral' speaking position. Likewise, there is no action that can be seen as totally separate from an individual or collective subjectivity or political position. There are, however, some contexts within which the politics of one's speaking position are more easily obscured than in others. This is particularly so within debates that focus on such 'natural' concerns as the welfare of our boys. Where the 'future of our sons' is at stake, it is difficult indeed to stand back and debate the agendas underpinning the various contributions to the 'solution'.

It is precisely because so much is at stake that we need to develop skills in negotiating this terrain. The first move is to acknowledge the complexity that is involved, and to recognize the consequences of an unproblematic acceptance of any dimension of the crisis discourse. The second move is to try to be clear about the 'real' issues facing boys (and girls) in schools. In the second section of this chapter we explore what it is we now think we know about the educational needs of boys and girls.

What's it all about? Boys and their schooling outcomes

We have argued that debates around boys, schooling and literacy are commonly couched in dramatic and alarmist terms and that this has the potential to generate further obstacles to meaningful reform (for boys *and* girls). We will now survey a range of common contemporary claims about boys' experiences in schools. In some cases the data are necessarily presented in comparison to the outcomes of girls in schools.

Who wins at school? Early differences between boys and girls

Concerns about the differential educational outcomes of boys and girls generally draw attention to both the early differences that appear in terms of their skills and abilities – particularly early literacy and numeracy abilities – and their 'final' or leaving results. Early differences in girls' and boys' achievements have been identified among children in England and Wales, with girls scoring higher on tests conducted at 5, 7, 9 and 11 (*Economist* 1996: 23). A similar pattern is identified within Australian data. Masters and Forster's 1997 report of a national survey of literacy levels in Australian Year 3 and Year 5 students found that 'the mean literacy achievements of girls were higher at these Year levels than those of boys and the differences were greater for writing and speaking than for reading' (cited in Collins *et al.* 2000).

The report on Australian national literacy testing in 1996 (DETYA 1999a, b), identified the fact that only 66 per cent of male students were able to meet the reading benchmarks set for Year 3, compared with 77 per cent of female students. Likewise, 65 per cent of all male students tested scored at or above the writing benchmark for Year 3, while 81 per cent of female students scored above and higher for the same benchmark. According to this report, the 'gap' between girls' and boys' performance repeats itself for the Year 5 test results conducted in the same year: 65 per cent of the boys tested and 76 per cent of the girls tested scored at or above the reading benchmark in Year 5; 59 per cent of the boys reached or went beyond the benchmark set for Writing in Year 5, whereas 74 per cent of girls met or exceeded this benchmark (DETYA 1999a, b).

Similarly, the combined results of the 1999 national testing in the United Kingdom for reading, writing and spelling (the Key Stage tests) for 7, 11 and 14 year old students indicate that 77 per cent of boys reached level 2 and above in reading, while 86 per cent of girls tested reached the same level and above. Similarly with writing, 78 per cent of boys tested and 87 per cent of girls tested performed at level 2 or above. In terms of spelling performance on the national test, only 65 per cent of boys tested at level 2 or above, whereas 76 per cent of the girls tested at level 2 and above (DfEE 1999a).

A recent Department of Education publication claims that, in the United States, '41 per cent of our 4th graders cannot read at the basic level and only 28 per cent performed at or above the proficient level, according to the 1998 NAEP Reading Report Card' (US Department of Education 1998). The test scores from the National Assessment of Educational Progress (NAEP) in 1996 have been analysed according to male and female performance in reading, writing and spelling tests and indicate what many see as 'dangerous' gaps between male and female performance in relation to sets of literacy skills.

These are not isolated cases. The pattern which identifies early differences between girls' and boys' literacy levels recurs in many countries. The reading literacy study conducted in 1990–1 by the International Association for the Evaluation of Educational Achievement (IEA) measured reading performance of 9-year-old students from 27 countries across the world. Secondary analysis of these data (Helbers 2000: 14) notes that there were significantly more boys than girls located within the 'low scoring' category. In Canada, boys comprised 56 per cent of the low scorers; in New Zealand, boys accounted for 64 per cent of those in this category; and in Trinidad and Tobago the figure was 53.8 per cent.

Kenway *et al.* (1997: 49) note that while once 'it never mattered much to boys, and to men generally, that girls succeed at things they despised, suddenly it matters that boys are not as successful as girls in the less prestigious subjects.' The current concern with boys' educational outcomes, however, has put these issues firmly on the agenda. There is a widespread insistence that basic and higher level literacy and numeracy skills are essential for full participation in academic, social and professional contexts, and that boys' needs in this area must be addressed. This concern is tied to an awareness that boys are occupying some less than prestigious spaces during their school lives.

Slow progress

Concerns about the lower literacy levels of boys are deepened when they are read alongside reports that identify less than desirable sets of experiences for boys during the course of their education. Researchers in a range of countries and across a variety of schooling sectors have presented evidence to argue that boys are:

- over-represented in remedial education classes (Prior *et al.* 1999) and more likely to be held back a grade (*Economist* 1996: 23);
- most likely to demonstrate behaviour problems (New South Wales Government 1994; Collins *et al.* 1996);
- more likely to be suspended (Lingard and Douglas 1999);
- the majority of counselling referrals (New South Wales Government 1994);
- three times as likely to receive a diagnosis of attention-deficit hyperactivity disorder (US Department of Education 1997).

Perhaps not surprisingly, there are also gendered patterns relating to subject choice, educational progress and school completion. At school boys are more likely than girls to enrol in high-level maths and science courses, and less likely to undertake studies connected to English and the humanities. This pattern continues into universities, with male students continuing to choose science, technology and engineering over humanities or education.

Leaving subject choice aside, boys are performing less well than girls when it comes to their final examinations or leaving certificates. A recent report into post-school options of Australian boys and girls provides information to demonstrate that:

> In Year 12 assessment, the average girl is performing better than the average boy over a larger number of subjects than vice versa in each of the three States we have chosen for illustration. Differences in average performance in major subjects in Western Australia and Victoria tend to be small – less than three per cent in most subjects. Excluding LOTE subjects where enrolments tend to be more erratic from year to year, in Western Australia in 1998 the average male who enrolled in these subjects out-performed the average female in computing, economics, geology, chemistry and physics. The average female out-performed the average male in approximately fifteen other major subjects. In Victoria in 1998 the average boy out-performed the average girl in literature, texts and traditions, music performance, accounting, international studies, chemistry and maths methods (the standard university entrance maths). The average girl did better in 35 other subjects. In New South Wales in 1998, the differences tend to be larger. Furthermore, in NSW the average boy outperformed the average girl only in 2-unit and 3-unit computing studies and in 'mathematics in practice'. That is all. The average girl outperformed the average boy in everything else.
>
> (Collins *et al.* 2000: 50)

A similar pattern has been found within the European Union, where data reveal that in 1995, 124 girls received leaving certificates to every 100 boys (*Economist* 1996: 23). Lingard and Douglas provide an excellent overview of the situation in the UK. Citing Elwood's analysis of gendered patterns relating to entry and achievement within the General Certificate of Secondary Education in England, Wales and Northern Ireland, they argue that 'in terms of the percentage of students getting A–C grades, girls outperform boys in all subjects (including chemistry and physics), except for biology and maths, and that the disparity in maths is minimal' (Lingard and Douglas 1999: 106).

And it's not just school

Concerns relating to boys' schooling experience are also linked to alarming (although hardly new or surprising) data relating to their out of school and post-schooling experiences. A variety of evidence suggests that young males are more likely than girls to appear in court, and to be convicted of a juvenile crime. For example, males account for 72 per cent of youth appearances in Canadian courts (statistics available from http://www.statcan.ca/english/Pgdb/State/Justice/legal14.htm and http://www. csc-scc.gc.ca/text/rsrch/briefs/b22/b22e.shtml). Similarly, 69 per cent of juvenile arrests in the USA relate to males (Snyder and Sickmund 1999: 81) and in the United Kingdom nearly one in four juvenile crimes is committed by girls (Teeside Probation Office 1999).

These are not the only risks negotiated by boys outside of school. They have a significantly higher chance of dying in motor accidents, of being murdered (Ryan 1998) and of committing suicide. In the United States it is generally conceded that boys are four times more likely to kill themselves than girls (Ryan 1998); in Australia the suicide rate for males aged 15–24 is four to five times that of women in the same age cohort (ABS 1997). These data, of course, are not unproblematic but there is enough of a pattern here to generate serious concern.

Boys and men are also seen to suffer from low level depression (80 per cent in the USA: Ryan 1998). Rising levels of unemployment, particularly for working-class men, are associated with poor health and psychological problems. This connection is graphically illustrated in the popular movie *Brassed Off* (1996). Set against the backdrop of the 1992–3 mining pit closure programme in the United Kingdom, the movie focuses on the experiences of members of a Yorkshire Colliery Band who struggle to keep their mine open, and to support themselves or their families. The emphasis in these and other movies is, understandably, upon the mental anguish experienced by men who lost a sense of purpose or direction. Australian data, however, indicate that 'by the upper years of schooling . . . girls' rates of mental health morbidity have increased and are on a par with boys' rates' (Collins *et al.* 2000).

Reflections and qualifications

It is difficult not to panic or be alarmed by such data. And it is easy to understand how discussions that explore these and related claims can quickly become emotional and hostile or descend into the 'competing victim' syndrome described by Eva Cox (1995). It is important, however, that we are not dazzled by the data, or reduced to emotive responses on account of their poignant or pathetic nature. Rather, we need to examine the data carefully and closely to identify some useful questions they challenge us to ask.

One important question, which is addressed in Chapter 4, concerns how 'success' or 'literacy' are measured. There are arguments to be made that evidence of boys' poor literacy is based upon particular and narrow understandings of what counts as literacy. The question we need to consider here has to do with *which* boys and *which* girls the data most accurately represent. Susan Bordo (1990: 139) reminds us that 'gender forms only one axis of a complex, heterogenous construction, constantly interpenetrating, in historically specific ways, with multiple other axes of identity.' With this perspective in mind – and without in any way wanting to detract from the seriousness of the statistics presented above – we therefore need to acknowledge the fact that *some* boys continue to do very well at school while *some* girls continue to fail (Kenway *et al.* 1997). A critical review of this research suggests the following points.

First, school failure increases among boys from low socio-economic or marginalized cultural/geographical communities: 'The higher the socio-economic status of parents on these measures [of household income, family structure, parental education], the higher is the literacy and English performance of their children, both boys and girls, on average' (Buckingham 1999: 7). Indeed, 'socio economic status makes a larger difference than gender to Year 12 performance even . . . where girls generally do better than boys' (Collins *et al.* 2000: 4) and it seems that socio-economic status appears to be the most salient factor in boys' (and girls') literacy performance in schools (ERO 1999).

Intersecting with socio-economic status as a factor in boys' troubles with literacy are indigeneity (Collins *et al.* 2000) and ethnicity (Metropolitan Life Foundation 1997; Kleinfeld 1998; Asch 1999; Cooper and Groves 1999; ERO 1999; Koerner 1999; Mahiri *et al.* 2001). Furthermore, according to Yunupingu (1995, cited in Alloway and Gilbert 1998), the same pattern of superior measured performance in literacy tasks by girls over boys occurs among Australian Aboriginal and Torres Strait Islander students as well.

Similar findings have been reported in Britain (see, for example, Foster 2000), the USA (Kleinfeld 1998) and New Zealand. The New Zealand Education Review Office clearly sees ethnicity and low socio-economic status as two dimensions of the same problem. According to the Office:

Because employment is increasingly based on knowledge and communication skills, the gender gap in educational achievement may be
reflected in future employment opportunities. For some groups of
boys, such as boys from low socio-economic communities and Maori
boys with few skills and qualifications, future employment opportunities are severely limited.

(ERO 1999: 5)

While this is not intended to be an exhaustive review of the literature
relating to the multiple ways in which literacy levels are affected, the kinds
of data cited here indicate that gender is by no means the only factor
influencing literacy attainment. Rather, gender intersects with a range of
other factors to create a network of disadvantage.

Lingard and Douglas (1999: 111) highlight the importance of acknowledging the multiplicities often concealed behind claims relating to the
'success' of girls or the 'failure' of boys via reference to apparent retention
rates: 'Any consideration of differential retention rates between various
groups drives home the point that . . . we must always disaggregate the data
and be clear about which girls and which boys we are talking about at any
moment.' Acknowledging the multiplicity of factors that combine with
gender to influence engagement and success in literacy classrooms is fundamentally tied to recognizing that neither 'boys' nor 'girls' is a homogeneous
category. Our primary goals are to identify ways in which school-based
literacy programmes can meet the needs of girls *and* boys. To this end, it is
necessary to be clear not just about the multiple factors that combine to
produce forms of educational disadvantage among *boys,* but also about the
ongoing existence of forms of educational (and post-schooling) disadvantage among *girls.*

We conclude this chapter by considering the implications of recognizing
that important challenges continue to face the education of girls. These
must be factored into any considerations about initiatives to be undertaken
on behalf of improving literacy levels for boys.

Challenges for girls

The first point to make is that not all girls are 'winning' at school. While
girls are generally performing better in literacy tests than boys from the
same socio-economic grouping and the same racial or ethnic background,
middle-class boys continue to perform better than working-class girls
(Alloway 2000).

Furthermore, girls continue to be under represented within the more highly
valued and prestigious subjects at high school and at university. Teese *et al.*
(1995) have made the important point that 'despite girls' increasing participation and continuing achievement – certain boys still top the high-status

subjects and stay on top in post-school life as a result' (cited in Kenway *et al.* 1997: 48). This results in the perpetuation of the gendered nature of the workforce and the location of women within stereotypically feminine spaces; particularly in the service industries, in 'caring' or nurturing professions such as teaching and nursing and increasingly in the peripheral labour market, as casual or contract workers.

Girls continue to report high levels of sex-based harassment at school (Australian Education Council 1991) and in the workforce. As Mills and Lingard (1997b: 52) remind us, there is 'a significant body of evidence . . . which suggests that boys as a social group make life very difficult for girls in co-educational schools (as well as for boys not conforming to stereotyped masculinity) and that this is often treated as normal.' Extreme and disturbing evidence of the attitudes that underpin day-to-day harassment of girls in schools was provided by an Australian study relating to the attitudes of Year 9 boys to forced or coerced sex. 'One in three boys believed it was "okay for a boy to hold a girl down and force her to have sexual intercourse" if she's led him on' (O'Connor 1992: 2).

In addition to this, girls are more likely than boys to suffer from some form of eating disorder, with recent estimates arguing that anorexia nervosa is the third most common illness among teenagers and that bulimia is the fastest growing disease among teenage females. Indeed, it has been estimated that 20 per cent of girls aged between 18 and 22 displayed symptoms associated with binge eating disorders (The Australian Longitudinal Women's Health Study, cited in Hutchinson 2000: 1–2). Over 80 per cent of females (and, importantly, 40 per cent of males) report a high level of dissatisfaction with their body image (Kostanski and Gullone 1998: 260). Equally troubling are data that reveal that the rate of smoking among young women is continuing to rise. A Canadian study revealed that the percentage of women between 15 and 19 who smoke rose from 21 to 29 per cent between 1990 and 1994, while the rate in boys rose from 21 to 26 per cent.

It is also important to note here that while there is increasing attention drawn to the suicide rates of young males, there is evidence to suggest that girls are attempting suicide at *five times* the rate of boys.

Women in the workforce also report high levels of overt and covert harassment and continue to enjoy less secure positions or permanent positions. Even when they possess the same qualifications as men, women earn, on average, less money (Lindsey 1994). As Rowan (2000: 154) has argued, 'women and men do not routinely occupy the same workplace territory *even if* they share the same office.' Women also continue to take responsibility for the majority of family and childcare responsibilities, working the infamous double shift (Davidson and Burke 1994; Townsend and McLennan 1995). Perhaps ironically, women are also more likely to be victims of domestic violence, and to spend time in sheltered or protected accommodation (Townsend and McLennan 1995).

We are trying to emphasize here that we cannot afford to focus exclusively on the needs of boys *or* girls. We cannot afford to get caught up in arguments which claim that all girls' problems have been fixed or others which insist women are now actually privileged over men. But nor can we afford to cling stubbornly to the belief that all boys experience the rewards of patriarchy in the same way. There are real challenges relating to the education of boys and girls that require us to consider experiences of boys *and* girls in attempting to formulate any cohesive or coherent response.

Ways forward

Moving forward in response to these challenges requires an appreciation of the following points. First, there *are* patterns relating to educational experience and achievement that indicate differences between boys and girls. Second, there are similar patterns relating to groups of boys and groups of girls, which indicate that there are many ways in which different boys and different girls experience and respond to the same educational context. Third, while there are serious in-school issues to be dealt with in relation to boys, there are equally serious, though different, issues faced by girls.

To those involved in schooling generally and literacy education specifically, these points raise serious challenges. How is it possible to meet the needs of boys *and* girls? How is it possible to respond to the diversity among *groups* of boys and girls? How can literacy classrooms support overall projects of gender reform? How can literacy lessons engage various groups of girls and boys, while remaining true to the goals of an overarching reform strategy? What do we already know about boys, or girls, that we can use to respond to this challenge? What do we already know about gender-based reform that we can draw on in designing these responses?

These are all complex questions requiring not only an understanding of what is at stake, but also a clear idea of what goals we are working towards, and what strategies we will use in the process. In this chapter we have tried to emphasize the fact that the educational experiences of boys (and girls) have a range of consequences, relating not only to their mastery of the kinds of literacies that continue to be highly valued within employment and post-school contexts, but also to what might be loosely regarded as quality of life, and sense of self. In other words, there is a lot at stake relating to their education. What we need to explore now are the various strategies available to us in formulating any response. This leads, once more, to a complex area. There are many different opinions concerning the best ways in which people should respond to the current boys' 'crisis', and equally diverse opinions relating to who should respond, and who should benefit. In the following chapter our aim is to provide an overview of these various mindsets relating to the how, who and why of gender reform.

chapter two

How, who, where, when, why and what way? Mindsets on gender reform in schools

Discourses of crisis surrounding issues associated with boys and school have helped to generate demands for urgent action. Our own view is that rather than leaping into hasty and ill-informed action, those wishing to make a real difference to the educational experiences and post-school lives of boys need, as a starting point, an informed understanding of assumptions underpinning many of the more commonly proposed interventions. They also need to be aware of the possible consequences or outcomes of these proposals. Short-term solutions often generate long-term problems.

The boys/education/literacy debate rocketed into the elite corps of educational crises during the past decade. On the other hand, issues associated with gender reform generally, and girls reform specifically, have featured prominently on social reform agendas for almost three decades now. Well established frameworks for making sense of and responding to gender-related crises already exist. Alongside them we find mindsets that counter and are in conflict with the goals of mainstream gender reform. These mindsets call instead for a return to 'basic' models of masculinity within which boys are just allowed to be boys. In this chapter we aim to provide an overview of the way these mindsets impact on what is and is not done in relation to gender-driven literacy reform in schools.

Before outlining dominant mindsets relating to gender reform in schools we need first to make explicit how we shall be using the term 'mindset'. For us, 'mindset' can be used to refer to a set of attitudes and dispositions held by a person that have grown out of their experiences in the world (e.g. by means of the discourses to which they are recruited, the people they talk to and hang out with, the cultures to which they have full access).

Mindsets are typically shared by groups of people or entire communities and are not innate. Rather, they are developed through meaning-making as one goes about interacting with others and the world. Mindsets are 'lenses' through which one receives, makes sense of and responds to one's experiences. They are 'determinant' in the sense that they shape and select the meanings we have available to us, while filtering out alternative possible ways of interpreting an event, ways of being, discourses, actions and so on. By their nature, mindsets can be altered, added to or abandoned in favour of others. Regardless of the kind of mindset in question, all mindsets enable *and* constrain the sense a person can make of an issue or state of affairs.

Three preliminary points are in order here. First, many of the mindsets relating to gender reform emerged out of an initial interest in *girls'* educational needs. Nevertheless, they are readily applicable to current issues associated with boys. Second, while these mindsets generally developed at particular historical periods, each one continues to flourish and can be found in operation within contemporary educational contexts. Third, while we will discuss the various mindsets in separate sections, it is important to be aware that few of the positions are so fixed or rigid as to be totally separate from the others. Indeed, there is a great deal of blurring between the mindsets and the following descriptions should be read as illustrative rather than absolute.

In our review of major gender reform mindsets we will emphasize what each mindset has to say about three issues relating to boys and their literacy experiences. First, we will identify the extent to which the different mindsets see the educational situation pertaining to boys as a *problem*. Second, we will explore what each mindset identifies as the source or origins of the problem, in so far as a problem is recognized. From this basis we will explore the various solutions advanced within each framework in response to identified problems. Underpinning the different mindsets explored here is the belief that there is, indeed, a need for *some* kind of response to the data explored in the previous chapter. For the most part, therefore, the mindsets we review take as their starting point a desire to provide boys with 'equitable' education. They accept that there are important reasons why it is valuable for boys to graduate with literacy skills. This motivates them to look for educational solutions to boys' current problems. In reviewing these mindsets, therefore, we are commenting not only on their key characteristics, but also on the extent to which we believe they are suited to producing the kind of gender reform that will, in fact, lead to different literacy experiences for boys in schools. We are also exploring the ways these mindsets will affect *girls'* education. Throughout the discussion we will work towards identifying a framework that will allow us to recognize and respond to the needs of boys without setting them up in opposition to, or in competition with, girls in schools.

A preliminary distinction

To begin, we can distinguish two broad kinds of mindsets associated with gender: namely, 'essentialist' and 'anti-essentialist'. Essentialist mindsets start from the belief that there are some *essential* and *natural* differences between boys and girls. They generally argue that there is something fundamentally different about the way men and women think, feel and act, and that these differences are tied to their different biological and psychological make-up. Anti-essentialist mindsets, in contrast, see differences in behaviour or interests displayed by some girls and some boys as being *produced* in particular social and cultural contexts, and not as *natural*. Whereas essentialist mindsets insist that gender differences are natural, that they cannot or should not be challenged, and must, instead, be accommodated, anti-essentialist mindsets perceive gender differences as *produced*. Hence, they could always be otherwise.

People starting from essentialist or anti-essentialist positions respectively will typically interpret the same behaviour in different ways. For example, in the early 1970s attention was drawn to the fact that girls were not participating in maths, science or engineering courses. Those who operated from an essentialist position interpreted this as a natural consequence of women's particular interests and abilities. This particular behaviour pattern was not regarded as a problem: it was just 'the way things were/are'. In contrast, those who began from the anti-essentialist position argued that girls had learned to develop particular interests, that they had been encouraged to display particular behaviours and to shun, among other things, mathematical and scientific ability.

Within contemporary schooling debates, it is possible to identify those located at one extreme of the essentialist camp who argue that differences observed in the behaviour, interest or abilities of boys and girls at school reflect natural and biologically determined abilities and thus pose no cause for concern. This is, perhaps, the only mindset that argues against *any* form of gender-based reform (for girls *or* boys). It is, nevertheless, a commonly declared position within debates around boys, schooling and literacy. The basic belief is that boys will be boys and girls will be girls and we should leave them alone and let them get on with it. Within the 'what about the boys?' discourse explored in previous chapters, however, this is a relatively uncommon claim. For the most part, people agree that there *is* a problem relating to boys' literacy levels but disagree about the origin of the problem and about the ways it should be dealt with. These differences reflect, again, variations on the fundamental distinction between essentialist and anti-essentialist perspectives and we will explore some of these variations in more detail here.

Boys will be boys: the essential masculinity approach to gender reform

If we continue with the broadly essentialist perspective, it is possible to identify groups of people who argue that there *are*, indeed, natural differences between boys and girls and that these differences need to be acknowledged and valued in classrooms so that boys and girls can achieve similar or equitable educational outcomes. Popularized during the early years of gender reform for girls, this extreme version of valuing difference generally argued that educational processes had traditionally disadvantaged girls by privileging male knowledge and 'masculine' modes of learning. This, it was argued, had resulted in an educational system within which girls were effectively marginalized and boys were routinely privileged. In order to work towards truly inclusive education, therefore, educators needed to identify and then value the different experiences, skills and interests of the girls in their classroom in order to help them to achieve positive or desirable educational outcomes. This involved not only adopting gender-inclusive language and incorporating material relating to women or girls within the curriculum (such as information about women in history, or women in war), but also attempting to make non-traditional subjects 'woman friendly' via the introduction of assessment and teaching strategies that were defined as 'feminine', including the use of group work, cooperative learning or 'creative' expression. In some cases, valuing difference was seen to be possible only in 'woman-centred environments' and these arguments were (and still are) widely used to support single sex schools or classes.

A similar pattern can be identified within current claims that schools need to learn (or relearn) how to value boys *as boys*. To those within this contemporary valuing difference framework, the problem currently facing boys is that 'masculine' interests or behaviours are *devalued* within schools generally and literacy classrooms more specifically. A recent article demonstrates this mindset well. Kerry Cue, a former teacher, writes:

> The big issue in education these days is boys. It should be, for the education system doesn't suit all boys. And I know why.
>
> It has a lot to do with Newton's first law of motion: a body will remain at rest (boys asleep) or in a state of uniform motion (boys awake) in a straight line unless acted upon by an external force (school).
>
> (Cue 2000: 18)

Cue, like many within the broadly essentialist mindset argues that boys and girls display their natural differences from an early age. She writes:

> When these boys first arrive at school, they're usually put at the end of the queue for a reason – to prevent the whole line disintegrating on the way into class.

A group of focused little Maggie Thatchers often leads the line into class in strict formation.

(Cue 2000: 18)

This 'boys will be boys' mindset, therefore, sees boys and girls as naturally suited to different kinds of activities: their future is to some extent *determined* by their biology or their psychology. These *determinist* arguments help to reinforce the belief that boys and girls can be understood as the negatives or opposites of each other. Where boys are active, girls are passive; where boys are loud, girls are quiet; where boys are mathematical, girls are literate; and so on. In relation to boys' literacy levels, therefore, this essentialist mindset regularly argues that boys are disadvantaged within literacy class-rooms because 'literacy' has been designed to suit the *natural* skills and abilities of girls. The solution, therefore, is either to place less emphasis on literacy as a desirable masculine skill in the first place (why do boys need to read anyway when we know that they are born to excel in maths?), or to change literacy classrooms so that boys' natural interests or skills are acknowledged and valued.

Common within this broad 'boys will be boys' mindset is the claim that educators – and parents and society generally – need to relearn how to value traditional masculine skills and abilities. These claims are supported by gestures towards biological and psychological research which aims to demonstrate 'natural' differences between men and women and are supported in some contexts by religious arguments about the natural ascendancy of men over women, an ascendancy ordained by 'god' (in 'his' various mani-festations). A brief example illustrates some of the different dimensions of this mindset.

> We recently had a conversation with a Member of Parliament who holds an education portfolio. During the course of this discussion, which took place over lunch in a café, the Minister sent back a glass of water which had been decorated with a slice of orange and a straw. This, he argued, was illustrative of what had gone wrong with boys in society generally: they were being 'sissified' and expected to give in to the feminization of the world. What schools needed to do in response, he argued, was to get back to celebrating masculinity as it really is. And if we want to get boys reading, he claimed, then we need to get them reading things they are interested in. And if that means reading about violence, or sex, then that's okay too.

At its most extreme, this kind of argument can be read as an example of what we describe as 'protest masculinity': a mindset that seeks to 'blame' women generally and feminists specifically for the current problems experi-enced by men. Within the protest masculinity framework, traditional understandings of what it is to be a 'real man' are highly valued, as are

traditional models of 'being a woman'. Those who depart from these traditional, patriarchal interpretations of the 'good bloke' or the 'good woman'
are regarded as unnatural, deviant or abnormal. Also described as the 'men's
rights' perspective (Kenway 1998: 158), or the 'poor boys' approach (Wearing 1996: 58), this kind of mindset is widely recognizable either by the
anger it directs at women and what might be defined as 'non-traditional'
men or by a denial of the kinds of power possessed and exercised by men in
relation to women.

It is also important at this point to acknowledge that the discourses
associated with various mindsets are not sex-specific. That is to say, not all
men are located within the protest masculinity camp. And some women
are. For example, Christina Hoff Sommers argues that 'We have allowed
socially divisive activists, many of whom take a dim view of men and boys,
to wield unwarranted influence in our schools' (cited in Jackman 2000: 40).
She advocates:

> a return to traditional styles of masculinity, with single-sex classes
> where competition between boys is encouraged and there are 'mascu-
> line' topics, such as war poetry.
> I admire masculinity, ethical masculinity . . . it's the most creative
> cultural force in history . . . I admire male stoicism and reticence. I
> think masculinity with morality is very powerful . . . Boys' natural com-
> petitiveness, their spiritedness, their rambunctiousness, and yes, their
> stoicism, I find these admirable.
>
> (Cited in Jackman 2000: 40)

From this point of view, letting 'boys be boys' involves getting to know more
about them – their interests, pastimes, learning styles, assessment preferences
and so on – and then modifying the literacy classroom to accommodate
those needs. Traditional ways of 'being a man' are thus reinforced, with
boys who depart from this norm being marginalized and devalued. In some
extreme cases, the needs of girls are regarded as irrelevant. These perspectives
reflect widespread, anti-feminist attitudes that assert men's natural 'rights':
rights to a hegemonic masculinity within which traditional male skills/
experiences are valued. The influence of this way of thinking is found in
discussions which assert a man's right to a job, to respect, to protect (and
have control over and access to) 'his' family and 'his' home (often through
the use of whatever force is deemed necessary).

A less angry but equally powerful dimension of this 'valuing boys' mindset
is provided by what has been described as the mythopoeic men's movement;
or what Mills and Lingard (1997a, b) have referred to as collections of
men's therapy groups, which encourage men to return to ancient traditions
and rituals in order to exorcise any feminine elements that may have found
their way into their identity and 'rebond' with their masculine heritage and
masculine mates. Within these groups men are encouraged to reconnect

with their 'essential' selves, often through various rituals (generally ones that have been appropriated from indigenous cultures: drum beating being a prime example). While some people read these rituals – and the male bonding they are intended to endorse – as a male equivalent of the feminist consciousness raising groups of the sixties in which women got to know their bodies, others read these as attempts to assert the naturalness of 'real' male instincts: instincts to hunt, command, dominate which are justified by reference to myths and legends that celebrate just such a role for men.

Another dimension of these biological determinist arguments represents men and women as different but complementary. Thus men and women bring to the family, the workplace and education distinct but compatible interests and abilities. A recent book released by Alan Pease (a man who made the analysis of body language into a big business) and his wife Barbara demonstrates this essentialist position well. The Peases argue that women and men are 'naturally' different with naturally different abilities that explain why men don't listen and women can't read maps (Pease and Pease 1998). Nevertheless, according to the Peases, men and women are still *equal* to each other, even though they are fundamentally different.

It is interesting to note here that determinist arguments generally reflect not only patriarchal beliefs – or beliefs in the natural authority of men – but also phallocentric beliefs. Phallocentrism, in this context, is an ideological framework which defines women always in some relation to men. That is to say, the male – and masculinity – is understood as the norm, the reference point against which women are defined. Women, therefore, exist only in relation to men. Elizabeth Grosz describes this phallocentric mindset well:

> patriarchal systems of representation always submit women to models and images defined by and for men. It is the submission of women to representations in which they are reduced to a relation of dependence on men. There are three forms phallocentrism generally takes: whenever women are represented as the opposites or negatives of men; whenever they are represented in terms the same as or similar to men; and whenever they are represented as men's complements. In all three cases, women are seen as variations or versions of masculinity – either through negation, identity or unification into a greater whole.
>
> (Grosz 1989: xx)

The power of these phallocentric arguments lies in the fact that because they have been circulated for such a long time they appear natural. It is perhaps because of their simplistic nature and their recourse to longstanding and powerful social myths that these essentialist perspectives on men and gender have tended to dominate media explorations of the issue. Newspapers report on the differences between men's and women's brains; they argue for a return to 'natural' family forms and so on. The solutions offered by these groups to problems faced by boys are based upon a return to the good old days when men and women knew their places and were comfortable and happy within them.

In summary, then, essentialist arguments generally share a belief that boys are biologically different to girls and that this biological difference is the cause of behavioural differences. To justify these claims, people in determinist mindsets will often posit a direct link between testosterone and activity or aggression levels; between boys' bodies and short attention spans; and between some biological boy-ness and an aversion to reading, writing and literacy generally. An example of this biological determinist argument is found within recent reports of a study designed to demonstrate that girls and boys have different predispositions concerning language use. The argument put forward is that girls are 'born to chatter' and that this is demonstrated by the fact that different-sex twins, raised in the same household, display different literacy levels in boys and girls as early as two years old. In an argument that contains more supposition and hypothesis than argumentation or evidence, Michael Galsworthy claims that:

> As early as two years old, girls out-perform boys on cognitive scores, particularly in verbal ability. Although this is not a big difference, it is even seen in opposite-sex twins, . . . it seems the way genes work for language development is different in boys and girls – it could be that this trigger is hormonal.
>
> (Cited in Rawstorne 2000: 14)

This article is typical of many of the determinist genre: there are many conclusions drawn, and lots of gestures towards the 'scientific' nature of evidence or the biological 'proof' that men and women are different, but there are absolutely no hard data. Rob and Pam Gilbert also demonstrate the point that despite the consistent ways in which boys are defined as the 'victims' of their testosterone, there is no conclusive evidence to demonstrate that testosterone has the impact ascribed to it (Gilbert and Gilbert 1998: 40). This kind of data interrogation, however, is seldom undertaken within essentialist discourses, which tap into 'received wisdom' or 'common sense' and thus appear as 'natural' or 'logical'. A similarly insightful analysis of the 'realities' of male bodies is provided by Bob Connell (1995) in his important work *Masculinities*.

From an essentialist or valuing difference mindset, therefore, the quest to improve boys' educational outcomes rests upon acknowledging the existence of differences between boys and girls and then working to accommodate them. The implications of the various strands of the valuing difference approach for the boys/literacy debate are significant. At one extreme are those who argue that poor literacy skills are a natural consequence of masculinity and that we shouldn't worry about it at all. This position, however, is rarely expressed – with people more likely to argue that boys will have a greater chance of developing necessary literacy levels if their 'natural' interests are acknowledged and valued in literacy classrooms. Solutions put forward within these classrooms range from allowing boys to focus their reading around traditionally male interests – sport, animals, the outdoors and so on – to ensuring that they are assessed in 'male friendly' ways, such as oral rather than written presentations (an assumption based on the belief that boys are better at talking than writing), through to using single-sex classrooms to ensure that boys' special interests are prioritized, and making use of male teachers (even if they have no particular literacy expertise) to try to maximize the attention and literacy success of the boys. Some have argued that benchmarks for literacy success need, in fact, to be lowered or changed for boys, and that it is fundamentally unfair to expect boys to produce the kinds of neat, written work that girls are so well suited to.

In relation to both girls' and boys' education, this mindset has several valuable dimensions. First, it highlights the fact that many boys and girls *do* come to school with different sets of skills, many of which provide valuable entry points into learning, if they *all* are recognized and valued. Second, it reminds us of the importance of gender-neutral or inclusive language, so that barriers are not automatically set up between some students and some disciplines. Third, it can provide us with insights concerning useful *starting* points for engaging boys or girls. We return to these points later in this chapter when we explore the ways in which people operating from anti-essentialist positions nevertheless make use of information concerning common patterns to boys' and girls' behaviours.

However, from an anti-essentialist perspective there are limitations with this approach. First, it regards unproblematically the *origin* of perceived differences between boys and girls. Alloway (1995: 32) reminds us of a key point within the valuing difference of gender inclusiveness model: 'Educators are encouraged to identify and accommodate the differences of gender without questioning the validity of their existence.' Second, the valuing difference model operates from the position that because these differences are 'natural' there is little that teachers can do to change them: teachers are required, instead, to work around these differences. Third, it works to homogenize groups of students – and represent all 'normal' boys as stereotypically 'macho' or 'masculine'. Pease and Pease (1998: 7–8) provide a good example of this kind of thinking.

> When weighing up the differences between males and females discussed in this book, some people may say 'no – that's not me – I don't do that!' Well, maybe they don't. But we will be dealing here with *average* men and women, that is, how most men and women will behave most of the time, in most situations and for most of the past.

In this framework *all* boys – and, by extension, their literacy needs or problems – are seen as fundamentally the same. But, as we noted above, not all boys are doing badly in literacy classrooms. And not all boys who *are* doing badly are failing for the same reasons. Differences relating to socio-economic status, ethnicity, sexuality and physical aptitude also impact upon how boys engage with and respond to literacy classrooms. For many boys, exposure to a reform project ostensibly designed to 'value their difference', which works, in fact, to value a very *specific*, narrow and hegemonic form of masculinity, can further inscribe feelings of alienation, separateness or otherness as they find themselves defined in relation to an artificial, but powerful, version of masculinity.

In contrast to these essentialist positions, the next group of mindsets to be examined begin from a different starting point. Instead of ascribing observed differences in behaviours, interests or abilities to biology or psychology (or even, in some cases, men's and women's different, inherent morality), mindsets operating from an *anti*-essentialist perspective emphasize the social production of gender differences. There are four main manifestations of anti-essentialist mindsets as they relate to gender reform in schools: those that emphasize the need to provide boys and girls with equal opportunities; those that see equal opportunities as something that may require the provision of different support structures specific to the needs of girls and boys; those that acknowledge the differences between groups of girls and boys; and those that work to examine the processes through which gendered identities and norms are constructed and, thus, the ways in which they can be contested and transformed.

These mindsets are not mutually exclusive. People regularly move in and out of the various manifestations of each one. The boundaries between all four are frequently blurred, and elements of each can be found today within many gender reform projects. In reviewing the major characteristics of these mindsets we hope to show the key concerns around which each one is organized, as well as the kind of developmental logic that leads to what we see as the most recent approach to gender reform. It is important to note that we are not arguing for abandoning insights associated with early mindsets, although our own preferences will be clear. Rather, we are trying to show that if the best of each mindset is taken on board they can collectively help us to head in new directions.

Even Stephens: the equal opportunity and 'sameness' approach to gender reform

Whereas the 'boys will be boys' model is premised primarily on the belief that boys and girls are fundamentally *different*, the first of the anti-essentialist mindsets which we review here is based on the belief that boys and girls are fundamentally the *same*, even though they have been conditioned to see themselves as entitled to different things. This shift to acknowledge that observed gender differences may be due, at least in part, to the different ways in which boys and girls are socially positioned led to a significant amount of work designed to 'even up' the educational (and life) opportunities available to girls and boys.

In the 1970s, those working within the liberal approach to girls' education (or what Nola Alloway (1995) refers to as the first tier of educational reform pertaining to gender) played an important part in identifying institutional or legislative barriers to girls' participation in schools and helped to create more opportunities for girls to take part in a full range of educational contexts and experiences. There are parallels here with the work of the early liberal feminists, who, during the first wave of feminism in the late nineteenth and early twentieth centuries, concentrated much of their effort on removing the social/legal obstacles which prevented them from contributing to social/political debate or from exercising the same constitutional rights as men.

A liberal/equal opportunity approach to educational reform for boys follows a similar line. Efforts are made to ensure that there are no structural barriers to boys' participation in, for example, the humanities area. Timetabling issues are therefore examined and boys are encouraged to see reading or literacy as something that they *can* excel at if they choose. Emphasis is placed upon 'equality of opportunity', with campaigns claiming 'boys can read too' providing an example of this kind of response. In this framework the emphasis is very much on the importance of individuals *choosing* to take up opportunities made available to them. Boys, like girls before them, are therefore encouraged to exercise their rights, to see themselves as free agents in charge of their own destiny, and to try 'new things' and reach their 'full potential'.

Equal opportunity mindsets have had a major impact upon schooling structures, and have improved the chances that boys *and* girls can exercise choice in the design of their school and post-school pathways. As is the case with most liberal approaches to reform, however, there is an emphasis on *individual* ability which generates a sense that it is really up to girls (or boys) to fit themselves into a pre-existing environment (such as a physical classroom or an engineering degree). In other words, equal opportunity approaches tend to leave relatively untouched the structures or the system within which girls or boys have been traditionally marginalized. They prefer to 'add in' the missing elements and believe that things will, thereafter, sort themselves out.

This approach means that nothing is changed culturally or socially; it relies instead on boys and girls adapting to the various cultures encompassing traditionally masculine and female domains. This can mean that boys, entering non-traditional areas, may find themselves subjected to value judgements that are 'the norm' within that area – values which see them as strange or unnatural for venturing into a 'feminine space' (and vice versa for girls). Not surprisingly, they may find this difficult to cope with. Relying on boys or girls to choose 'new pathways' is not, therefore, a particularly efficient means of achieving gender-based reform, for the choice does not take place in a vacuum and boys understand very well the social risks associated with choosing a 'non-masculine' pathway.

Similarly problematic is the assumption that boys and girls make their choices on a 'level playing field'. This is not the case. Within most societies the traditional gendering of careers, life choices and behaviours has mostly placed men in privileged or culturally valued positions. While it is easy to see the appeal for women of a reform framework which argues that they should do less housework, earn more money, exercise greater freedom, have more leisure time and so on, it is harder to find ways to sell what are often seen as the necessary corollaries: that men should do *more* housework, earn the same amount of money as women, have less leisure time and so on.

Although there will always be exceptions to gendered patterns of behaviour, if we wait for the majority of boys to express a spontaneous interest in literacy we may be waiting a very long time. Indeed, teachers working within equal opportunity or liberal frameworks who also possess a desire to make the world a more equitable place for boys and girls regularly express a sense of frustration that the girls or boys they are targeting aren't taking up the opportunities they are provided with. Glenda MacNaughton describes the experiences of a teacher in an early childhood centre who felt that her attempts to involve girls in what she regarded as valuable play with blocks appeared to come to nothing. The teacher comments: 'I've given them [the girls] space, I've given them encouragement, I've given them reinforcement, I've given them everything, but they are not perceiving those blocks as being relevant to them' (MacNaughton 2000: 15). This sense that nothing is changing can lead to a situation where teachers who were originally committed to gender reform actually begin to feel that you can't, in fact, change nature. That is, they find themselves drawn to the kinds of essentialist arguments outlined above, in an attempt to account for their 'failure' to disrupt traditional gendered practices. This can lead, in turn, to a situation where the teachers may resent being asked to continue to work on gender-related projects. Let's give another example.

Bronwen, a physics teacher in her third year of teaching at a suburban, middle-class high school, expressed frustration that she was still asked to think about gender issues when it was patently obvious that girls just weren't interested in physics. 'I've spoken to the girls, I've invited in guest speakers to tell them about the ways physics can be, or is, useful in a lot of professions. And they just don't want to do it. I'm not stopping them. Their parents aren't stopping them. But they just won't do it. What more am I supposed to do? I guess in a lot of ways I'm abnormal because I like it but clearly other girls are not like me.'

These two examples remind us that while an equal opportunity mindset may alert us to some of the obvious barriers to boys' participation in literacy classrooms, and encourage us to be aware of the ways in which, although we see literacy as something they are entitled to want and to pursue, there are other factors that need to be attended to, including the extent to which boys and girls come to school with different knowledge and different experiences.

Horses for courses: valuing gendered knowledge and experience

This second mindset is based on the belief that it is necessary to acknowledge that in many cases boys and girls *do* come to school with different sets of experiences. In many cases, they also come with pretty fixed ideas about what it means to be a good girl or a good boy, and with learning patterns that appear to predispose them to respond positively to different teaching strategies. Many girls, for example, *will* begin school with an appreciation of group work. Many boys *will* begin school with a preference for noisy, active behaviour. Many girls *will* express an interest in animals, dolls, dressing up, shopping and so on, while many boys *will* show a strong commitment to physical sport, computers or the outdoors.

These differences remind us that for a very long time girls and boys, men and women have experienced the social world in different ways. More than this, patriarchal beliefs as mediated by such key institutions as the family, various churches, workplaces, governments, sporting groups and the media have helped to sustain gendered patterns concerning what it is men and women *do*, and how these behaviours are *valued*. This means, among other things, that there are histories relating to women and men that are markedly different. Women's experiences in the two world wars, for example, were greatly different from those of men. Similarly, boys' experiences of bullying may be different from those of girls.

Andrea Allard, Maxine Cooper, Gaell Hildebrand and Eileen Wealands argue that, in terms of girls' education, teachers are challenged to value female knowledge and experience. Working from this perspective, they offer several suggestions as to how teachers can negotiate a number of gender issues (Allard *et al.* 1995). In particular, they suggest that this approach draws attention to the kinds of skills and values that females may have developed as a result of their lived experiences (for example, skills associated with 'women's work', including domestic and family-based work). Allard and her colleagues highlight differences in preferred approaches to learning (and assessment models) for girls, and draw attention to the ways 'female' skills may be excluded from or devalued within traditional curricula in which masculine experience is predominantly centred, privileged and engaged. More than this, attention is drawn to the way traditionally female-dominated school subjects such as English or arts are devalued within school structures against traditionally male-dominated subjects such as maths or science.

When applied to the education of boys, this valuing female/male knowledge approach encourages us to identify the ways in which the skills and preferences which boys bring to school can be valued. This seems, at first, rather a peculiar task, for most gender reform in schools has been based upon the belief that boys in schools have almost always been valued over girls: within curriculum that centres and emphasizes male experience, assessment practices based upon male models, reward systems that privilege masculine interests (including sport and competitiveness) and a myriad of informal and formal practices that emphasize everything represented as or associated with the masculine in a superior relationship to whatever is seen as feminine. It is no accident that one of the worst insults that can be directed at a boy in school is that he is acting 'like a girl'.

Consequently, recognizing the differences that boys and girls may display is read as a valuable strategy for engaging them in various learning environments. This does not mean that we are endorsing the essentialist perspectives on boys' and girls' *natural* differences explored earlier in this chapter. It does mean, however, that we can't just ignore or 'wish away' the fact that many girls and boys have been socialized to prefer different learning strategies, different subject areas, different activities. It also means that trying to make connections with boys – of the kind necessary to involve them in literacy activities – may necessitate beginning from where they are at: even if that place is traditional, narrow and limiting in what it has to say about what it means to be a boy.

We have no interest in arguing that the unproblematic valuing of boys over girls in traditional schooling practice is something to be continued (or reintroduced). It *is* important, however, for us to acknowledge that some discipline areas – including literacy – have a decidedly feminine image, and appear to value female knowledge and experience over male. Indeed, it appears that – at least for students in developed and overdeveloped countries – literacy education in primary and secondary schools has come to be associated largely with women and women's business. Elaine Millard reports a variety of studies that show that even by the first year of formal schooling, boys and girls have very clear notions about what is 'proper' for them to read:

> Primary teachers in England have . . . reported significant differences in boys' and girls' reading interests, often citing this as one of the major factors in boys' weaker all-round performance in the literacy curriculum . . . Osmont reports that children brought to the classroom their perceptions of what adults at home were reading, describing

considerable differences between men's and women's reading matter. She reports that a majority of mothers were observed reading mainly fiction, whereas fathers read newspapers, information books and documents brought back from work.

(Millard 1997: 11)

As Millard and many others (e.g. Clark 1976; Heath 1982; Alloway and Gilbert 1996) have pointed out, most teachers of early school classes value and foster an interest in reading fictional and-they-lived-happily-ever-after stories, rather than factual or 'real life' accounts or the epic, lone adventurer stories many boys seem to prefer (Millard 1997: 12, 16). Moreover, many educators refer to what they call the 'feminization' of English and literacy education because it is a school subject where girls achieve more highly than boys and which is being taught more often by women than by men (Millard 1997).

As boys themselves put it in relation to English lessons (Martino 1995, cited in Cordukes 1997: 77):

English is more suited to girls because it's not the way guys think . . . this subject is the biggest load of bullshit I have ever done. Therefore, I don't particularly like this subject. I hope you aren't offended by this, but most guys who like English are faggots.

Boys don't read as much as girls because of sport.

I think English is boring. We know how to talk so why do we have to learn more? Also reading is lame, sitting down looking at words is pathetic. Watching TV and playing sport and the computer is way more interesting.

The irony here is that a great many literacy programmes centre masculine texts and male authors, and work to reinforce traditional gendered patterns of behaviour. Nevertheless, while the content of key literacy/literary texts – from Shakespeare to Hemingway, European fairy tales to *Goosebumps* – may be reinforcing traditional gendered patterns that associate activity with boys and passivity with girls, boys are not, in many cases, finding material within those texts (or in the teaching/learning strategies or assessment practices used) to encourage them to align themselves with literacy *per se*.

Attempts to value masculine knowledge, therefore, can lead to a situation where literacy teachers make greater use of male-friendly texts, including the non-fiction resources commonly associated with boys and other popular culture texts: comics, computer games and so on. In addition to this, teachers might adopt what they see as 'male-friendly' assessment strategies and allow boys to complete the majority of their assessment in verbal rather than written form, even though there is little evidence to suggest that this will lead to positive outcomes.

It is possible to identify here a fine line between this 'valuing male knowledge' approach and the essentialist valuing difference approach outlined above. While those operating from this anti-essentialist position may well believe that this is the best way to achieve a transformation of gender norms associated with literacy, there are real risks associated with an uncritical endorsement of this approach. For example, it is possible to further promote traditional models of masculinity; it is similarly possible that the content of the English curriculum will become even more 'male-centred' than it usually is. A related risk is that English – one of the few areas where girls currently feel valued, will become another site within which masculinity and specific, narrow versions of masculinity are celebrated. And, of course, any approach that rests upon categorizing some kinds of experiences/interests/learning strategies as 'masculine' or 'feminine' can fall easily into the practice of treating all girls and all boys as fundamentally the same.

This last insight has led to the emergence of a now widely cited mindset: that of acknowledging differences among groups of girls and groups of boys.

Ain't I a woman? Ain't I a man? Valuing multiplicity in gender reform

In 1851, former slave and well known abolitionist Sojourner Truth spoke at the Akron Women's Rights Convention against the idea that women were not the equal of men. In the process she drew attention to the fact that the 'privileges' this inequality brought to women – male support, protection, assistance – were not universally experienced and that she, as a black woman, experienced none of the comforts of a woman who is white:

> That man over there says that women need to be helped into carriages, and lifted over ditches, and to have the best place every-where. Nobody ever helps me into carriages, or over mud-puddles, or gives me any best place! And ain't I a woman? Look at me! Look at my arm! I have ploughed and planted, and gathered into barns, and no man could head me! And ain't I a woman? I could work as much and eat as much as a man – when I could get it – and bear the lash as well! And ain't I a woman? I have born thirteen children, and seen them most all sold off to slavery, and when I cried out with my mother's grief, none but Jesus heard me! And ain't I a woman?
>
> (Truth 1851: 250)

Truth highlights here the fact that gender is not the only factor that determines an individual's life experiences. Race, ethnicity, economic status, physical appearance, physical ability and many other issues influence the ways in which people are valued or devalued within educational settings. Over the past decade, people working within school contexts to construct gender reform projects have increasingly acknowledged that the needs of 'boys' are not simple. Boys are not all the same. Not all boys experience privilege in the same ways, or to the same extent. Not all boys are disadvantaged. And of those that are, not all have been brought to a disadvantaged state in the same ways or for the same reasons.

We have learned, in other words, to recognize that 'being a boy' relates not only to experiences of a male body, but also to factors associated with race, ethnicity, economic status, physical ability, sexuality, religion, first language, physical appearance and so on. In other words, many factors combine to determine the ways in which an individual boy will be ranked within a particular gender hierarchy. Audre Lorde (1990: 282) argues that most people find themselves lacking in some way when they compare themselves to a socially coded version of 'normal':

> Somewhere, on the edge of consciousness, there is what I call a mythical norm, which each one of us within our hearts knows 'that is not me' ... this norm is usually defined as white, thin, male, young, heterosexual, Christian and financially secure.

Lorde draws attention to the existence of powerful images about what constitutes normal and desirable behaviours and characteristics and the impact that these images have on people who understand that they do not 'fit' this mythical norm. This is as relevant for boys as it is for girls. While some boys are ranked very highly within dominant social structures, other boys who are not part of what might be regarded as mainstream or hegemonic masculinities find themselves marginalized and devalued. Within what Connell (1987) describes as 'the gender order' there are hierarchies among and between various versions of masculinity and femininity. Josephine Peyton Young (2000: 316) summarizes the point to argue that:

> Discourses of masculinity – some hegemonic, some marginalized, and some stigmatized – interact with institutional and societal relations to construct and negotiate differences and hierarchies. These differences and hierarchies are influenced by interactions with race, class, and age.

This returns us to the points made in the previous chapter, where we acknowledged that socio-economic status and race had a close relationship with gender when it comes to the development and demonstration of literacy skills. This insight reminds us that it is not enough to offer boys choices: not all boys are in the same position to exercise choice. Some boys who choose to step outside of normative models of masculinity are routinely punished – in a range of direct and indirect ways. Nor is it a simple matter to value boys' knowledge or experience: for boys do not all have the same experiences. And identifying the diverse ways in which boys can be devalued or marginalized within mainstream models of masculinity challenges us to consider how our gender reform practices can actually effect a transformation of these practices.

While the equal opportunity and valuing boys' knowledge approaches can both be read as ways of coping with existing models of masculinity, recognizing the differences among boys challenges us to think more carefully about the way these differences are produced in the first place. Thus the next mindset we will consider is the first of two major approaches for accounting for the production of gender differences – and all the variations among and between masculinities and femininities.

Made not born: gender as a social construction

In 1949, Simone de Beauvoir made the famous claim that 'one is not born a woman, but rather, becomes one'. This statement captures the basis of gender reform that interprets gendered behaviours not as natural, but as socially produced. While determinist arguments generally ascribe observable differences between boys and girls to natural or biological differences, anti-essentialist arguments maintain that gendered behaviours are learned. While the mindsets we have reviewed to this point constitute responses to learned behaviour, they have not outlined in any detail theories concerning the *ways* these behaviours are learned. Coupled with approaches that 'value male knowledge' or work towards 'equal opportunity', therefore, are attitudes about where knowledge about 'being a man' comes from in the first place. The socialization model that we deal with here sees gendered behaviour as a social product. The argument is that boys and girls are socialized from an early age to act, think and live in different ways, and to get pleasure from different activities and experiences. If we want to change the way boys or girls act, therefore, all we need to do is 'reprogram' them to enjoy or desire *new* and *different* ways of being.

Thanks to socialization frameworks, girls' education – and, indeed, boys' education – moved in new directions from the 1980s. Attention was drawn to the value of providing girls with alternative pathways, role models, choice. The impact of individual teachers upon what students would regard as natural or normal gendered behaviour became the subject of discussion. Teachers were encouraged to think about the ways they could open up new pathways for girls and emphasis was placed upon the benefits associated with 'non-traditional' careers. Schools began to develop comprehensive programmes focused on girls' education which attended not only to issues of subject choice and career paths but also to the various school locations and the status of girls within them. Sexual harassment became an important issue for discussion. Girls and teachers developed a language to talk about the way people were socialized – in overt and covert ways – to adhere to gender norms.

For the education of boys, the socialization model has been used to identify the diverse ways in which boys are taught to 'act like a man'. Key agents of socialization such as families, peer groups, sporting clubs, TV, movies and games have been identified as places that help to circulate understandings of 'normal' masculinity: norms that boys negotiate in their day-to-day school life. In this framework, boys are exposed to different role models: they are shown men who read, men who teach, men who work in non-traditional fields.

The value of the socialization approach lies in the way in which it draws attention to the constructed nature of so many of the processes and behaviours commonly represented as normal.

Within the socialization literature, however, children tend to be represented in unnaturally passive ways. If girls are socialized to wear dresses and play with Barbies, the argument goes, then they can be socialized to wear Doc Martens and fine tune cars. Anyone who has tried to implement these kinds of programmes will know that things aren't as simple as this. All the role models in the world do not necessarily lead to girls becoming engineers. For this reason, this framework is described by MacNaughton (2000: 19) as one where children are seen as 'sponges' who 'soak up' ideas about gender identity. She argues that while consciousness of gender norms has encouraged teachers to be aware of the ways they 'socialize' kids, many of these frameworks position kids in passive relationship to their teachers or schools: as 'social dupes' (Heckman, cited in MacNaughton 2000) who will take on board whatever their teachers model for them. Sex role theory or socialization literature has encouraged educators to provide children with a range of 'socialization' experiences: to ensure that they are exposed to men and women in non-traditional areas, to make certain they are constantly told of their rights to pursue non-traditional pathways and so on. But it has been unable to account for the fact that boys and girls do not always take on board the preferences of their teachers.

One of the issues here is that the differential power attached to various displays of 'normal' or acceptable behaviour for girls or boys is not always fully recognized. Within the socialization literature in the early 1980s it was common for teachers to try to encourage girls into non-traditional areas by linking them to the skills associated with that area. Attempts to encourage girls into engineering, for example, drew upon a popular campaign exhorting people to 'hand a girl a spanner'. While popularly embraced, this campaign did not necessarily attend to the more widespread and powerful stories that circulate in a culture about being a girl, and whether or not 'normal' girls had any kind of relationship at all with spanners. The problem, therefore, is that to feel safe, valued and legitimate within some engineering contexts, many girls don't simply need spanners. They need also to have their use of the spanner acknowledged and valorized.

In the following example, a girl demonstrates technological competence: the kind of skill which we are regularly told is valued within both schooling and 'male' cultures. The girl who displays this skill, however, does not appear to be valued herself:

> *Anita was recognized by her teachers and classmates as being the resident 'computer expert'. The students in this classroom were rostered in pairs for using the computer during class time. A pair of boys, Todd and Grant, had just sat down at the computer and had decided to try out a new maths game. They inserted the disk and tried a few commands but couldn't get the game to run. They spent some time arguing over what was wrong, then Todd told Grant to go and get Anita so that she could show them what to do. Anita was deep in the middle of her school work, but put that aside at Grant's request and came over to the computer. She asked what game it was, then pressed a few keys and – presto! – the game burst into life on the screen. She showed them which key combinations they needed for this particular game. Both boys looked really pleased. Grant turned to Anita and said, 'Thanks, stupid,' echoed by Todd, 'Yeah, thanks, stupid.' Anita simply turned and went back to her desk as though being addressed like that was nothing out of the ordinary.*

It is not just masculinity or masculine qualities, such as strength aggression or intelligence, that are valued in Western cultures, therefore. *It is hegemonic masculinity performed by a white, physically able, masculine body that is the most privileged of all gender performances.*

This leads us to the final point on our journey through various gender reform mindsets: one which takes on board and learns from the ideas and insights developed within the models that proceeded it, and which has, as a fundamental aim, the belief that gender norms impact in significant and often negative ways on the lives of girls and boys, and that these norms can be successfully transformed. For this reason we refer to this as the 'transformative' mindset.

Making it not so: transformative mindsets on gender reform

The first point to be made is that the transformative mindset as we discuss it here is based upon a theoretical field known as feminist post-structuralism. This framework has explored diverse and complex issues associated with the production, naturalization and contestation of gender norms. The distinguishing feature of the transformative mindset, therefore, is that it places the production of gender norms at the centre of analysis. Rather than starting from a position that seeks to accommodate and value differences between boys and girls, or between some boys and others, the transformative mindset seeks to understand *how* and *why* some gendered patterns of behaviour have come to be so powerful, while others have been marginalized. It focuses on the production of gender-based inequalities and examines, as a result, the fundamental ways in which the structures that are associated with gender inequity – schools, families, governments, religions and so on – actually work to produce, circulate and naturalize gendered norms. Emphasis is therefore placed not just on the *structures* that sustain women in an oppositional and generally negative relationship to men, but also to the *processes* through which these structures construct and secure their legitimacy.

There are elements of post-structural theory which we explore in more detail later in this chapter. For immediate purposes it is worth spelling out several principles relating to post-structuralism and transformative approaches to gender reform.

First, in common with earlier anti-essentialist mindsets, the transformative approach to gender and schooling has rejected the idea of a masculine or feminine essence which determines girls' and boys' behaviour and highlighted, instead, the way in which gender norms are constructed, naturalized and valorized particularly through language and discursive practices. It seeks to identify the various stories or narratives about gender that are circulated within particular social/cultural contexts. Thus 'gender identity' is read more as a construction – even a fiction – than as any kind of natural truth.

But while talking about gender as a story makes it sound rather harmless, or even entertaining, the stories are also attached to powerful institutions which make them appear as natural and legitimate. According to Walkerdine (1990: xiii), 'femininity and masculinity are fictions linked to fantasies deeply embedded in the social world which can take on the status of fact when inscribed in the powerful practices, like schooling, through which we are regulated.' In other words, while understandings about what it means to be a 'woman' or a 'man' may be culturally produced and thus more like fiction than fact, some of these fictional stories are more powerful than others as a result of the institutions that support, endorse and circulate them. Powerful institutions, in other words, help to produce what can be seen as *normative* and *dominant* models of masculinity and femininity. These present individuals with messages about the differences between men and women, as well as messages about the relative value of different versions of masculinity and femininity.

Accordingly, post-structuralist feminism has worked to acknowledge not only the ways in which gender norms are circulated, but also the differential power attached to competing understandings about what it means to be a boy or a girl. Furthermore, post-structuralist feminism acknowledges that stories about gender intersect with stories about race, ethnicity, sexuality and economic status to determine the particular ways in which any individual experiences 'being a man' or 'being a woman'. Attention is therefore drawn not just to the processes through which gender norms are produced, but also to the consequences of these norms for individual and groups of men and women. This is not to produce new, discrete categories of 'white men' or 'Indian men', for example. As Connell (1995: 76) reminds us:

> To recognize more than one kind of masculinity is only a first step. We have to examine the relations between them. Further we have to unpack the milieux of class and race and scrutinize the gender relations operating within them. There are, after all, gay black men and effeminate factory hands, not to mention middle-class rapists and cross-dressing bourgeois.

Because of this appreciation of the diverse factors impacting upon boys' sense of 'masculinity', those working within the post-structuralist tradition tend to articulate a more complex understanding than the previous mindsets we have discussed of the challenges facing those who wish to explore, for example, boys' literacy needs. Essentialist mindsets seek only to have boys' 'natural' interests and skills valued; equal opportunity mindsets seek to provide boys with the freedom to 'choose' to be literate; socialization models see that boys need only to be provided with different socialization experiences, and the multiplicity model encourages us to see that these different socialization experiences may also need to be different for individual boys and girls. A post-structural feminist model, however, takes on board all these aims, but seeks, as an opening move, to develop a detailed under- standing of the complex and multiple ways in which gender norms are produced in the first place. This involves examining the ways in which institutions and the discourses – ways of speaking – associated with them circulate, legitimate and naturalize some stories about gender at the ex- pense of others. It is only when one has a clear understanding of the diverse and powerful ways in which gendered behaviour is produced that one can reasonably attempt any intervention or transformation of these behaviours. To borrow a medical image, this is the difference between treating a symp- tom, and treating a cause.

Hence, by referring to this approach to gender reform as a transformative approach we are signalling our interest in working to transform both the ways boys and girls interact with literacy classrooms and the ways broad concepts of masculinity and femininity are conceived in the first place.

To this end, we recognize the importance of operating always at two levels: at the first we must identify the processes whereby narrow and limiting versions of masculinity or femininity are produced. In Elizabeth Grosz's (1995: 59) terms, this is the necessarily 'negative' or 'reactive' dimension of feminist theory: 'the project of challenging what currently exists, or criticising prevailing social, political, and theoretical relations' – work that is about developing what she describes as anti-sexist theory.

Equally important, however, is the constructive, positive dimension of feminism: energy directed into the development of creative alternatives to mainstream, patriarchal practices (Grosz 1995). This dimension celebrates women's *and* men's abilities to resist, challenge and transform phallocentric systems of thought and their material consequences. Traditional narratives about gender are therefore challenged by *counternarratives* which offer new ways of imagining gender and gender relations.

Underpinning the belief that patriarchal systems can be *transformed,* therefore, are two vital points. First, while gender norms may appear to be natural they can, in fact, be changed. Second, while individuals must negotiate multiple (and often competing) discourses concerning what it means to be a 'boy' or a 'girl', they are neither passive nor helpless in this process and are able to exercise their own power in making choices.

MacNaughton (2000: 28) summarizes these points when she argues that five themes emerge from the 'post-structuralist terrain' focused on gender identity formation:

- there is not a fixed, coherent immutable gender identity to be learnt;
- the child is an active player in gender identity formation, but not a free agent;
- the child does not receive messages through one single process;
- the child selects her or his messages from a highly controlled market place of ideas;
- interaction with others is central in forming identity.

This means that educators concerned with boys' literacy levels must move beyond frameworks that see boys or girls as naturally suited to the development of particular skills. We must similarly let go of frameworks that assign the teacher – or the parent, or the peers – as sole determinants of gender identity and recognize that there are multiple forces which children negotiate in developing their own sense of self. Consequently, we must acknowledge the significance of providing kids with opportunities to reflect upon this negotiation, and with an environment that is able to provide them with support as they move in and out of traditional and non-traditional gender performances.

We must also acknowledge ways in which literacy lessons and texts – along with every other educational and cultural context – are complicit in the production of gender norms. Attention, therefore, shifts away from reading boys unproblematically as the 'victims' of over-zealous gender reform and towards more sophisticated frameworks. These are frameworks capable both of attending to issues relating to the relationship between masculinity and femininity and of identifying ways in which boys are variously positioned in school contexts. This point is made strongly by Mahony (1998: 37), who writes:

> My argument is not that the education of boys is unimportant but that the assumptions and purposes underpinning the current obsession with their academic performance are misconceived. As a consequence, key questions concerning the role of schools in the social construction of

masculinities are omitted; the practices and consequences of different masculinities in relation to women become invisible; and the effects on different groups of boys of the internal orderings of masculinities are obscured.

Post-structuralist frameworks also draw attention to the fact that literacy classrooms are much more than sites within which boys' literacy problems can be fixed. They are, in addition, places – like so many others – where gender norms are produced. For this reason, any attempt to restructure literacy classrooms in ways that respond to consistent underperformance of groups of boys and groups of girls must be aware of the ways in which they also contribute to the circulation of gender norms. The extent to which these norms are prescriptive or transformative is, finally, the most significant question of all.

Post-structuralist feminism has had a dramatic impact on how people think about gender and its transformation in schools. It has given us a language to identify gender as something that is produced, but also experienced individually, within individual and different bodies. It has helped us to recognize that gender alone does not determine an individual's position in particular historical/social/contexts: that not all women (or all men) inhabit the same gender territory (Jones 1990).

Moreover, with its emphasis on the social production and regulation of gendered meanings, post-structural feminism has highlighted the regularly unacknowledged point that boys are gendered too. That is to say, it is not only girls who must negotiate powerful social understandings about what it means to be born and to live in a particular body. Boys, too, experience the pressures (and joys) of hegemonic gender norms. Boys, too, negotiate diverse and conflicting discourses concerning their role and their 'natural' place in various social/cultural groups.

As a result, post-structuralist research into gender and schools has consistently (though sometimes only *implicitly*) focused on the ways in which gender – as it relates to both boys and girls – is discursively constructed, individually and collectively experienced, and continually negotiated, resisted and transformed. A representative example of this interest in boys and girls as gendered subjects is provided by *Gender Equity: A Framework for Australian Schools*. This policy provided the first clear indication in Australia that gender reform in education related to girls *and* boys:

> Gender equity in schooling is based on understanding that explanations for the differences in experience and outcomes in education for girls and boys arise from the ways in which the construction of gender impacts on the expectations, interests and behaviours of both sexes. It acknowledges that the impact is often one which constrains and limits, rather than expands, options and possibilities for girls and women,

and boys and men. It also acknowledges that, as with other areas of human experience, the construction of gender is able to be understood, and is capable of change.

(DEETYA 1995: 3)

As this extract makes clear, transformative approaches to gender have focused on issues to do with both masculinity and femininity. This is an important point. Extreme examples of the 'what about the boys?' discourse explored in the previous chapter tend to represent 'gender equity experts' in a hostile and oppositional relationship to boys; they also tend to assume that all these 'experts' will be women, and that gender reform for the most part has been, and continues to be, 'women's work'. This view is reinforced by the protest masculinity voices referred to above. They regularly argue that everything will be OK if we get back to basic boyness.

Although protest masculinity is sometimes the *loudest* position espoused by men with respect to boys and schooling, it is not the *only* position taken up by men. Men as well as women have embraced the transformative approach. Indeed, a very significant contribution has been made to gender debates by men working within a variety of positions which we group together here under the heading 'progressive masculinity'. These men work against essentialist and protest positions and seek, instead, to identify the ways in which masculinity is constructed socially. They are, in Connell's words, 'actively engaged in resisting hegemonic masculinity and those other "complicit" masculinities which provide a support base for this valorised masculinity' (cited in Mills and Lingard 1997a: 277).

Progressive and pro-feminist men accept the legitimacy of the work undertaken by feminists (although, as we have mentioned before, there is significant debate about which 'feminism' they are 'pro'), and seek to focus their own energies on investigating the ways in which masculinity (like femininity) has been culturally constructed. This involves recognizing the ways in which normative and new ways of being a man are produced within various social institutions and discourses, identifying the consequences this has for all men (and women) and exploring ways out of these narrow and restrictive gendered norms.

Proponents of this position have drawn on the influential literature from sociology, and particularly on post-structuralist resources in sociology and other fields. Emphasis is placed upon the ways in which various social institutions and discourses represent natural and normal ways of being a man. Thus, both hegemonic (culturally endorsed and rewarded) masculinity and marginalized versions of masculinity are identified and explored. Attention is also drawn to the consequences for men/boys who relate to particular forms of masculinity. Recognizing the existence and significance of progressive masculinity frameworks is an important part of reviewing attitudes towards gender reform. As previously acknowledged, debates about boys' education all too often represent men and women in oppositional ways. According to David Jackson (1998: 82),

> At the moment we seem to be locked into a dichotomized, confrontational model of the girls' disadvantage discourse versus the boys' disadvantage discourse. These competitive, binary divisions are getting in the way of a more open dialogue emerging between men and women working in the field.
>
> To be concerned about what is happening to boys today does not mean that one is automatically anti-woman. Also to be concerned about some boys' distress at school (distress about physical violence from other boys, fears about being bullied and intimidated, fears about being savagely mocked as effeminate or a 'poof', fears about stepping out of line) does not mean that one is wanting to betray the feminist agenda in schools. To acknowledge that white, heterosexual men, collectively, possess power over women and subordinated men, does not mean that some men cannot oppose patriarchy for the collective interests of women and men.

A similarly significant point concerns the fact that both men *and* women are involved in the processes of constructing, circulating and critiquing understandings of masculinity just as they both have a role to play in the education of girls. Connell (1998: v) captures this point well and articulates an

> important point about masculinity-making: it is not all done by men. Women are important in the shaping of gender practices and gender meanings for boys as well as for girls – as mothers, sisters, lovers, workmates, entertainers, service workers, and so on. Women as teachers have a lot to do with the shaping of gender regimes in schools that impinge on boys as well as girls.
>
> This is important to recognize, because the pop psychology of masculinity currently circulating in Australia as well as the US, typically assumes that the making of masculinity is 'men's business' and needs men's rituals, initiations, etc. to make sure it is well done. That men should be more involved in the care of children, I wholly agree. That would be one of the most progressive things we could do in gender relations. But men should be involved in the care of girls as much as boys; and they should be involved *together with* women, not apart from them. To think we will improve the current mess in gender relations by *increasing* the psychological separation of boys and girls is lunatic.

Post-structuralist resources are, then, of use to men and women alike because they accommodate several integrally related concerns. These are concerns about *gender* – masculinity and femininity – and the diverse processes through which gender norms are constructed, the multiple ways in which they are negotiated, the role of men and women in these processes, and the value of transformative projects. This sets post-structuralist resources apart from essentialist perspectives and from the protest masculinities reviewed earlier. The day to day tensions that must be negotiated by those within progressive masculinity frameworks are illustrated by the following story.

> I was asked to address the topic 'what about the boys?' to a large private school in Australia. This school had begun life as a boys' school but had become coeducational about 15 years earlier. The teachers in the school expressed concern that boys were not coping as well as girls, and that there were particular boys in the school who seemed at risk. Over the course of the presentation the teachers raised the issue of the school's proud sporting history and, eventually, the ways in which boys in the school were all expected to take part in sporting activities and the after match rituals, including a communal shower, some good natured slapping and thumping, and so on. When one of the men present suggested that perhaps this was one of the ways in which some of the boys in the school were actually made to feel uncomfortable a teacher replied, 'That's nonsense. Boys love to get together, to whack it out and wave it about, that's part of being a real man.'

Setting aside the ways in which this could easily be read as an endorsement of boys' 'natural' homosexual tendencies, this point of view illustrates the belief that there are some 'macho' and 'butch' behaviours naturally associated with boys. Traditional teachers leave these behaviours unproblematized and may, indeed, actively endorse them. Proponents of gender reform operating within progressive masculinity frameworks work to problematize the notion that 'traditional' models of masculinity are somehow better or superior to others. They encourage critical reflection on the origins and consequences of masculine behaviour patterns and the development of new and multiple ways of being a boy, and new and multiple ways of being a man, which can exist alongside new and multiple ways of being a girl and being a woman.

Thus the transformative mindset to gender reform embraces both men and women who work to contest fixed and rigid understandings of gender associated with masculinity or femininity, who recognize and legitimate multiple ways of being a 'boy' or a 'girl' and who see schools – and literacy classrooms – as places where gender norms can be explored, rendered problematic, denaturalized and transformed.

For all these reasons – and many others to be explored in subsequent chapters – we (the authors) align ourselves with the transformative mindset. This means we make use of a range of concepts associated with post-structuralist feminism, some of which need further explanation. In the next chapter we will illustrate how these theoretical resources – and others that resonate with them – may be used in a practical way to begin the process of analysing a particular educational or literacy context. We will, in particular, outline ways in which concepts like transformation, discourse, multiplicity and subjectivity can be used on a day-by-day basis to help us make sense of, evaluate, respond to and initiate a range of literacy practices designed to improve and extend educational experiences of girls *and* boys.

Gender reform proponents working within a post-structural feminist framework emphasize the ways in which an individual's sense of self – commonly referred to as subjectivity rather than identity – is shaped at the intersection of various social/cultural practices and discourses. Our use of the term 'discourses' likewise draws on a post-structuralist rendition. 'Discourse' is used to stand for a way of speaking that is consistent with the beliefs/values of a particular context and that, in the process, helps to produce the context. To talk of the discursive construction of femininity or masculinity is, then, to draw attention to the vast range of ways in which a particular culture circulates meanings about what it is to be a boy or a girl and, more specifically, to be a *valued* boy or girl. Within concrete discursive contexts, boys and girls may be valued (or devalued) for different things. An aggressive boy may be spoken about as 'rugged' or 'macho' in contexts which see these terms as complimentary for a man. An aggressive girl, however, is more likely to be described as 'butch' or 'pushy': terms most commonly intended as insults when addressed to a woman.

While discourse is commonly associated with language – with words – it also refers to the ways of communicating produced within particular contexts. Within a masculine discourse, for example, it is not just *words* like 'tough' or 'bloke' that are valued. In addition, certain behaviours, appearances, interests, relationships and so on are regarded as natural and desirable. In our use of the term 'discourse', therefore, we are referring to a way of communicating, often produced by a particular context, that reflects the beliefs and values of that context. 'Context' comprises patterns of inter-actions that are socially recognized (even enforced in many cases) as being of 'a particular type'. In some cases the relationship between discourse and context is obvious. The Catholic Church, for example, supports particular ways of speaking and acting that are directly tied to being 'at church' as well as to being 'a member of the Church'. Similarly, there are discourses – ways of speaking, acting, dressing and so on – that are seen as appropriate and valued within less formal contexts, such as a soccer match or a Fijian beach.

Precisely the same action or behaviour can be valued differently within different discourses. Wearing a bikini in Honolulu, for example, might be regarded as natural behaviour. But wearing a bikini in an Indian mosque would be regarded as highly undesirable behaviour. And it is not just a particular behaviour or use of language that discourses value. Instead, discourses are gendered, so that it is a *female* body in a bikini that is celebrated in Honolulu, while a male body in the same costume would be at best regarded as a joke, and at worst seen as evidence of inappropriate and undesirable effeminate and ungodly behaviour.

The point here is that in their day-to-day lives boys and girls encounter many discourses. These include: discourses associated with formal institutions, such as schools, religions and governments; and discourses produced by less formal but by no means less powerful social institutions, such as the family, sporting clubs or peer groups. Each child, in other words, negotiates what Weedon defines as a discursive field which may 'consist of competing ways of giving meaning to the world and organising social institutions and processes' (cited in Kenway *et al.* 1997: 67).

This negotiation does not, however, happen on anything remotely resembling neutral territory. Some discourses – such as those associated with the family and gender norms within it – are supported by longstanding cultural practices and often are quite difficult to negotiate, let alone resist or challenge. Nevertheless, a fundamental tenet of the post-structural feminist philosophy is that social and cultural change *is* possible. This is evinced through the diverse ways in which girls in society generally, and schools more specifically, have been able to take up 'new' options and pathways without automatically giving up elements of 'traditional' femininity.

The significant matter here is the ability of post-structuralism to recognize that while powerful and regulatory social fictions about gender are endorsed and circulated by a wide range of institutions, it is also possible for other, less restrictive understandings of being a girl and being a boy to be constructed, circulated and validated.

Within the post-structural framework for gender reform, then, a key project involves identifying dominant narratives associated with gender and then working to introduce and validate counternarratives. These are alternative ways of being and alternative modes of representation. First and foremost, this involves working to show that in their educational and wider life contexts there is more than one way to be a boy or a girl. It also involves helping young boys to see that they can align himself with more than one version of masculinity in the course of their life, or, indeed, in the course of a single day. Likewise, it involves helping young girls to understand their parallel options with respect to femininity.

Where does this leave us?

We have reviewed to this point a significant – even bewildering – range of positions relating to various ways of analysing the experiences of men and women, girls and boys. We have also identified some of the ways in which these frameworks have influenced practices in schooling, and made valuable contributions to how we think about education for girls and boys.

The articulation between perspectives on men/women and society and gender reform in schooling is not always clear cut. There are many men within both protest and progressive masculinity frameworks who pay only cursory attention to boys in schools; there are many women with significant experience in gender reform who see boys' educational needs as located within the broad post-structuralist approach and who pay little attention to literature arising from men's work on gender; there are many men concerned with boys in schools who pay little attention to the work that has already been done by committed feminist and pro-feminist teachers. The list goes on.

We are trying to highlight here the fact that the terrain associated with gender reform is both complex and characterized by a curious scarcity of connections among and between various groups.

One of our primary goals here is to help to forge some connections among diverse groups of people who share a common concern with the educational experiences of boys. In some cases this will involve forging alliances between groups of people who, if they have not exactly been estranged, have certainly not hitherto been on first name terms. Underpinning our work is a conviction that the work of post-structuralist feminists and pro-feminist masculinity researchers has the most to offer people struggling with complex issues associated with boys and their education and literacy. Our next goal is to spell out what it is that these perspectives can offer us in thinking through the complex task of responding to boys' educational and literacy experiences. In the following chapter we will outline the pragmatic nature of the theoretical resources introduced here, and use this as a basis for conceptualizing transformative literacy practices.

chapter / **three**

Some really useful theoretical company for transforming and transformative literacy education

This book is primarily concerned with identifying ways in which literacy educators can make a difference to the lives and literacies of boys, while also attending to the needs of girls. We are committed to identifying a range of ways in which literacy classrooms can be redesigned to problematize traditional conceptions of being a boy, and contribute to a broad-based political project of extending and transforming understandings of 'normal' gender roles.

We are also concerned about the ease with which 'well intentioned' intervention projects can actually work to reinscribe traditional understandings about gender and to widen the gap between some boys and some literacies.

The following chapters will use the transformative mindset introduced in the previous chapter to identify ways in which four common literacy interventions can work either to *reinforce* or to *problematize* normative understandings of masculinity. This, of course, isn't as simple a challenge as it may sound. Most literacy practices have strengths and weakness relating to the way literacy skills can be acquired (see Chapter 4). Similarly, most gender reform mindsets have strengths and weaknesses. Gender reform designed to address literacy levels, therefore, needs to operate not only at the operational level of helping students to develop functional literacy skills, or at the cultural level of helping students to understand the relationship between literacy and context, but also at the critical level of ensuring that students understand the relationship between literacy, gender and context.

With this in mind, we will be making use of the transformative mindset introduced in the previous chapter to illustrate ways in which literacy practices can work *transformatively* to open up new possibilities relating to schooling for boys and girls, or else to work *traditionally* and reinscribe patriarchal gender norms. To do this we must first explain how we distinguish between what is seen as transformative and what is seen as traditional. Accordingly, this chapter has two goals:

- To explore the role of schools in producing traditional – or hegemonic – masculinity that represents boys in an oppositional or uneasy relationship with literacy practice.
- To identify a framework for determining the likelihood that particular literacy interventions will work to denaturalize and resist these traditional performances of masculinity.

Being a boy, becoming a man: traditional masculinity in schools

Over the past twenty years authors representing diverse positions within the broad field of education have identified a variety of common ways in which masculinity is performed within school sites. They have also distinguished between performances regarded as mainstream, or normal ways of being a boy, and performances understood as deviant, or 'unnatural'. This work has drawn attention to the existence of both normative and marginal ways of 'doing masculinity' within schools and the consequences – for boys and girls – of these various masculinities.

Authors like Bob Connell, Máirtín Mac an Ghaill, Debbie Epstein, Jane Kenway, Bob Lingard, Martin Mills, Rob and Pam Gilbert are among the many writers who have drawn attention to the ways in which educational institutions participate in the construction of masculinity in both hegemonic and subordinate forms. Students negotiate implicit and explicit discourses associated with what it means to be a man, and what it means to be a woman through the 'three message systems of schooling' – curriculum, assessment, pedagogy – as well as through multiple informal and formal contexts, including playgrounds, sporting activities, speech nights, graduations, field trips, community service activities, school fetes, fund-raisers and so on. As Gilbert and Gilbert (1998: 205) note, 'The schoolchild has to learn how to construct a school "self" – how to perform as a schoolchild – and this learning is not disassociated with gender.' The challenge here is that even before they get to school, boys and girls bring with them understandings about how they are supposed to act, interact and learn:

> Whereas much of a girl's social learning has introduced her to performances of submission, passivity and courtesy, much of a boy's learning has been different. His learning is more likely to have introduced him to performances of activity and maverick individualism.
>
> (Gilbert and Gilbert 1998: 205)

This early perception of one's particular – different – status, and, by extension, one's particular and different relationship with school processes and content, is reinforced from the earliest days of school. Rollo Browne sums up a common belief when he writes:

> It is in schools, during the formative years, that notions of masculinity (often linked to such images as strength, cleverness, winning, power and status) are reinforced daily. Schools are a potent site for young people to absorb messages about what it means to be male and female.
>
> (Browne 1995: 225)

These messages are circulated in a range of ways. Linda Lindsey makes the point that from kindergarten onwards, males are given greater status within curriculum material, with male characters, male experiences and images of masculinity dramatically outnumbering appearances of women. She writes: 'over thirty years of research demonstrates that girls are virtually invisible or, at best, play insignificant roles in a variety of such material' (Lindsey 1994: 264). Similarly, evidence suggests that teachers interact with boys and girls differently, expecting and rewarding or tolerating different kinds of behaviours from the two sexes and bestowing different kinds of attention on the males. Arguments have also been made that dominant assessment systems emphasize what are represented as masculine models of learning and thus disadvantage girls who may not have learnt to excel in examinations or various competitive situations (Allard *et al.* 1995).

Along with all the other social institutions, schools participate in constructing, circulating and naturalizing gendered norms. They do so through the direct ways they speak about and celebrate particular manifestations of masculinity and femininity, and in the multiple ways various behaviours, interests and performances are viewed as normal or deviant.

According to Holland *et al.* (1993: 2),

> Since men are born into male bodies, but not into the successful accomplishment of culturally appropriate versions of masculinity, becoming a man is a complex process of learning and doing within shifting sets of social constraints.

Schools play a vital role in inducting boys into these 'culturally appropriate versions of masculinity'. As Connell (1995) reminds us, they also reflect the wider patterns associated with normative masculinity and value boys for displaying particular qualities such as reason, strength and courage, as well as for performances relating to their independence, reserve and heterosexuality.

Rob and Pam Gilbert and Máirtín Mac an Ghaill provide excellent illustrative examples of the ways various school settings help to produce and sustain a variety of masculinities. In a study based in England, Mac an Ghaill (1994) identified four masculine typologies worth reviewing here for the ways they illustrate multiple variations on a central, masculine theme.

First, he identified a 'fighting, fucking and football' type of masculinity associated with Macho Lads, whose 'vocabulary of masculinity stressed the physical ("sticking up for yourselves"), solidarity ("sticking together") and territorial control ("teachers think they own this place").' He identified a second group defined as Academic Achievers, who had a 'a positive orientation to the academic curriculum' and were reminiscent of the grammar school boys who saw academic achievement as a pathway towards post-school successes. A third group was identified as the New Enterprisers. About these, Mac an Ghaill (1994: 63) writes:

> Working within the new vocationalist skilling regimes of high-status technological and commercial subject areas, the New Enterprise students were negotiating a new mode of school student masculinity with its values of rationality, instrumentalism, forward planning and careerism.

Mac an Ghaill identified a fourth group that he called Real Englishmen. Like 'modern-day high-priests positioned themselves as the arbiters of culture. From this self-appointed location, they evaluated both teachers and students in terms of their possession of high-status cultural capital' (Mac an Ghaill 1994: 65).

Gilbert and Gilbert also report a range of similar and related masculine typologies identified in various studies of boys in schools. These are, respectively, the 'competitors' and 'footballers' fundamental to Australian masculinity, as discussed by Jim Walker; gothic punks identified by Abraham; Haywood's distinction between 'wankers', 'gays' and 'poofs'; and Denborough's identification of 'cools' and 'squares' (cited in Gilbert and Gilbert 1998: 124–9).

These classifications are not exhaustive, and do not relate unproblematically to all or even most school systems. They none the less illustrate the important point that within any educational setting there are multiple ways in which 'being a boy' is understood and performed. This multiplicity, moreover, is not uncontested, for there are differences between what can be defined, in Connell's terms, as hegemonic, subordinate or complicit masculinities; and there are consequences for those boys located within these various frames. Most highly valued are hegemonic versions of masculinity; any performance which, in Connell's (1995: 77) terms, 'embodies the currently accepted answer to the problem of the legitimacy of patriarchy, which guarantees (or is taken to guarantee) the dominant position of men and the subordination of women.' Hegemonic masculinity, then, is the most culturally powerful image of masculinity in a particular cultural and historical time-space, even if the majority of men may not be easily aligned with that image.

This necessitates acknowledging the existence of what Connell (1995: 79) refers to as complicit masculinities: he argues that 'masculinities constructed in ways that realise the patriarchal dividend, without the tensions or risks of being the frontline troops of patriarchy, are complicit in this sense.' Kenway (1998: 162) expands on this point to argue that:

> Hegemonic forms of masculinity provide various 'standards' about what it means to be a 'real' man or boy. Many males draw inspiration from the cultural library of resources provided by such standards, although few men can live up to them. Many may try and many may not but either way . . . they benefit.

In contrast to hegemonic masculinity, there exist also a range of subordinate masculinities. These include forms associated with masculine performances that are explicitly devalued. Here, clearly, issues to do with sexuality are significant. In addition to this, those whose performance of masculinity is not convincingly hegemonic risk being aligned with subordinate masculinities. And it is important to acknowledge too that, within subordinate or complicit masculinities, there are further hierarchies, so that some subordinate men are more powerful than others.

Hegemonic, subordinate and complicit masculinities work to naturalize not only masculine behaviour patterns in schools – including those associated with competition, aggression, noisiness, argumentativeness – but also 'masculine' discipline areas. By this we mean that schools have long worked to produce some subject areas as complex, demanding or sophisticated (and more appealing or suited to boys); others as physical, practical and trade-oriented (and thus appealing or suited to boys); and still others as social, 'soft' or domestic (and thus of more relevance for girls). This reflects different cultural expectations about the 'future' for girls and boys and thus the education which they need. As Debra Hayes notes, 'differential provision in education played an important role in preparing girls for domestic duties' (Hayes 2000: 49). Similarly, boys have long been educated within frameworks that imagined particular futures for them: futures that positioned them in 'masculine' trades or professions, that granted them a wife and family to support and that offered them the status that comes from performing as 'real men'.

We are not suggesting that in contemporary schools every boy reads maths or technology as 'masculine', while seeing typing or history as 'feminine'. As Hayes (2000) and others have made clear, however, there are ongoing differences between the ways females and males participate in school curriculum. Many students continue to differentiate between subjects which are 'meant' for boys, and those intended for girls. Davies (1996: 214) captures the spirit underlying this difference when she writes:

> Proper hard, non-subjective subjects like maths, science and technology provide a haven of acceptable (male) knowledges which confirm that true knowledge lies outside oneself and independent of any subjectivities, independent of those emotions which need to be held in check. They are rational, cool, controllable, abstract, distant, and unquestionably hegemonic.

Similarly, traditional literacy practices are associated with behaviours and interests that do not sit easily alongside dominant models of masculinity. Alloway and Gilbert make the point that hegemonic masculinity 'is not done in terms of self-disclosure, introspection, personalised and creative expression, but rather in terms of an outside-of-self, objectified expression' (cited in Gilbert and Gilbert 1998: 214). Skills relating to English and science or maths, therefore, are routinely produced as mutually exclusive. It is an either/or situation within which English is linked to understandings of traditional femininity – or subordinate masculinity – while science and maths are associated with hegemonic and complicit masculinities.

Returning to a theme introduced in Chapter 2, an explicit link exists between identification with hegemonic or complicit masculinity and the rejection of traditional school literacy practices. In a widely cited example, Wayne Martino (1995: 354) quotes a secondary school boy who argues that 'most guys who like English are faggots'. This attitude also helps to explain the fact that boys are still more likely to enrol in scientific or mathematical subjects even if they do not have particular strengths in these areas. This, in turn, helps to account for the lower average performance outcomes among boys than girls within some 'masculine' areas. Girls are more likely to take up a subject only if they think they have skills in that area, whereas boys appear to enrol because of the subject's image, and its importance to them as 'normal' boys.

Within and across schools, therefore, it is possible to identify varieties of masculinity which have varying relationships with traditionally 'masculine' behaviours and subject areas, as well as varying degrees of authority, influence or power. Normative masculinity is often linked to the following kinds of characteristics, spaces or behaviours: intelligence, technology, science, invention, rationality, stoicism, independence, assertiveness, aggression, sporting prowess, the outdoors, confidence, humour, objectivity, activity, money, leadership, toughness, discipline, physicality, competition, argumentativeness, risk taking and so on.

In our own research relating to gender, schooling, literacy and masculinity we have identified a wide range of masculinity varieties, which can be seen as manifestations of some combinations of these behaviours. Some of these masculine varieties are regularly read positively, others are interpreted negatively. For example, the boy who links with technology, science and technology could be read as a techno geek or a techno guru, depending upon the other connections he is able to make. Similarly, a boy who talks back to his teachers could be interpreted as a larrikin or a trouble maker, depending upon the other associations that are made between him and particular characteristics or behaviours. We would argue that it is regularly possible to identify boys in schools who are aligned with the following kinds of labels: techno gurus, techno geeks, stars, fans, larrikins, trouble makers, losers, wimps or heroes. These labels indicate both their relationship to each other – in the form of a complex set of relationships and hierarchies – and their connection with particular characteristics that are commonly linked to boys.

As the labels suggest, therefore, there are 'positive' and 'negative' outcomes associated with various masculine behaviours. For some boys, taking risks, arguing and being competitive can lead them to be seen as heroes. This can result, in turn, in them receiving particular social rewards. For other boys, very similar qualities will see them branded as trouble makers or losers. This reminds us that all manifestations of masculinity are produced and interpreted in specific contexts, and that the same behaviour, performed by a different body, may be read and valued in different ways.

For example, while academic ability may be valued in an overall school context, only some boys can carry off performances of academic excellence without being branded as a 'nerd' or a 'geek'. Some boys who display technological expertise will be seen as 'techno-gurus' while others will be branded 'tech-less'. This points to the fundamental interconnectedness of the various masculine behaviours: for the boy who is technologically competent, as well as active, aggressive, popular, 'attractive' and so on, will command a different kind of respect from the technologically competent boy who 'looks different' and has few other cultural resource to draw on.

Underpinning our recognition that there are different ways of 'being a boy', supported or critiqued within school contexts, is the awareness that both the positive and the more negative meanings ascribed to boys who behave in various ways depend upon a differentiation between the masculine and the feminine.

Studies of gender norms – and their production and critique – have long drawn attention to the ways in which women are routinely defined in a binary relationship with men. Pythagoras put forward the following list of opposites (McManaman 2000, n.p.):

limited	unlimited
odd	even
one	plurality
right	left
male	female
resting	moving
straight	curved
light	darkness
good	bad
square	oblong

The ambivalence of Pythagoras was absent when Aristotle expressed an opinion relating to the differences between men and women; a view that echoes in contemporary debates:

Man is full in movement, creative in politics, business and culture.
Woman, on the other hand, is passive. She stays at home, as is her
nature. She is matter waiting to be formed by the active male principle
. . . Man consequently plays a major part in reproduction; the woman
is merely the passive incubator of his seed.

(Cited in Lindsey 1994: 85)

Within this Aristotelian and fundamentally patriarchal framework, therefore,
men are read as active, women are read as passive. Where men are rational,
women are emotional. The list goes on: culture/nature; public/private. Such
has been the legacy of the ways of thinking represented by Pythagoras and
Aristotle throughout the history of the European tradition that cultural constructions relating to masculinity continue to differentiate men from women,
boys from girls. Boys are more likely to be devalued if they deviate from
traditional models of masculinity towards more 'feminine' behaviours or
interests. As Connell (1995: 68) reminds us, ' "Masculinity" does not exist
except in contrast with "femininity".' As we noted above, one of the worst
fates for a boy in school is to be labelled with the insulting descriptor 'girl'.

Moving beyond traditional gender norms, therefore, is a real risk for
many boys. It exposes them to assumptions about their 'masculinity' and
regularly leads to situations where they are branded as 'sissies', 'wooses',
'poofs', 'faggots', 'queers' and so on. But staying within traditional masculine
norms does not guarantee a happy ending either. Some boys may perform
the 'star' or 'legend' masculinity, and display skills and abilities in science
or technology, on the sporting field or in leadership that are valued explicitly
and implicitly in schools, universities, workplaces and social settings. Others
may enact various 'bad boy' masculinities – for example, as 'larrikins' or
the less institutionally popular yet socially endorsed 'trouble makers'. Which-
ever masculinity boys associate with (and we are conscious here that boys
move in and out of various models of masculinity on a regular basis), the
key concern is that many of the most common masculinities have consequences, and these consequences are not always good. As we discussed in
Chapter 1, this whole book is premised on an appreciation that boys – and
men – are experiencing a range of negative personal, social and professional consequences that can be linked to expectations – of themselves and
others – and evaluations of their manliness.

Normative masculinity has generated boys and men who have taken on
very specific and prescriptive messages about what it means to be a good
bloke. These messages relate not only to subjects studied, exams passed,
sports played, but also to relationships established or destroyed, to self-
esteem and well being, to the futures that the boys can imagine for themselves, their friends and their families.

Furthermore, we argue that traditional models of masculinity – even in
their most valorized versions – do not automatically secure for boys positive

school experiences and desirable post-school lives. For example, while it is routinely acknowledged that schools privilege masculine models of learning, male-centred curricula and male achievements, this uncritical reproduction of various masculinities does not always lead to the traditional patriarchal rewards. Men are no longer guaranteed untroubled careers and schools do not always prepare boys well for contemporary labour market conditions. While boys have traditionally been educated for a range of labouring, trade or professional careers, there are few guarantees now that positions within the blue collar or even trade-based areas are secure. And while the service industry continues to flourish (Edwards and Magarey 1995), girls are more likely than boys to conceptualize a career for themselves within that field.

Personal interactions, too, are changing. Families are no longer organized around traditional patriarchal assumptions, and relationships are no longer conducted on male terms. This is not to suggest that many households do not continue to follow gendered divisions when it comes to labour or household responsibilities. Certainly they do. These patterns, however, are quite commonly called into question, and women are far more likely than ever before to initiate and follow through with divorce.

In short, the data and issues discussed above, associated with declining male confidence, esteem, health, employment, educational attainment and literacy, suggest that traditional patterns of masculinity are not working well. Consequently, those wishing to engage with boys, schooling and literacy are confronted with the challenge of finding pathways out of traditional models, towards new frameworks within which an association between boys and literacy is not seen as unusual, problematic or unnatural.

In relation to the current literacy debate, we suggest the following points.

First, masculinity and femininity have been oppositionally defined within traditional schooling structures. Within these structures subject areas and disciplines have been differentially constructed as masculine or feminine: a construction that reflects the broader based and widespread systems of interpretation that characterize Western patriarchal societies. In accordance with frameworks that interpret men as rational, scientific and logical, subjects like science and mathematics have been coded as masculine, whereas subjects like English, drama and history have been seen as sites for the natural location of the emotional, communicative and interpersonally motivated girl. Similarly, 'hands-on' trade-oriented subjects – graphics, manual arts and so on – have been seen as male, whereas similarly hands-on but 'domestic' subjects, such as home economics or typing, have consistently been read as feminine. These interpretations reflect, of course, the different roles that schools have long been expected to play for boys and girls.

Second, traditional models of masculinity no longer position boys or men well when it comes to accessing, and keeping, jobs or, indeed, relationships.

Even where traditional models of masculinity *do* lead to boys following traditional and valued career pathways – and there are still many boys who enter culturally valued and 'masculine' professions as doctors, lawyers, mechanics, football players and so on – there are other social costs paid by many of these boys, and the people they have relationships with. This is a key point. We are not arguing from the position that we need to restore to boys access to the kinds of resources most valued in Western contexts in order that they may, once again, feel 'equal' (or superior) to girls. We are arguing instead that boys – and girls – have the right to access various cultural resources, and to have their use of these resources read as legitimate and appropriate. To this end, boys need opportunities and space to reflect upon what it means to be a male, and the chance to have multiple masculinities valued and supported.

Third, and most importantly, transformative approaches to boys, school and literacy are fundamentally concerned with critiquing, destabilizing and moving beyond the dominant understandings of femininity and masculinity which inevitably produce and reproduce different – and dangerous – gender patterns. Steve Biddulph (1995a: ix) argues that 'Boys will change when they are helped to understand themselves better, are affirmed and valued "as they are" and are given the tools to feel safe and equal around girls.' We argue that attempting to value boys as they 'are' will work ultimately only to reinscribe limited and limiting conceptions of masculinity. We aim to resist any temptation to revalue 'traditional' boys or to 'masculinize' literacy classrooms or schools and seek, instead, a systemic interrogation of schools, masculinity and literacy. We are committed, particularly, to critiquing the costs for boys, not of the loss of masculine certainty, but of the endurance of normative masculinity. This – as we have already discussed – involves identifying the ways in which gender norms are circulated and naturalized. We are also committed to advancing multiple and diverse masculinities. This involves identifying the ways in which dominant norms can be challenged, transgressed, exceeded and ultimately displaced. By extension, we need the ability to think about boys not as victims of their biology or the passive products of their socialization, but as active individuals who negotiate their sense of self – their subjectivity – at the intersection of multiple and competing discourses.

In the following section we discuss the ways in which we conceptualize this process of both critiquing and departing from gender norms and their associated social and cultural limitations. We aim to build on a transformative mindset with respect to gender reform in schools in order to develop an overarching framework. This framework will help us to state our concerns about schools, boys and masculinity. It will also provide a vocabulary for articulating our goals, visions and beliefs about the future as far as gender reform, boys and literacy are concerned.

Practical theory and theorized practice

This section outlines three practical theoretical resources that provide the basis from which we will discuss the design and delivery of gender-based literacy reform.

Multiple mes: subjectivity, discourse and gendered performance

To work within a transformative framework it is necessary first to acknowledge that there are multiple ways of being a boy. It is also necessary to recognize that every individual boy accesses, performs and transforms multiple versions of masculinity in various contexts or at various times.

Boys, like girls, are exposed to a range of influences, a range of social institutions and a range of discourses which tell them what it means to be a good, natural, normal little boy. These discourses have different kinds of power at different stages in a kid's life. Early on, a child's world may well revolve around his or her parents. Nothing is as normal as what mummy or daddy (who whoever the relevant kin or caregivers are) do. But it isn't very long before kids start making regular contact with people outside the family. There are friends, neighbours, play groups and kindergartens. Soon there are pre-schools and primary schools. And there is the wonderful world of television, video games and computers that kids interact with for longer and longer, at younger and younger ages.

Just as the family (whatever form it takes) is a powerful force in the life of kids, so, too, are these other social institutions. For any little boy, making sense of the world around him involves making sense of his *role* in the world: what he needs to do to belong, what he needs to do to be accepted, what he needs to do to be rewarded. Regardless of whether or not boys conform to these cultural norms, they *are* negotiating them: to reject, accept or locate themselves in some middle ground boys develop not a fixed identity but a fluid, changed and changing sense of self. Or, to put it another way, boys – from a very young age – are involved in negotiating a subject position or their *subjectivity*.

Subjectivity refers to our sense of ourselves, our sense of who we are. It is based on the recognition that there is more than one possible self for all of us. Glenda MacNaughton (2000: 97) describes subjectivity – from a post-structuralist perspective – as 'our ways of knowing (emotionally and intellectually about ourselves-in-our-world. It describes who we are and how we understand ourselves, consciously and unconsciously.' Importantly, subjectivity is neither fixed nor determined at birth. Rather, it is fluid and changing from time to time, context to context. Gender is not written on to passive bodies by active 'society'. Instead, individuals negotiate cultural understandings about femininity and masculinity, in shaping and reshaping their own sense of themselves (Wearing 1996: 38).

These cultural understandings about gender are sustained by 'discursive practices'. Post-structuralism has drawn attention to the role of language constructing gender and gender norms (Wearing 1996). Discourses, however, relate not only to language, but also to a full range of social practices that reflect and are produced by sets of beliefs, assumptions and theories about how social worlds are 'meant' to operate. Discourses are largely the product of belief systems and, in day-to-day enactment, they help also to reproduce, and naturalize, these systems of belief. MacNaughton (2000: 50) argues that discourses around gender involve more than the language we use to speak about men, women, masculinity or femininity. They also involve:

- the social practices that constitute masculinity and femininity in our society, such as dressing, acting, thinking, feeling and being;
- the emotional investments people make in their gender;
- the social practices and structures that are organized on the basis of gender, such as family, work, religion, sexuality, education and law.

Hence, hegemonic discourses of masculinity in school comprise both the language used to speak about or to boys and the overt ways in which boys are rewarded or censored, the spaces boys are expected or encouraged to be, the way they walk, the nuances in their speech, their non-verbal language, their clothing, their assumptions about others, their relationships and so on. These discourses around masculinity reflect beliefs about the 'nature' of boys, as well as concerns about what is *not* appropriate for boys.

A post-structuralist position draws attention to these various discourses, the oppositions they sustain and their links to an individual's subjectivity or status as a speaking subject. The differences between this approach and a more essentialist framework which seeks to insist upon a biologically produced and essentially fixed subject position is made clear by Davies:

> Poststructuralist theory thus opens up the possibility of seeing the self as continually constituted through multiple and contradictory discourses that one takes up as one's own in becoming a *speaking subject*. One can develop strategies for maintaining an illusion of a coherent unitary self through such strategies as talking of roles or through denial of contradiction, or one can examine the very processes and discourses through which the constitution of self takes place.
>
> (Davies 1992: 57)

Patrick Hopkins demonstrates the ways in which a post-structuralist perspective can be used to highlight contradictions, which he identifies as the ways in which dominant discourses of masculinity work to construct the idea of 'masculinity' as natural, but also as performance which can 'go wrong', if boys aren't careful.

Essence: You (the little boy) have a natural, core, normal, good, essential identity; you are a *boy*, a *young man*, male, not-a-girl. This is just what you are. You were born this way. Little girls will like you. You have buddies. You're lucky. You are our *son*. It's natural and obvious that you will grow up and get married and be a *daddy*.

Performance: But even though you just *are* a little boy, even though it's perfectly natural, you must make sure you do not act (how? why?) like a girl. You must always make sure that you exhibit the right behaviour for a boy (but isn't it natural?). Don't ever act like not-a-boy! Don't betray that which you are naturally, comfortably, normally. Don't not-be what you are. Perform like a man.

(Hopkins 2000: 137–8)

In this passage Hopkins highlights two dimensions of post-structural perspectives on masculinity. First, there is always more than one possible way of being a boy – there are always multiple 'mes' (Moore 2000). These options are not, however, presented in a value-free context. Rather, each is located within a wider social and discursive framework that attaches differential value to various performances. Individual boys, therefore, negotiate various understandings about what it means to be a 'good' or 'natural' boy and may, as a result, perform quite different versions of masculinity when they are with their mother, with their father, with a friend, with a sports coach and so on.

This poses a challenge to the determinist idea that girls and boys have in-built gendered identities that predispose them to act like our stereotypical images of boys or girls. It also lets us acknowledge that, while each one of us has more than one potential self, how we actually *do* define ourselves (and how we act and interact) often reflects dominant cultural understandings about what it means to be a boy or a girl. So instead of us seeing 'boy' and 'girl' as simple, discrete categories, we can see various cultural versions of 'boy' and 'girl' that people may align themselves with in negotiating their own sense of self, their own subjectivity.

This position has some practical implications. Adopting the idea that gender – masculinity – is produced, and not natural, that it is performed and not determined, and that it is multiple and not singular, allows us to make some important moves.

- It allows us to recognize that there is more than one way of 'being a boy' and that not all boys experience literacy – or the current literacy crisis – in the same way.
- It encourages us to look at the ways in which some versions of masculinity may endorse greater connection between masculinity and literacy than others.
- It reminds us that the various ways of 'being a boy' which position literacy and masculinity in opposition to each other are no more natural

or permanent than any other form of masculinity. This means it is almost impossible to base a gender reform programme on any notion that there is an 'essential' male identity. Instead, we need ways of thinking about gender that allow us to recognize and respond to both existing and potential differences between and within boys.

• It emphasizes the fact that while various agents of socialization have a powerful impact upon the way individuals and groups of boys view themselves and their understanding about what it means to be a boy, they are not necessarily passive recipients of these socializing messages. Boys, instead, are able to negotiate and resist even the most powerful socializing agents and to align themselves with marginal, rather than hegemonic, forms of masculinity.

This means we can begin to imagine new – *and literate* – performances of masculinity.

This is both a theoretically and a practically significant point. If we view biology as destiny, or if we see socialization as an all-powerful force, then there is very little that we, as educators, can do to challenge or transform understandings of masculinity held by individuals or groups of boys, for our work will always be 'undone' by other, more powerful, socializing forces. In this scenario, all we can do is 'fit in' with what would be seen as natural or inevitable versions of masculinity and make do. Similarly, if we seek to produce *one* model of masculinity within which all boys will access and enjoy literacy education in the same way, we are surely doomed to failure. If, however, we view gender as something that is produced and negotiated, and if we acknowledge that there are multiple ways in which boys can identify with and depart from gender norms, then there is endless potential for us to disrupt dominant, narrow and limiting versions of masculinity and to circulate, validate and celebrate alternative ways of being a boy. Instead of making do, we can participate in the process of constructing and circulating new masculinities.

It ain't necessarily so: from traditional narratives to counternarratives

To begin to move beyond the limitations of hegemonic versions of masculinity we need to experiment with ways of making connections between traditionally masculine and traditionally feminine characteristics. Unfortunately, when we face a crisis, such as the one which has sprung up around boys and literacy, there is a lot of pressure which makes us say let's get to know boys better and then bring literacy into this 'masculine world'. This leads us to identify the things that are traditionally associated with boys, and to try to use those to get boys into literacy or the humanities. This is the classic essentialist pattern: looking for the essence of boys so that we may 'masculinize' literacy or humanities or schooling.

If, however, we keeping looking *inwards* to this same set of characteristics in order to come up with a solution to the 'problems' produced by traditional discourses around masculinity, we run the risk of *reproducing* rather than *critiquing* those discourses that produce the problem. From a transformative perspective, we need skills for moving outside the limitations of traditional discourses around masculinity. We need the ability to make connections between ideas and people that are usually kept apart. We need to be able to imagine the new: new possibilities, new masculinities, new ways of being and performing as a 'boy'.

This is not to say that we want to devalue or do away with the association between, for example, sport and masculinity. It means, instead, that we recognize the danger of allowing *all* our activities to be confined to this set of possibilities. If we do allow this we are effectively helping to stabilize the traditions at the heart of the problem. Consequently, we need to look at other ways of being in the world – emotions, activities, places where boys are not expected to be, not expected to excel, which they are not expected to desire or enjoy – and to work towards making connections between these spaces and traditionally masculine places.

We are, then, challenged to look for new configurations of masculinity: new masculinities; transformative masculinities that render the divisions between different 'types' of boys, as well as the divisions between boys and girls, problematic, and which endorse and celebrate complex, contradictory and changing ways of being a man. Feminist research focusing on the productive value of alternative representations of girls or women has introduced a number of terms to capture the political and personal significance of new images or being a woman: what Donna Haraway described as new figurations. The importance of these figurations is captured by Rosi Braidotti (1994b: 181), who writes: 'Figurations are not pretty metaphors: They are politically informed maps, which play a crucial role . . . in that they aim at redesigning female subjectivity'; a point also explored in detail by Hills (1998b: 125–35).

A famous example of such a new figuration – an image of female subjectivity that moves beyond and works against gendered discourses – is Haraway's (1985, 1991) cyborg. Braidotti offers the term 'post-"Woman" women' to capture the image of female subjectivities operating against normative and restrictive images of 'Woman'. Identifying multiple figurations – 'political fictions' (Braidotti 1994b: 181) – of 'woman' has been the project of a great many feminists. Only recently, however, has attention been turned to the importance – indeed, the possibility – of conceptualizing equally transformative figurations of masculinity and 'man'. This is not surprising, of course. Traditional discourses around 'being a man' are extremely powerful as a result of how they are connected to key social institutions and discourses. They also come with a range of rewards, even though some men have easier access to these reward systems than others. While a reconceptualization of what it means to be a 'woman' is easily motivated by a desire to link women to the kinds of places, resources and experiences that have been previously coded as 'masculine' and understood as 'valued', it is harder to reverse the logic and argue that men will benefit if they are linked to that which is dominantly understood as 'feminine'.

This transformative logic, however, has the greatest potential to lead schools – and boys *and* girls – beyond the limitations of dominant gender discourses. From our point of view, gender-based literacy reform in schools is fundamentally about the creation, circulation and celebration of stories that run counter to traditional narratives about gender. If left uncontested, traditional narratives will continue to possess a factual air. As Judith Butler (1990: 139) writes:

> Gender is . . . a construction that regularly conceals its genesis; the tacit collective agreement to perform, produce, and sustain discrete and polar genders as cultural fictions is obscured by the credibility of those productions and the punishments that attend not agreeing to believe in them; the construction 'compels' our belief in its necessity and naturalness.

Teachers concerned with moving beyond the limitations of these cultural fictions are fundamentally involved, therefore, in the production of stories that run counter to normative understandings of masculinity. This can be understood as the process of constructing, circulating and legitimating *counternarratives*. The term 'counternarrative' has been used by feminist theorists bell hooks and Trinh Minh-ha, among others. They define counternarratives as stories, histories or representations that stand in opposition to and, as such, implicitly critique the legitimacy of mainstream texts (hooks 1990; Trinh Minh-ha 1990). Counternarratives about women, in other words, provide alternatives to authorized, mainstream, normative enactments of 'womanhood' and work to disrupt the culturally dominant understandings of what a 'good' or 'natural' woman is or does. They provide, instead, evidence of women's multiplicity, diversity and power.

Similarly, counternarratives about men can work to provide alternative understandings about the multiple ways of being a man. Importantly, counternarratives are not necessarily radical departures from everything that boys know, but work to create links between the traditional and the alternative, between the familiar and the new.

Michael Peters and Colin Lankshear (1996: 2) emphasize this link between the traditional and the new in their work on counternarratives. They distinguish between two dimensions of counternarratives: one that functions generally as a critique of 'the modernist predilection for "grand", "master" and "meta" narratives', and the other which counters legitimating narratives that still shape our lives and actions. Their championing of this second 'sense' of counternarratives is worth quoting at length:

> Even in a postmodern age, where citizens retain some sense of the critical exhibiting an 'incredulity towards metanarratives', there remain

'official' narratives, whether grand or otherwise. Counternarratives, then, in [the] second sense counter not merely (or even necessarily) the grand narratives, but also (or instead) the *'official'* and *'hegemonic'* narratives of everyday life: those legitimating stories propagated for specific political purposes to manipulate public consciousness by heralding a national set of common cultural ideals. The notion of counternarratives in this sense carries with it Foucault's 'counter-memory' and the idea of counter-practices, but in a specific and local sense.

(Peters and Lankshear 1996: 2; emphasis in original)

Some theorists regard postmodernism and its associated counternarratives as a complete and radical break from modernism (for example, Lyotard 1984) whereas others – like Peters and Lankshear – argue that postmodernism is characterized by *flows* within various 'scapes' (e.g. the flow of images and ideas in mediascapes, the flow of tourists, immigrants, refugees, exiles etc. in ethnoscapes), and that much of the modern can still be identified within these flows.

Similarly, when we speak about the kinds of counternarratives that can characterize attempts to broaden out conceptions of masculinity, we are thinking of stories that may connect the old with the new – the traditionally masculine with the traditionally not-masculine – in a process that begins with the familiar and stretches out to the new.

In conceptualizing this process – or what counternarratives about masculinity, for example, might look like, we have found the image of the rhizome. This image was put forward within a particular theoretical framework outlined by Gilles Deleuze and Felix Guattari in 1987, and has been used in a range of contexts since that time (for explication see Hills 1998a). While we have no space here to enter into detailed discussions of the Deleuzian framework, the image of the rhizome is nevertheless extremely helpful for thinking through issues associated with gender-based literacy reform. Rhizomes are parts of plants that grow sideways through the ground. Ginger root is a good example of a rhizome. In contrast to rhizomes there are arboreal structures or, simply put, trees. While the rhizome reaches out, and travels away from where it starts, the tree, for the most part, stays put, growing bigger and stronger, but not travelling very far. The distinction is not hard and fast and there are some exceptions but the notions of rhizomatic or arboreal structures is useful for thinking about different approaches to gender. Let's consider this in more detail.

I'd rather be a rhizome than a tree: beyond normative masculinity

We can see all of the traditional understandings about what it means to be a guy as part of an arboreal, tree-like structure. Year after year the tree has new layers added to it and each new layer reinforces the idea that boys are rational, aggressive, independent, scientific and so on. Eventually the tree becomes so large and so strong that it is almost impossible to imagine trying to move it. Indeed, it can seem almost criminal to think about doing so. The tree becomes an object of beauty, and the 'good bloke' becomes an object of cultural admiration.

Many discussions around boys, boys in schools and boys and literacy in schools work arboreally. They add another layer to existing core knowledge about what it means to be a 'real boy' and do absolutely nothing to tackle the limitations associated with this discourse. At the risk of pushing this metaphor too far, it might be worth remembering that it is often the biggest, strongest and most established looking tree that suffers the most in turbulent conditions. And the 1990s and beyond have brought significant troubled times for men.

In contrast to the patterns of thought that add layer after layer on to our tree there are rhizomatic ways of thinking. Grass, for example, grows sideways rather than up, and is hard to confine to any one location. It moves outwards and beyond the limitations of a specific place. The rhizome makes connections across territories and thus joins together areas which may otherwise be considered distant or distinct.

Thinking rhizomatically about gender generally and masculinity specifically encourages us to identify the existence of arboreal like, dominant forms of masculinity or femininity, and then to think of ways in which we can make connections between so-called masculine and feminine characteristics, spaces and interests.

A transformative agenda

Bringing the concepts of multiple subjectivity, counternarratives and rhizomatic thinking together gives us a basis for thinking about the relationship between gender reform and literacy. We recognize the political importance of stories, histories and representations that stand in opposition to and, as such, implicitly critique the legitimacy of mainstream stories about such things as gender, race or class. And we embrace the possibility of making connections between ideas, people and places that are commonly kept apart. Bronwyn Davies provides support for this position with her idea that 'poststructuralism opens the possibility of encompassing the apparently contradictory with ease – even, on occasion, with pleasure' (Davies 1992). We see our task here as one of working to identify, create, circulate and legitimate new stories around boys, girls, literacy and school.

A vast range of strategies fit within this framework, some of which we explore in subsequent chapters through a series of counternarratives. These counternarratives make connections between traditional masculine *and* feminine characteristics and spaces. This can involve making connections that

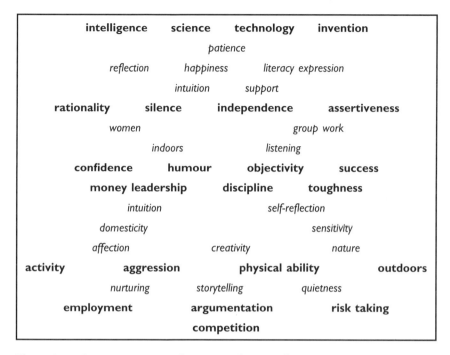

Figure 3.1 Counternarratives about masculinity make connections among and between any of these terms

are familiar in the boys' education context – between boys, science and technology, for example – while also making connections between science, technology, boys, self-reflection, creativity and so on. In other words, all those traditionally 'masculine' characteristics (shown in Figure 3.1 in bold) need to be mixed or linked or connected to other more traditionally 'feminine' characteristics (shown in Figure 3.1 in italics). The characteristics or behaviours shown in Figure 3.1 are not depicted in a specific order, or in a representational hierarchy; taken together, the figure includes some of the diverse ideas that have traditionally been associated with the masculine and the feminine. Counter-narratives resist the distinction between masculine and feminine spaces and seek to combine commonly distinct fields and to cross boundaries into new transformative spaces.

When we talk about rhizomatic connections or counternarratives, then, we are imagining practices which make links between the masculine and the feminine: practices which encourage, for example, boys to combine humour and assertiveness with reflection and creativity; or the outdoors with group work and self-expression.

In the following chapters we explore a range of ways in which literacy practices have aimed to meet the contemporary and future needs of boys.

We explore the extent to which these function as traditional narratives or counternarratives. We consider the ways they can or do work rhizomatically, and the potential literacy practices have for opening up, expanding and transforming our conceptions of masculinity, while working to support, endorse and celebrate multiple figurations of the feminine. Before taking up these tasks, however, we need to clarify our view of literacy. Chapter 4 reviews a range of literacy mindsets and advances a literacy framework tailored to the approach to gender reform we have been developing.

chapter four

Mindsets matter: an overview of major literacy worldviews

Most of the 'deficit' and 'essentialist' arguments outlined in Chapter 1 have been so widely circulated that they have had a disproportionate, and at times dangerous, impact upon the ways in which literacy intervention strategies have been designed and implemented in classrooms. Indeed, if we look closely at the debates surrounding boys and literacy discussed in the previous chapters, we can see a number of well defined worldviews or mindsets underpinning each. Thinking about the various boys and literacy positions and arguments in terms of mindsets enables us to identify those ways of thinking that do not attempt to essentialize boys' (or girls') literacy practices and propensities, that do not set up false 'gender competitions' between girls and boys (and men and women) in term of literacy achievement in school and that are most productive in constructing transformative approaches to literacy education for all students.

This chapter is organized in two sections. The first focuses specifically on literacy mindsets in order to argue for a particular worldview that is consonant with the transformative approach to gender reform we argued for in the previous chapters. In the second section we bring together our position on gender reform – a transformative mindset – and our position on literacy – a new literacies studies mindset. This pairing is argued for, and used to frame the remaining chapters in this book.

'See Dick. See Jane. Run Dick, run': literacy mindsets at work in the boys and literacy debates

As used here, the term 'mindset' refers to the 'world view' or the 'lenses' with which an individual makes sense of a particular issue or context. To be able to move the boys/literacy debate in a productive direction we need to be aware of the major (and often competing) mindsets relating to the nature and purposes of literacy in schools. To explore the boys and literacy debate it is helpful to consider the current literacy scenes in Australasia, Britain and North America in the light of a complex web of current and resurrected mindsets evident in education policy, everyday 'common sense', literacy theory and educational research. These include, but are not exhausted by, the following:

- The 'old' basics.
- The 'new basics': applied language, problem solving and critical thinking.
- 'Elite literacies': higher-order scientific, technological and symbolic literacies.
- Emotional literacy: learning to read and talk about feelings.
- Technological literacies: operational understandings of technology.
- Critical literacies: critiquing power relations through language.
- 'The new literacy studies' and the study of new literacies.

Each of these mindsets is discussed in turn below.

The 'old' basics

Constructions of the 'old' basics in schools frame literacy in terms of mastering the building blocks of code breaking: knowing the alphabetic script visually and phonetically, grasping the mechanism of putting elements of the script together to encode or decode words and separating words or adding them together to read and write sentences. Literacy conceived as mastery of the fundamentals of encoding and decoding print texts (including elementary math operations) has an interesting status within education at present. On the one hand, it is believed that survival-level reading and writing competencies are no longer enough for effective participation in the economic and social mainstream (NCEE 1983: 14; Reich 1992). Paradoxically, on the other hand it is acknowledged emphatically that integration into public life demands, minimally, the ability to decode and negotiate texts encountered in the course of everyday routines.

Ironically, however, the emphasis in national policy statements around the world appears to be on a skills-based notion that breaks literacy down into specific components: reading, writing, spelling, speaking and listening. This is evident, for example, in the wording of the national literacy goals of various countries:

- 'Commonwealth, State and Territory Education Ministers [of Australia] have agreed to a national literacy and numeracy goal: That every child leaving primary school should be numerate, and able to read, write, and spell at an appropriate level' (DEETYA 1998: 1).
- 'By 2005 every child turning nine will be able to read and write, and do maths for success' (Ministry of Education, New Zealand 1998: 1).

- The first general requirement of English in the National Curriculum, United Kingdom, states: 'English should develop pupils' abilities to communicate effectively in speech and writing and to listen with understanding. It should also enable them to be enthusiastic, responsive and knowledgeable readers' (DfEE 1996: 1).
- The US Department of Education and President Clinton set seven priorities for education. The first of these is that students will be able to 'Read independently by the end of the third grade'. Some policy documents add 'read *independently and well*' to this priority (US Department of Education 1997: 1; original emphasis).

The figures regarding boys and literacy presented in the previous chapters are part of a more general 'literacy crisis' hysteria at present sweeping over-developed countries (see Freebody and Welch 1993). This is not to say that the boys and literacy test results from around the country are being ignored – far from it. They have simply added fuel to the fire of governments' zeal to 'get kids literate', which in many cases has meant a 'back to the old basics' push. And much of the old basics has translated into national testing and standards-setting against which all students are measured, and by which 'winners' and 'losers' are identified absolutely. For example, key strategic components of the recently developed National Plan for Literacy in Australian schools include: assessment of all students by teachers as early as possible in their schooling; early intervention strategies for learners assessed as having difficulty with literacy learning; development of literacy 'benchmarks'; progress toward reporting student and school achievement against the benchmarks (DEETYA 1998: 10). This policy and its accompanying suggestions for literacy education practices replicate procedures and trends already well established in Britain and many of the North American states.

Literacy is framed here as 'basic literacy competence' construed as mastery of generalizable techniques and concepts that are presumed to be *building blocks for subsequent education*. Within the 'old basics' mindset, then, literacy is defined in terms of decontextualized decoding tools that serve as means for accessing subsequent content and more complex literacy skills. This conception of literacy has interesting – if not worrisome – effects on remedial literacy education, whose main recipients have long been boys (Gilbert and Rowe 1989; Alloway and Gilbert 1997; Pollack 1998).

Working with an 'old basics' mindset means that approaches to remedial literacy work for school students focus heavily on phonemic processing, accuracy and self-correction in reading aloud exercises, and on correct spelling in written work. Advocates of a return to the basics typically recommend that remedial learners be subjected to batteries of word recognition and dictation activities and tests, as well as to letter and phoneme identification and book concept exercises, claiming that reading success relies heavily if not exclusively on mastering phonological processing. Teachers or tutors are expected to maintain accurate and detailed records for diagnosis, validation, accountability and reporting purposes.

The issue with the 'old basics' is that literacy involves very much more than simply being able to encode and decode alphabetic script. Testing students by means of pencil and paper reading and writing exams often fails to measure what students actually *can* do in terms of literacy. Many educators know of boys who are failing at school literacy, but who can strip and rebuild a motorbike with the help of a thick, written manual (Rowan *et al.* 2000); or as in the case of Jacques, a 13-year-old boy who had a history of school literacy failure but who produced a sophisticated flier advertising his new mowing business and who rapidly developed a thriving business (Knobel 1999); or the case of inner-city African American youths who have long had a history of literacy failure in school but who outside school write mature and eloquent poems and rap chants (Mahiri and Sablo 1996; Mahiri 1997). These examples suggest that remedial education in particular and perhaps literacy education in school in general is doing more harm than good in terms of constructing 'literates' and 'illiterates'.

In many ways the old basics mindset may actually contribute to boys' seemingly dismal performance in literacy and English classes. The piecemeal approach to teaching reading and writing underpinning this mindset, and its accompanying pedagogical strategies that rely heavily on decontextualized and repetitive practice, can serve to alienate boys who are not motivated by a desire to 'please the teacher' (as are many girls; Walkerdine 1990), or who are not already able to read before they reach school. The 'old basics' mindset is a far cry from being a transformative approach to boys and their current literacy crisis.

The 'new basics': applied language, problem solving and critical thinking

The 'new basics' pick up on the widely acknowledged fact that 'old' basics are no longer sufficient for effective participation in modern societies (A. Luke 1993; Lankshear 1997; OECD 1998a, b). Alleged qualitative shifts in social practices are variously associated with the transition from an agro-industrial economy to a post-industrial information/services economy; from 'Fordism' to 'post-Fordism'; from more personal face-to-face communities to impersonal metropolitan and, even, virtual communities; from a paternal (welfare) state to a more devolved state requiring greater self-sufficiency; and so on. These are seen to call for more sophisticated (smart), abstract, symbolic-logical capacities than in the past. Some see this in terms of a generalized shift towards a more 'meta-level' way of operating, which they talk about in terms of higher-order thinking skills as the norm (e.g. 'critical thinking'). Within this context, it is argued, 'old' approaches to teaching reading and writing and spelling need to be brought into line with current times.

This mindset argues that for almost two decades schools have been over-emphasizing such rudiments as reading and numerical computation at the expense of other essential skills, like comprehension, analysis, solving problems and drawing conclusions (e.g. NCEE 1983; DEET 1991a, b). 'Critical thinking' is often used in this sense as a grab bag for metacognitive skills like comprehension, problem solving and analysis, and conjoined with reading, writing, speaking, listening – or, in short, 'communications' – to encapsulate the 'new basic literacy' (see Maxson and Hair 1990; Brandon 1998).

For example, Australia's language policy throughout much of the 1990s – *Australia's Language: The Australian Language and Literacy Policy* (DEET 1991a, b) – identified its primary objective as working to ensure that all Australians 'develop and maintain effective literacy in English to enable them to participate in Australian society' (DEET 1991a: 4). Effective literacy was defined as 'intrinsically purposeful, flexible and dynamic and involves the integration of speaking, listening, and critical thinking with reading and writing.' It 'continues to develop throughout an individual's lifetime', with 'the support of education and training programs' (DEET 1991a: 5, 9).

In terms of schooling, the 'new basics' have generated a range of programmes and approaches to literacy, such as the Learning to Learn through Reading movement in Australia, Brain Gym or Brain Dancing teacher handbooks, imagery training, Learning and Study Inventories and reciprocal teaching strategies in the USA, the Somerset Thinking Skills Course or Philosophy for Children programmes in England and Wales, and the Activating Children's Thinking Skills (ACT) project in Northern Ireland, among countless others. These approaches focus on enabling students to become reflexive and reflective in their thinking and – in particular – in their thinking about their reading and writing (Brown and Palinscar 1982; Bondy 1984; Anstey 1998). Key strategies include direct teaching, where the teacher makes some aspect of, say, reading or writing explicit to students by means of teaching them explicit text strategies, such as compare and contrast, list and describe, cause and effect. Explicit teaching also means showing students how to make use of a range of 'higher order' thinking strategies, such as analysing, synthesizing, extrapolating and evaluating. Strategies also include providing students with meta-level 'supports', such as prior knowledge charts, concept maps and advance organizer diagrams (see Turner 1992; Creenaune and Rowles 1996).

Although the new basics mindset certainly embraces a wider conception of literacy than its old basics predecessor, it remains at heart a predominantly *psychological* conception of effective literacy. As such it does not aim to contribute to social transformation, but focuses instead on the individual as a thinking and learning being. This mindset does not entertain the possibility of changing or even challenging school literacy or English content, concentrating instead on how to improve students' cognitive performance within existing subject boundaries and definitions of literacy.

Very often in classrooms, it seems that these strategies and supports become ends in themselves. Nicholas, a 12-year-old boy in primary school in Brisbane, illustrates this point well. Nicholas knows full well that his teacher wants the class to develop analytical composition skills needed in high school, as demonstrated by regular lessons that focus on identifying the main ideas in paragraphs, summarizing passages of text and the like (see Knobel 1999). However, Nicholas is also keenly aware that the criteria set for his latest assignment were drawn directly from the class textbook on government in Queensland: 'I've got what he's done, he's just copied [the criteria] out of this book. See look, "Making Laws" and he's just put it all together.' Judging from comments Nicholas made to his mother when they began discussing his written text to date, Nicholas appeared to have interpreted the task as a large 'cloze exercise' whereby he was required simply to fill in text beneath his teacher's criteria-as-headings until the set word limit was reached. Indeed, at this stage of his assignment he seems more interested in constructing a glossary (his own idea) than in engaging with the concepts of government in Queensland.

'Elite literacies'

Reform proposals based on 'education for excellence' affirm that post-elementary education must emphasize *academic* learning and pursue greatly increased academic subject standards (Toch 1991: 1; see also OECD 1998b). The key notion underlying this mindset is that high impact innovation comes from applications of theoretical knowledge. Claims like the following, advanced in UK reform proposals, are common throughout (post)industrialized countries:

> Competitive pressures are intensifying. Ours is an increasingly complex and technologically driven world. As a country we need the effort and skill of all our people to compete and succeed. The sheer pace of change is adding to the pressures. In today's job market, people have to constantly adapt – train and re-train – to stay ahead. Those who lack the skills to do so – those who, through lack of a basic education, are not even on the first rung of the training ladder – will become increasingly vulnerable.
>
> (Blunkett 1999a: 2)

'Elite literacies' comprise high-level mastery of subject or discipline literacies, understood in terms of their respective 'languages' and 'literatures' (Hirst 1974). The *language* of an academic subject/discipline is basically the 'logic' and process of inquiry within that field. The *literature* of a subject/discipline consists of the accumulated attainments of people working in the field, who have brought its language to bear on its existing literature in order to extend knowledge, understanding, theory and applications within everyday life.

Elite literacies have played a major, albeit supporting, role in many of the gender reform movements applied to education in the past twenty years. As analysed in Chapter 2, liberal/equal opportunity approaches to gender reform have critiqued the relative absence of girls from elite literacies such as advanced mathematics, chemistry, physics, computer science and geometry. None the less, elite literacies are not grounded in a concern for challenging normative gender roles – just the opposite in fact. Arguments raised in response to initiatives that encourage girls to become fluent in an elite literacy often include biological determinism in the form of girls' lack of ability to be rational, to think logically and to be unemotional and object-ive. As two examples among many, both Allucqure Stone (1996) and Ellen Ullman (1997) have sobering stories to tell about women working in the field of computer programming and the initiations, harassment and deni-gration they receive from males (see Chapter 6 below).

Of course, this kind of treatment is not the sole purview of women and girls – boys, too, are given a hard time by peers if they happen to prefer writing stories for English classes to setting up genetics experiments with *Drosophila melanogaster* for biology classes or to spending hours of after-school time coding a complex computer program. As we argued in Chapter 2, simply getting girls to enrol in the 'elite literacies' is not enough in terms of them being accepted as being full and fluent practitioners of these literacies or, indeed, in terms of changing the gender 'make-up' of elite literacies.

Emotional literacy: learning to read and talk about feelings

A concern with emotional literacy does not yet pervade public and educa-tion policy documents. In recent years, however, a large literature has emerged around the concept. Educators and commentators have attempted to provide insights into the nebulous processes of 'character education', 'self-regulation' and, more recently, the more serious issues of suicide, bullying at school, violence in schools and in workplaces and domestic violence. Increasingly, in fact, emotional literacy is taking centre stage in school-based discussions of 'managing' or 'rescuing' boys (Pollack 1998; Taylor and Larson 1999; Kindlon and Thompson 2000).

The person most closely identified with drawing attention to emotional literacy is Howard Gardner (e.g. 1983, 1989, 1994), whose theory of intelligences includes interpersonal and intrapersonal intelligences. These constructs have been developed by others as 'emotional literacy'. This has come to mean 'having the skills to understand and manage emotions, to communicate effectively, and to become an autonomous person' (Bocchino 1999: 1).

Most educators and education-related commentators view emotional literacy pragmatically and attribute to it such dispositions and capacities as the following: life skills, self-direction, reflection, respecting others' feelings and perspectives, developing healthy personal relationships, avoiding dangerous situations and relationships, accepting responsibility for own actions, being able to work cooperatively, controlling impulsive behaviour, the accurate appraisal of emotion in self and others, and mood self-maintenance. However, just as many others imbue emotional literacy with deeper meanings – and more troubling outcomes for boys if they do not become emotionally literate. Howard Taylor and Susan Larson (1999: 331), for example, claim that

> Without social and emotional competence, students lack the skills to manage life tasks such as working cooperatively, solving everyday problems, and controlling impulsive behavior . . . Additionally, without being able to identify and manage their emotions effectively, students are vulnerable to 'emotional hijackings' (Goleman 1995), that is, being unable to think clearly because they are emotionally overwhelmed.

Even worse things wait in the wings for children struggling with emotional problems. Linda Ryan (1999) summarizes a 1999 Mental Health Foundation report in England which found:

> around one in five children and teenagers suffers mental health problems. Children experiencing increased stress at home and at school are manifesting anxiety, disruptive behaviour, attention deficit, developmental disorders, bed-wetting and substance misuse. Attempted suicides are said to be on the increase among teenagers. The report, entitled 'Bright futures', claims that children are failing to thrive emotionally, and suggests that we all face a grim future unless they are taught the skills of 'emotional literacy'.

Less apocalyptic, but none the less serious, is the issue flagged earlier in this chapter in relation to the old literacy basics: namely, the 'emotional element of literacy' and how many lads will do anything in their power to avoid having to write or read about feelings (Buckingham 1999: 6). Wayne Martino argues that the macho culture in schools also means that boys avoid anything even remotely to do with self-expression or emotions – especially those encountered in the 'dangerous' intimacy of literacy lessons or English classrooms (Martino 1998).

Many educators hold fast to emotional literacy education as a panacea (or talisman) for most of the social ills troubling boys and young men; however, more often than not, emotional literacy has been used to reinforce hegemonic stereotypes and to promote white middle-class values. Examples include claims that:

- Asian students' 'emotional trait' or enthusiasm and persistence leads to 'the superior' academic success of these students (Goleman 1995);
- students who are able to self-regulate from an early age and delay gratification will be more academically successful (Shephard *et al.* 1999);
- students with emotional literacy problems will have a greater range of problems in and out of school (Goleman 1995).

In her analysis of emotional literacy programmes in schools and the assumptions which underpin them, Megan Boler (1999: 61–2) makes the important point that

> None of the representations of emotional intelligence analyse how people are taught different rules of conduct for emotional behaviour according to their gendered, racialized, and social class status. Instead, we are all supposed to feel the same 'empathy' and 'optimism'. Gender is powerfully ignored.

There is a clear need, in other words, for a cautious approach to any discussion around 'emotional literacy' or an emotion quotient, so that the risks of ascribing certain emotions naturally to boys or girls are kept at the forefront of one's mind. The contradictions in what is claimed on behalf of emotional literacy on their own are enough to ensure that emotional literacy will never become a truly transformative method for dealing with boys and literacy issues.

Technological literacies

Current educational policies and agendas abound with talk of harnessing new digital and communication technologies to literacy practices and integrating new technologies into literacy education. In many cases, this talk simply recognizes the growing importance of digital-electronic information processing and adds a new technology dimension to already familiar literacy constructions. Indeed, until recently, the most obvious contender for a different mindset on literacy based on new technologies was the notion of 'computer literacy'. As Chris Bigum and Bill Green (1992a: 5) point out, however, 'computer literacy' typically serves as a shorthand for the idea of possessing an appropriate or acceptable amount of computer-related knowledge or technical know-how, rather than providing a cogent construction of *literacy*. In other words, computer literacy is more a notion of technology proficiency than a conception of literacy.

In 1996, President Clinton's announcement of America's 'technology literacy challenge' brought talk of 'technological literacy' to official policy prominence in the USA. Here again, however, the central concept is severely limited as a mindset on literacy. Technological literacy can be defined loosely in terms of 'communication, math, science, and critical thinking skills essential to prepare [students] for the Information Age' (Winters 1996).

This move towards 'technological literacy' is re-emphasized in the US government's Educational Excellence for All Children Act of 1999, which emphasizes information technology as a means of supporting educational reform initiatives aimed at addressing disadvantage (Clinton 1999). Communication skills, according to Winters, include the ability to learn by means of using computers and the Internet, and to handle modern computers efficiently. Framed in these ways, 'technological literacy' appears to be little more than 'the new basics' harnessed to information and communications technologies.

As a further example, the British government has established what it calls the 'National Grid for Learning'. This grid, or online network of interconnected web pages, is regarded by the government as an 'architecture of content' (Blair 1999: 1) because its main role is to provide links to information, advice and learning resources. The purpose of the grid is to help to take Britain 'swiftly and successfully into the Information Age':

> This year has seen the launch of digital television bringing the closer integration of Internet and TV technology. Not only will digital technologies become a normal part of everyday life, but Britain's international competitiveness will increasingly depend on the way in which we adopt them . . . In parallel, the Government is investing very substantial new resources in a programme to raise standards in schools and increase opportunities in lifelong learning. The National Grid for Learning will play a crucial part in this process.
>
> (Blair 1999: 1)

The ministry's scenarios of students using the Grid suggest that the main use of the Grid will be archival. It will mainly involve students and teachers posting and accessing information related to homework, school projects and the like (DfEE 1999b).

Outside education policies, technological literacies have been writ as 'information literacy', which in turn has become largely the purview of librarians, who in many ways have been reinventing themselves as information archivists or brokers in relation to managing and accessing information in digital forms. Information literacy refers to the ability to 'recognize when information is needed and have the ability to locate, evaluate, and use effectively the needed information' (American Library Association 1989: 1). This includes being able to analyse key concepts in what is being read or searched for, use Internet search engines effectively, evaluate returns or 'hits' from a search engine or entries in an e-mail inbox, evaluate the quality of information gathered, sort information according to relevancy, judge the 'authenticity' of an article or web page and so on (see for example, Jones 1996; LaTrobe and Havener 1998). In many ways, this conception of technological literacy and the mindset that accompanies it is old library research practices dressed up in technodrag.

Many media subject teachers have also embraced 'information literacy' and shape it around teaching students to 'think critically about information once it's been found and decoded' (Quesada and Summers 1998: 30). To this end, media teachers have developed a swag of strategies for getting at the meanings and/or value of information accessed through broadcast media such as television and magazines. These strategies include: distinguishing between relevant and irrelevant information; judging reliability of sources; differentiating between fact and opinion; and identifying persuasive techniques (Quesada and Summers 1998; Yucht 1999). Information literacy in a media sense also draws heavily on key aspects of the 'new basics'.

With respect to the boys and literacy debate, 'information literacy' proves troublesome in terms of constructing a transformative literacy which addresses the needs of both girls and boys in schools. Most schools find themselves in a difficult position; given their historically central role in the task of educating members of society for their roles as users, producers and assessors of information, opinion, understanding and knowledge, schools have been recruited aggressively in countries like Australia and elsewhere to promote information literacy. At the same time, most teachers continue to struggle with the (merely) technical aspects of using new communications and information technologies, with the result that principles and practices of sound information retrieval, evaluation and application are typically conspicuous by their absence in classroom work (Burbules 1997a, b; Lankshear *et al.* 1997; Comber and Green 1999). Very little space for transformative practices appears to be made in the conventional information literacies found in most schools; that is, students are still constructed as *consumers* of information, rather than active processors and producers of information, knowledge, culture and so on (see Doneman 1997; Duncombe 1997).

A further variant of a digital technological literacies mindset is beginning to emerge. This position defines technological literacies as 'social practices in which texts (i.e., meaningful stretches of language) are constructed, transmitted, received, modified, shared (and otherwise engaged), within processes employing codes which are digitized electronically, primarily (although not exclusively) by (micro)computers' (Lankshear and Knobel 1997a: 141). This broadly conceived definition deliberately sets out to challenge 'operational' definitions of computer literacy and information literacy. Conceiving (digital) technological literacies as *social practices* means that spaces are opened up for much broader definitions of literacy as envisioned from old basics literacy, new basics literacy and even emotional literacy.

In other words, within this mindset, literacy is not conceived solely as 'literacy *for* technology' as in operational skills, or 'technology *for* literacy' where computers are used to 'teach' or 'enhance' literacy, or even solely as 'technology *as* literacy' when young people become fluent navigators of computer and game interfaces and the like (see Bigum and Green 1992a; Cummins and Sayers 1995; Lankshear and Knobel 1997a). Rather, a socio-cultural mindset on technological literacies encompasses all these conceptions of literacy and technology, and – in many cases – adds a *critical literacy* dimension as well. In particular, this mindset on literacy focuses on the actual use of digital technologies – and the social practices that shape and are shaped by them. This is evident in the work of Colin Lankshear and colleagues, who employ a three-dimensional model of literacy and technology (Green 1988; Lankshear *et al.* 1997; Lankshear and Snyder 2000). This model differentiates among three intersecting and co-present dimensions of literacy and technology use and can readily be summarized as a table (see Table 4.1).

This three-dimensional framework is useful for evaluating practices at the nexus of boys (and girls), literacy and digital technologies, as well as for planning meaningful classroom experiences for students. In particular, this approach emphasizes the non-neutrality of digital technologies, which is a subject we discuss in greater detail in Chapter 6. Included in this discussion are the often hegemonic masculinities enforced and valued within the realm of digital technological practice and use.

Critical literacies: critiquing power relations through language

The mindsets we are discussing in this chapter are not necessarily discrete entities with separate histories and theoretical genealogies. We have already touched on critical literacy in the previous section, but need to explore it a little more on its own. There are any number of critical literacy definitions available, but we choose to define it as 'the process of reading and writing the world such that the relationships between power, social practice and language are explored and evaluated.' Educators who subscribe to critical literacy have a stake in social change or transformation – no matter how small – and aim to encourage students to investigate, question and even challenge taken-for-granted assumptions about how the world *is* or *should be* (Lankshear 1994).

Critical literacy approaches to literacy education assume that meanings of words and texts (and by texts we mean 'stretches of language' which can be verbal, digital, printed, iconographic, symbolic etc.; anything that is 'coded' and/or belongs to a system of meaning) cannot be separated from the cultural and social practices in which – and by which – they are constructed. In other words, this mindset posits that language is used by all sorts of people to get all sorts of things done on a moment-by-moment basis, as well as in a more enduring sense, so that language – and literacy – is *fully* involved in social, historical, political and economic practices. Language is never neutral or value-free (Lankshear and McLaren 1993; A. Luke 1993, 2000; Gee 1996, 2000; Muspratt *et al.* 1997).

Table 4.1   Three-dimensional framework for analysing technological literacies

	Dimensions of digital technologies	Dimensions of literacies
Operational	This dimension is concerned with the 'how to' of digital technologies. This dimension focuses on the digital technology itself, and involves developing an operational sense of how it works (Lankshear and Snyder 2000: 45). It is concerned with the development and consolidation of computing skills and capacities.	The operational dimension of literacy principally refers to competence with regard to the language system: 'To refer to the operational dimension of literacy is to point to the manner in which individuals use language in literacy tasks in order to operate effectively in specific contexts' (Lankshear et al. 1997: 17).
	For example, an internet-based treasure hunt to teach search engine skills.	For example, group cloze activity that focuses on pronouns.
Cultural	This dimension relates more specifically to the specific knowledges and contexts that digital technologies are used in, and 'is always in the service of "authentic practice"' (Lankshear and Snyder 2000: 45). Using digital technologies in literacy activities should be as life-like – if not real-life – as possible.	The cultural dimension of literacy principally refers to competence with the meaning system: 'literacy acts are not only context specific but also contain specific content' (Lankshear et al. 1997: 17). It is about understanding texts in relation to their contexts. It includes authentic purposes for participating in text making activities and is closely related to 'how things are done' in the world outside school.
	For example, developing a database of historically oriented oral recounts and a website to contain it.	For example, interviewing older people about their childhood and writing up these recounts as texts that will be made available to the local community through the library and/or printed booklets.
Critical	This dimension is constituted by 'internal' and 'external' elements of discourse critique. 'It involves seeking to (analyse and)	The critical dimension of literacy has to do with the socially constructed nature of all human practices and

Table **4.1** (*cont'd*)

Dimensions of digital technologies	Dim ensions of literacies
understand the contexts within which current forms of educational computing are meaningful, and to contribute to enhancing social practice as a whole by acting in and/or on educational computing discourse in accord with this understanding and the standpoints from which it is attained' (Lankshear *et al.* 1997: 52). This also includes being able to access and critique software and other types of digital programs in a 'spirit of informed scepticism' (Durrant and Green 1998, cited in Lankshear and Snyder 2000: 46). Optimally, the critical dimension of technology and technological practice includes using digital technologies 'against the grain' (Lankshear and Snyder 2000: 46) – to use them in ways not necessarily intended by the manufacturer (e.g. using HTML programming language to build websites that critique transnational computer companies; developing a free computer operating system – Windows is an operating system – such as Linux that grows through donated labour and skills and not through a company owning it). In other words, to engage in production and transformation rather than in just consumption of digital devices or programs. **For example,** critiquing the portrayal of indigenous people in CD-ROM based encyclopaedias and producing alternative portrayals that are posted on a website	meaning systems. This dimension is the basis for ensuring that participants cannot merely engage in a practice and make meanings within it, but that they can in various ways transform and *actively* produce it. **For example,** creating postcards with appropriate captions of your local area that show the things students are interested in and not necessarily the things the town council might be (e.g. the local skateboard rink, people in the aged residents' home, old abandoned chairs artfully arranged at the local rubbish tip).

Critical literacy, then, is about evaluating something. Wayne Martino (1998, 2000), for example, uses critical literacy to assess and challenge dominant discourses of masculinity operating in schools, as do Grant Webb and Michael Singh (1998). Pam Gilbert (1993) uses critical literacy to critique the construction of gender in advertising, as do Jenny O'Brien (1994) and Barbara Comber and Anne Simpson (1995). Popular culture is another area where critical literacy is used to show how communications media construct and promote certain discourses, gender roles, identities, or social positions (Janks 1993; Buckingham and Sefton-Green 1994; C. Luke 1997; Giroux 1997; Alvermann and Hagood 2000).

As with most, if not all, established mindsets on literacy, one increasingly common problem with critical literacy is that it often becomes an orthodoxy in classrooms and teachers fall into the trap of scheduling critical literacy for wet Friday afternoons when they can read 'feminist' picture books to students and critique traditional gender roles. More insidiously, perhaps, critical literacy often becomes divorced from its generative theories – critical theory, discourse analysis, cultural studies, philosophy – so that it comes to mean simply critiquing texts alone by means of a set list of criteria, rather than critiquing something in respect to relationships, discourse, social practices and structures of power (see LeCompte and de Marrais 1992; Lankshear 1997). At worst, critical literacy is reduced to sets of 'tricks' to do with texts – a stock of 'moves' to be performed on the texts themselves without further exploration of what these may entail socially or politically. Such 'tricks' might include simply identifying patterns of male and female pronouns in a text or rewriting *The Three Little Pigs* from the point of view of the wolf. Such 'tricks' have little or no transformative import on their own. At best, however, critical literacy can work actively to challenge a range of taken-for-granted assumptions about boys, girls, literacy and schooling. For us, however, critical literacy works most effectively when it is tied to the new literacy studies and conceptions of 'new literacies'.

'The new literacy studies' and the study of new literacies

During the past 10–15 years an interdisciplinary body of work has coalesced into what is now sometimes called 'the new literacy studies' (or NLS for short). The NLS focuses on language, literacy and learning in conjunction with their many interacting social, institutional, cultural, political and cognitive contexts (New London Group 1996; Gee 2000; C. Luke 2000; Bigum 2001; Lankshear and Knobel 2001a). Strictly speaking, the NLS is not a mindset in and of itself, but is grounded in a mindset that seeks to integrate the kinds of dichotomies prevalent in other kinds of research and comment on language and literacy (Gee 1992, 1996, 2000; Lankshear 1997). These include dichotomies: between cognition and culture; between written and oral language; between language and other symbol systems; between learning inside and outside schools; between children and adults as learners; between 'native' and 'non-native' (second, bilingual and ESL) language development; and between language and human (inter)action. In short, the NLS are anti-essentialist in nature and practice. Unlike the old and new literacy 'basics', the NLS mindset conceives literacy not as singular or monolithic, but as many litera*cies* which are variously embedded and situated within diverse institutional and cultural practices within formal and non-formal settings. Distinct from critical literacy – which is often text-based in its application – the NLS actively engage with literacy practices and social ideologies *along with* the social practices and contexts constructing (and being constructed by) them. In this sense, we could readily call NLS part of the 'post-critical literacy' movement (see Lankshear *et al.* 1996; A. Luke 2000).

So, working within a NLS mindset, we can say that every meaningful text we read and write is an integral – embedded – element of some *discourse* (as we defined it in Chapter 3). In James Gee's words, every meaningful text we read is an integral or embedded element of some 'lived, talked, enacted, value-and-belief-laden practice which is engaged in under specific conditions, at specific times and in specific places' (Gee 1996: 3). Therefore, within the ambit of the NLS it is impossible to abstract or decontextualize 'literacy bits' from the larger practices in which they are embedded and for them still to mean what they mean in real life. For example, it would make no sense to this mindset to present students with a pro-forma that structures how an argumentative essay should be written (i.e. state thesis, argument 1 in support of thesis, argument 2, argument 3, conclusion and restating of thesis) without the students reading/hearing lots of examples of such texts and having a real need to write an argumentative essay (e.g. writing in protest of the closure of the council skateboard park, arguing on behalf of teenage mothers and their need for strong support, requesting funding from the council to start a tree-planting programme in the community). Seen in this way, it suddenly seems very odd to think that we could teach people to read and write by 'attending to their heads'; by teaching literacy 'skills' and so-called 'basics' outside contexts of authentic social practices.

Many subscribers to the NLS mindset take the 'new' in the new literacy studies very seriously, focusing on:

- what it means to be literate in 'new' times (Gee 1996; Rowan and Bigum 1999);
- new technologies and media and the possibilities they hold for teaching students effectively (e.g. Rowan *et al.* 2000; Bigum and Green 1992b; Lankshear and Knobel 2001a; C. Luke 2000; Bigum 2001);
- new forms of expression in youth culture and what they signify within and for 'new' times (Rushkoff 1996; Duncombe 1997; Mahiri 2001);

- developing new tools for understanding and conceptualizing of these new literacies (Doneman 1997; Johnson 1997; Rowan and Bigum 2000; Lankshear and Knobel 2001b).

In this way, what children and young people are able to do successfully with language and literacy is given a wider purview, which automatically includes out-of-school literacy practices not normally valued in schools. For want of a better term, we call this the 'new literacies studies' mindset.

An excellent example of new literacies as embodied enacted practice is evident in the original incarnation of the *Digitarts* project during the period 1997–9. *Digitarts* (http://digitarts.va.com.au) is an on-line multimedia project space constructed by young women for young women, exploring alternative perspectives on style, food, everyday life and commodities, and expressing different conceptions and constructions of female identity through poems, narratives, journal pages, 'how-to-do' texts and digital images. The project is 'dedicated to providing young women who are emerging artists and/or cultural workers with access to the knowledge and equipment necessary for the development of their arts and cultural practices in the area of new technologies' (see http://digitarts.va.com.au/welcome.html). It aims to challenge 'the "boys' toys" stigma often associated with electronic equipment', and to 'provide young women with access to information technology in a non-threatening "girls' own" space, to encourage involvement in technology based artforms.' *Digitarts* provides a venue for emerging multimedia artists to showcase their work, and seeks to attract young women to the field by providing 6–8-week 'web development' courses for beginners. Other training provisions have included a 12-week advanced web development course, a 12-week digital animation course and the collaborative production of four issues of *grrrowl* (an electronic zine, or ezine: http://digitarts.va.com.au/ grrrowl), using 'only two machines [computers] augmented by a scanner [and] a printer'.

Much of this *Digitarts* work is project-based. Each project engages its participants in developing a range of 'operational' technology and literacy skills needed to produce effective web pages (e.g. becoming fluent in web page design skills, HTML and VRML, scanning images, hyperlinking files, digital photography and image manipulation, embedding digital video clips in web pages). Items in the *Digitarts* portfolio are steeped in cultural analyses of everyday life, as well as in processes that properly blur the relationship between effective web page construction in cyberspace and meaningful social practices in meat (or 'real') space. This includes broadcast publishing of on-line zine-type commentaries, the use of the Internet to establish and nurture interactive networks of relations between like-minded people and the exploration and presentation of cultural membership and self-identity through writing, images and hyperlinks. *Digitarts'* work has an overt critical literacy dimension in virtue of its keen-edged critique of 'mainstream'

Australian society. For instance, the editorial in the third issue of *grrrowl* explains how to override/subvert the default settings on readers' Internet browser software, and encourages young women to override/subvert other socially constructed 'default settings' that may be operating in their lives. It challenges social scripts which allocate various speaking and acting roles for young women that cast them as passive social objects or as victims (e.g. 'This is not about framing women as victims – mass media vehicles already do a pretty good job of that': *Girls in Space*), and that write certain types of girls (or grrrls) out of the picture altogether. *Digitarts* offers a coherent alternative to the commodification of youth culture – i.e. youth as a market category – by making space for young women to become *producers*, and not merely consumers, of culture in the way it privileges the personal over the commercial (see Doneman 1997: 139; Duncombe 1997: 68, 70).

We have not, of course, discussed every possible and available mindset on literacy – cultural literacy (e.g. Macedo 2000) ecological literacy (e.g. Orr 1992), environmental literacy (e.g. Bowers 2000), media literacy proper (Kellner 1995), school subject literacies (e.g. Green 1988) and so on. We have nevertheless discussed key mindsets in relation to the boys and literacy debates currently circling the English-speaking world. And, for us, the mindset associated with the new literacy studies – the version which includes new and emerging literacies and digital technologies – is a potentially transformative approach to understanding and enacting critiques of power and social relations. A focus on new literacies, too, opens up unmapped, unregulated and not-yet-orthodox ways of being literate that create space for and promote a rhizomatic approach to teaching literacy to boys and girls. The old basics, new basics, elite literacies and even at times critical literacies and technological literacies, on the other hand, are often shaped by pedagogies of control that ensure the teacher remains the authorized literacy expert in the classroom.

Rewriting male order catalogues: the intersection of new literacies studies and transformative gender reform mindsets

The transformative mindset on gender reform discussed in Chapters 2 and 3 and the new literacies studies mindset and approach outlined above are compatible in terms of their respective theories and goals. Both aim at challenging taken-for-granted assumptions about 'the way things are', and at addressing inequalities in useful and practical ways. To recap, the transformative mindset scrutinizes the production of gender norms and is committed to understanding and ultimately changing for the better gender inequity. The new literacies studies approach offers educators and others a theoretically supported position for looking at the boys and literacy 'problem' in ways that do not exclude girls, but that aim at enhancing the possibilities of literacy success for *all* students. When we meld a transformative mindset with a new literacies worldview, we generate a useful position from which to make sense of and productively respond to gender-related challenges within education contexts.

From this new position we are able to develop strategies for both mapping and *rewriting* hegemonic narratives about 'being a bloke'. These strategies include a hypersensitivity to binaries – e.g. one is *either* a girl *or* a boy – that can be critiqued by asking 'what is missing from this equation?' or 'who or what is silenced or made invisible by this binary?' Strategies given to us by post-structuralist feminism also include asking what other possibilities exist in addressing an issue such as the boys and literacy crisis. For example, one of the most recognized taboo-breaking moves in post-structuralist feminism is the distinction made between 'gender' and 'sex'. That is, by troubling taken-for-granted assumptions about what gender *is*, post-structuralist feminists are able to distinguish between physical elements and social elements that make up who we are – and who we are accepted as being – in any society or social group. By making 'gender' a much more fluid category than traditionally conceived, new ways of being and of seeing others have been brought into discussions of boys' and girls' literacy education outcomes and school performances (Davies 1993, 1994; Alloway and Gilbert 1996, 1997). As we have discussed in previous chapters, thinking of gender as something that is 'constructed', 'enacted' and 'changeable' enables us also to imagine and act on new performances of masculinity and new ways of being literate that are not constrained by gender norms.

In complementary fashion, the new literacies studies mindset and theoretical frame gives us a number of strategies for analysing and critiquing discourses surrounding and construing gender issues, as well as for generating possible approaches to literacy education that address the fallout of gender debates in equitable ways. These are discussed briefly in turn below.

Historical analyses of social assumptions and norms

A useful approach to critiquing those narratives that confine what it means to be 'female' or 'male' is found in historical analyses of social assumptions or storylines about men and women, boys and girls. For example, Margaret Wertheim provides an excellent model of how to use historical texts and events to launch a critique of current claims that women are much less rational or scientifically minded than men when she writes:

> Soon science itself was enlisted to the complementarian cause [a movement in the 1700s which claimed men and women were different, but complementary] as practitioners in the emerging field of anatomy searched for scientific evidence of women's intellectual inferiority. After

careful measurement, anatomists 'discovered' that women's skulls were smaller in proportion to their bodies than men's. Thus, they said, the facts demonstrated that, as thinking beings, women were inferior to men. The problem with this deduction was that women's heads are actually larger in proportion to their bodies than men's. When anatomists were forced to concede this point in the nineteenth century, they did not thereby conclude that women had better brains; instead, they interpreted the relatively larger head as a sign of incomplete growth. Cranial size was seen to indicate that women were closer to children, whose heads are also proportionately larger. Thus, again, women were constructed as mentally inferior to men.

(Wertheim 1997: 148)

Identifying key historical factors in the development of 'myths' about males and females enables us to argue from an informed position and more easily enables us to see the 'constructedness' of gender norms.

Cultural or discursive decoding

Hegemonic discourses can be identified and unpicked at the seams so that their lining or stuffing shows by means of focusing on the meanings encoded into social and cultural texts and practices. Popular culture generally proves the most instructive when culturally decoded, and much work has been done in analysing the ways in which cultural norms and hegemonic discourses have been reinforced. This work includes analyses of gender and:

- romance books and other texts written specially for girls and women (Frazer 1987; McRobbie 1991; Christian-Smith 1993a, b);
- television soap operas and movies (Gilbert and Taylor 1991; Aidman 1999);
- advertising (Sofia 1996; Merskin 1999);
- music and fashion (McRobbie 1994; Jennings 1999);
- fandom (Alvermann and Hagood 2000);
- toys and software (Steinberg 1997; Murray and Kliman 1999).

Emphasis within this discourse analysis strategy is on identifying the ways in which patterned cultural assumptions or *discourses* are 'encoded' or 'naturalized' in relation to how the world is or how it should be in terms of gender practices – and in relation to the effects these discourses have. Admittedly, much of this work has for a long time been devoted to analysing the cultural norms and practices associated with 'being a girl/woman' – although, as we demonstrate in this book, it is slowly beginning to include analyses of masculinity and 'being a boy/man'.

Discourse analysis helps us to think of new and perhaps unbounded ways of being a boy, of being a girl, and to work rhizomatically to produce new stories – or counternarratives – about, and performances of, masculinity and femininity, and in turn as literacy learners and users.

Socio-cultural analysis

A frequent criticism of both critical literacy and post-structuralist feminist theories is that both approaches tend to value texts over practices, or that they directly extrapolate findings from textual analyses to larger social contexts. By emphasizing a socio-cultural analysis of the various dimensions of the boys and literacy crisis debates by mean of the mindsets we have chosen to work with, we hope to circumvent such criticisms. A socio-cultural approach – such as that advocated within the new literacy studies approach outlined above – requires us to pay attention not only to verbal interactions but to gestures, body positions, presence and absence, beliefs, habits, mannerisms and the like in our analysis.

Moreover, a big-picture socio-cultural approach to analysis makes it possible to trace rhizomatic links between *disrupted* 'masculine' and 'feminine' practices, spaces and interests. For example, tracing changes in the ways a group of boys approach a literacy-related task at the start of an intervention programme and how they approach similar tasks when the programme has finished can provide us with many insights into the efficacy or otherwise of the programme. Alternatively, documenting the ways in which a group of boys is perceived and *treated* by teachers can tell as much about the ways in which normative masculinities (or non-normative ones) are maintained and promoted in a school. In this way, we are also able to evaluate boys and literacy interventions. Our analyses in Chapters 5–7 provide the acid test here.

New literacies focus

By deliberately focusing on the fluid and generative nature of literacy practices we remain open to the emergence of *new literacies* – ones that arise out of engagement with digital technologies in particular. In addition, because most – if not all – new literacies are being constructed outside school contexts, our hybrid approach to understanding and responding to the boys, literacy and schooling 'crisis' will necessarily go beyond the confines of school contexts which often limit both boys and girls in terms of what they can actually *do* with literacy.

New literacies at present and in most cases are not yet deeply gender-encoded, and as such create spaces for envisioning and practising new ways of being literate that lie outside normative masculinities (and femininities). A good example of what we are on about here lies in the area of web page design, where creative and artistic uses of language (most often associated with women) blend seamlessly with the rational logic of programming language (most often associated with men) to produce roughly equal gender representation in web page design employment.

These four strategies – historical analysis, discursive decoding, sociocultural analysis, new literacies focus – help us to map the way gender norms are produced in schools (and beyond) and to recognize dominant narratives about gender operating around us. These strategies also help us to think beyond the limitations of traditional notions of appropriate masculine or feminine behaviour and to imagine ways in which gender norms – in relation to literacy practices in particular – can be resisted, denaturalized and perhaps changed. The following chapters outline our work in these directions.

Conclusion: not in Kansas any more ... Making the familiar strange

Bringing together the gender transformative and new literacies studies mindsets enables us to excavate a new route through the boys, literacy and schooling debates by equipping us with strategies for analysing claims and arguments made from the standpoints of a range of mindsets. This will also provide us with room in which to 'step back from' the hurly-burly of the boys, schooling and literacy debates in order to see them clearly and to trace their origins. This is not such an easy task, given that we have been immersed in the debates for quite some years now; nevertheless, we need to look at the debates anew in order to understand better what is at stake and whose interests are being served best by the various debating positions. As Cathie Wallace (1992) puts it, we need to work at 'making the familiar strange'. Taking the familiar, taken-for-granted, this-is-how-it's-always-been stuff of everyday life and making it strange and unfamiliar opens our eyes to things we may have never noticed before. This also enables us to think outside the box in relation to boys, literacy, masculinity and schooling and to create and enact our own counternarratives.

chapter five

Making it not so: transformative literacy practices for girls and boys

The new literacy studies mindset is well suited to the kind of gender reform advocated in Chapter 3. This is because it is committed to educational programmes that locate literacy practices in social and cultural contexts, and emphasize cultural and critical dimensions of literacy as well as operational capacities. Practices and programmes based on a new literacies perspective have the potential to:

- problematize taken-for-granted assumptions about what it means to be a girl and a boy;
- link this problematization to widespread beliefs about boys' and girls' different literacy abilities and potential;
- promote literacy classrooms that work rhizomatically to provide multiple figurations of masculinity and femininity;
- generate links between boys and elements of school literacy practice;
- work to make links between girls, elements of school literacy practice and non-traditional spaces.

A new literacies perspective is inherently compatible with the pro-feminist perspective we outlined in Chapter 3 and the task of conceptualizing the kinds of literacy practices that can identify and respond to the needs of boys and girls. This is a vital point; all too often gender reforms are couched in 'either/or' terms, with the understanding that teachers can prioritize the needs of boys, or girls, but possibly not the needs of both groups simultaneously.

This perspective on literacy is also able to accommodate the post-structuralist commitment to:

- recognizing the differences between some girls and some boys;
- acknowledging the similarities between some girls and some boys;
- identifying the diversity within groups of girls and boys;

- highlighting multiple forms of literacy and literate practice;
- celebrating multiple figurations of masculinity and femininity.

These latter distinctions are crucial ones, for the rush to develop responses to a declared boys and literacy crisis makes it easy for educators to conceptualize boys and literacy in unproblematic terms. We have written in previous chapters about the dangers of ascribing, without reflection, traditional masculine characteristics or interests to whole groups of boys. We have discussed ways in which teachers often assume that the boys in their classrooms will be more interested in literacy, for example, if they are able to read or write about 'boy things' like violence, sport, machines or the outdoors. From our point of view this kind of practice runs the grave risk of essentializing boys and further naturalizing the kinds of masculine behaviours that keep boys in a tenuous relationship with education in the first place.

Nevertheless, while we are wary of educational programmes, which assign 'masculine' interests to boys without any reflection, we also recognize that many boys *do* come to school with interests that reflect hegemonic masculinity. Many boys in schools *are* interested in computers; many of them *are* interested in sport; many of them *do* find it difficult to sit still, to be quiet, to express their feelings or emotions; and all of this impacts upon the way they respond to English and literacy lessons.

Out of the essentialist trap

The challenge for educators, therefore, is to find a way to make a connection with boys, and where they are at, while also keeping in mind where it is that each teacher wants to go. David Shores (1995: 101) describes three initial steps for working with boys in schools that capture the nature of the challenge:

Principle 1: find where they're at without putting them offside.
Principle 2: teach them where they're at.
Principle 3: affirm them for where they are at (and move them on).

In responding to the challenge implicit in all three of these principles we find – in seeming contradiction to our arguments against essentialism in the earlier chapters – a particular perspective on essentialism to be quite useful. First, Gayatri Spivak, and many others since (including Elizabeth Grosz, Chilla Bulbeck, Bob Lingard and Peter Douglas), have distinguished between the kind of essentialism we outlined in Chapter 2 (an essentialist mindset that ascribes gendered behaviour to sexed identity and sees either no possibility for or no benefit to be had from problematizing these behaviours) and a more pragmatic and partial essentialism. A certain degree of *strategic essentialism*, in Spivak's terms, allows us to recognize the similarities between groups – women, men, boys, girls – in order to draw upon the power that this acknowledgement supports. Feminism as a broad category, for example, takes much of its cultural power from its ability to refer to and distinguish between the experiences of the cultural groups 'Woman' and 'Man'. While we are increasingly aware of the need to speak not of a homogeneous 'Woman', but of a diversity of *women*, there are sufficient connections *between* women to ensure that a degree of essentialism is necessary and useful. Spivak (1985: 184) encourages feminists to 'pick up the universal that will give you the power to fight against the other side', and sees this as a necessary precondition of any attempt to politicize debates around women's lives.

Elizabeth Grosz takes Spivak's words as a reminder that women and men are positioned within cultural contexts that routinely privilege men over women, and hegemonic masculinity over subordinate masculinity, and that it is therefore practically useful to draw upon sets of similar or shared experiences in the process of moving beyond these patriarchal structures (Grosz 1995: 57). Susan Hekman takes this point further and argues that 'feminists today are less in danger of the totalizing theories feared by the gender sceptics than by increasing paralysis at the fear of being essentialist.' She goes on: 'If the paradigm of differences precludes any discussion of gender as a general category or, for that matter, any general categories at all, then it is seriously deficient. It will thwart rather than foster the development of feminist theory' (Hekman 1999: 53).

Taken together, the arguments made by Hekman, Grosz and Spivak remind us of the need to be cautious about uncritically essentialist positions – whether these relate to understandings of masculinity or femininity – while at the same time acknowledging the existence of gendered patterns of behaviour that operate within and external to classrooms. These are patterns that we can – indeed must – attend to if we are seeking to move beyond them and if we wish to avoid, in Hekman's (1999: 53) terms, throwing the baby of general analysis out with the bath water of essentialist practice.

In a sense, what we are acknowledging here is that we will use almost any tool if it helps us to shift entrenched understandings of what it is to be a school boy. The corollary to this is, of course, that the worth of any tool is fundamentally tied to its ability to help us in this process. Biological determinist attitudes which argue that boys are not suited to literacy in the first place do not help (although discussions relating to the kind of Darwinian natural selection process that had led to an association between Y chromosomes and poor literacy levels would certainly be entertaining!). Strategic essentialist perspectives which argue that it is possible, OK and, indeed, *important* to acknowledge where kids are positioned before trying to shift them, on the other hand, do allow us to move forward.

This commitment to imagining the world – and attendant understandings of masculinity and femininity – in new ways is fundamentally tied to the rhizomatic agenda established in Chapter 3. With regard to the boys and literacy agenda, we can make use of almost any strategy and almost any model of literacy if we have a clear understanding that we are doing so in order to stretch beyond the set of characteristics associated with normative masculinity (such as aggression, competitiveness or an anti-literacy mindset). Working rhizomatically, we aim to make connections *outside* of this set to other characteristics, including those commonly conceptualized as 'feminine' or 'not masculine'. This involves much more than simply reading books to students that show men washing dishes or changing nappies, or shopping. Instead of trying to make boys be 'more like girls', working rhizomatically means that a range of alternative ways of 'being a boy' are modelled, opened up and valued in school and community settings. In this way what it means to be a man or a woman is challenged and the rigid policing of the boundary between the two begins to be challenged.

The stories we explore in this chapter illustrate both the rhizomatic application of strategic essentialism and the less transformative adoption of biological determinist attitudes in action in a literacy classroom. We will demonstrate the way that one response operates rhizomatically to exceed the limitations of the class's understanding of dominant masculinity, while the other works, fundamentally, to reinscribe opening positions. The two cases are compilations of research conducted in a range of primary and secondary schools throughout Australia during the past two years. While the examples and anecdotes included here are taken from extant data, the stories are an amalgamation of experiences documented over this time and in these various contexts. They are intended, therefore, not to represent all literacy practices or all 'real' classrooms, but to illustrate the ways in which different mindsets impact upon literacy lessons.

Back to basic boyness: an essentialist fantasy

Montague High School is a coeducational, suburban, middle-class state-funded high school located in a relatively new suburb of a relatively affluent town. In terms of socio-economic status, the student group is relatively homogeneous, but there are at least four significant ethnic groups: Indian, Chinese, Vietnamese and Euro-Australian students.

In recent times, a group of teachers at the school have begun talking about the apparent differences between the educational outcomes of the girls and boys. Recent analysis of the Year 8, 9 and 10 results shows that boys are, on average, scoring 9 per cent lower than girls on testing associated with reading and writing. In addition to this, 33 per cent of the boys (as compared with 18 per cent of the girls) are failing to reach the Year 9 literacy benchmarks introduced by the government during the previous year. Three teachers in the group are especially vocal about the problems this can lead to. They see the failure of many boys to achieve basic literacy levels as indicative of the kind of post-school options they will be able to access. These boys, the teachers argue, are being set up for a series of under-paid, short-term, insecure and dead-end jobs.

These teachers believe that the failure of boys within literacy contexts is tied to a broad school-based 'culture of defeat' for boys. One of them, Tracey, attended a workshop several months ago, where the guest speaker argued that boys today were being discriminated against by a school system which rewarded only feminine and feminized behaviour. Boys, the speaker insisted, were being victimized by an overly feminized workforce and a sissified curriculum.

While Tracey didn't agree with the part about female teachers being tough on boys, she and her colleagues – Roger and Rubin – shared a common belief that literacy teachers were failing to connect with the 'real world' of boys, and that perhaps they needed to start taking arguments about boys' learning styles more seriously. Rubin was particularly passionate about this point. He believed that the boys he had taught – in a teaching career spanning more than fifteen years – had become increasingly uninterested in school generally, and literacy particularly, because it had become a place where only girls' needs were catered for. Boys at Montague High were discouraged from indulging in naturally masculine activities. Sport had less of a profile than it used to and there was no longer any special parade for the footy teams as had existed in the past. Orienteering classes had become coed and the computer lab had been 'feminized'. Girls spent nearly as much time as boys on computers during lunch breaks and refused to let groups of boys have the space to themselves even occasionally.

Rubin has nothing against the educational reforms put in place for girls; he has daughters himself and is pleased that they have both gone on to tertiary education, one into teaching, the other into law. But he is worried about his son. He can't compete with his sisters and doesn't appear to be given any incentive to do well at school. Surely, Rubin states, we need to find ways to re-engage boys in school. Surely that's our role?

Roger couldn't agree more: as far as he is concerned schools have really lost the plot when it comes to meeting the needs of boys. Coed schools are fine as an idea, Roger claims, but we have missed the chance to create schools where boys and girls can complement each other; instead we have created artificial places where only some male interests are valued and girls' skills reign supreme. While he is reluctant to say this out loud – after all, half the teachers at the school are women – he really believes that the gender reform movement has gone too far. Boys don't know who they are any more; and he doesn't think the school has done girls any big favours either. One day, after all, they're going to have to go out in the real world, and compete with boys on level territory. They think they have it tough now. They really don't have a clue.

Roger, Rubin and Tracey decided that the school needed to start looking seriously at boys' educational needs. They agreed that, as a first step, they needed to organize some broader discussion within the school. Because none of the three felt confident enough to deal with what they thought in advance would be some negative feedback or resistance from the women in the staff, Tracey volunteered to contact the speaker at the workshop she had been to and see if he would be available to come and speak at a staff meeting. In the meantime, Rubin negotiated with the principal, who agreed to allocate some professional development money to the workshop.

The 'boys and literacy' workshop was scheduled for a two-hour, after-school session. The guest speaker began by displaying statistics that showed the same kind of gap between girls and boys as was present in Montague. He went on to cite research that demonstrates boys' fundamental difference from girls. At least, he cited people who claimed or argued that boys were different from girls because of their testosterone, their differential use of right and left brain and a quality he referred to as their 'basic boyness'. This, the speaker argued, was what we needed to take as the starting point in any serious attempt to engage boys with school or literacy or anything else: what are they basically all about? And how can we build on this?

After the session the teachers' discussions ranged around a lot of issues. While there was a group who argued strongly that this emphasis on boys' 'essence' would not help any gender reform project, by the end of a couple of weeks there was a cohort of Year 9 teachers committed to trialling a new way of teaching boys. The principal – who had recently been getting a lot of anxious questions from parents about their sons' progress – decided that it was worth trying out the new project.

And so it went ahead. The premise underpinning the proposal was simple: work to value 'masculinity' within traditionally feminized spaces (such as literacy classrooms). This was focused on Year 9 English classrooms. Three moves were made:

- Boys and girls were broken into single-sex groups for English lessons.
- All the boys' groups were taught by men (even though a shortage of male English teachers within the school meant that one class was taken by a manual arts teacher and another by a maths teacher).
- The boys were to be given the chance to focus on traditionally masculine texts. The starting point would be comics; from this point kids would move into studying *Harry Potter* or *Goosebumps* books. Later in the year the boys would have the chance to make web sites based around their favourite book. The girls would follow a similar programme, but be taught only by women and read books that catered specifically to 'girls' interests'.

This curriculum was presented to boys at the start of term. They were not given any real choice within the programme, except in terms of the specific book from within a given set that they chose to read. The assessment for all the work would be 'masculine': they would be assessed on their oral presentations more than their written work, and particular emphasis would be placed upon their computer projects. In terms of particular literacy activities, lessons were organized predominantly around the operational and cultural dimensions of literacy.

Boys were encouraged to practise their reading and summation skills. They worked in teams to discuss the plot for each story, and to transform sections of some books into dramatic performances. In relation to the cultural dimension of literacy, for example, the boys researched comics within different cultures (e.g. Japanese manga comics compared with Mexican cartoon novellas and the superhero cartoons of Marvel Comics in the USA). The boys who began with limited reading skills were provided with additional tutoring by parental volunteers – all men – who were encouraged to talk to boys about other 'blokey' things and were regularly engaged in debates around football, cricket and other sporting events.

During one of these lessons the topic of Shane Warne was raised. Warne is a well known Australian cricket star recently accused of sexual harassment by a British nurse; an allegation which Warne seemingly admitted to be at least partially true. Perhaps as a result of his admission Warne was stripped of the Australian cricket team's vice-captaincy and this was what prompted debate among the boys and one of the fathers supporting the group. One boy argued that Warne had been ripped off, and that it was just another case of whinging girls. Another boy agreed and said that even if he did make a few 'dirty phone calls' no one was forcing her to listen to them, but a third, quieter boy said that he thought Warne had asked to be dumped if he was going to act like such a wanker. At this point Clint, the father, joined the discussion saying that what Warne did in his private time was no one else's business and that he was a 'damn fine cricketer who'd been the victim of sexual harassment'.

Discussion then moved in a different direction. It is possible to identify here a lost opportunity for opening up debate around gender roles, sexual harassment and the 'rights' of men to force their attentions upon unwilling women. This is a particularly important opening given the well documented relationship between sport, sporting cultures and very traditional and patriarchal masculinities.

Lindsay Fitzclarence and Christopher Hickey (1998) make the valuable point that sporting discourses often work to justify what might otherwise be read as inappropriate or anti-social behaviour. Citing several publicized cases relating to censored behaviour of football players, Fitzclarence and Hickey (1998: 71) argue that:

within the culture of football there exists a wide array of behaviour rationalisations associated with *retributive justice, temporary disfunctionality, containment and provocation.* Used independently or collectively, these rationalisations act to dissolve individuals of their self-responsibility. (Emphasis in original)

Consistent with this example, there was no discernible attempt to incorporate critical literacy strategies within the programme. The boys were not encouraged to reflect upon the origins or nature of the kinds of practices they studied; nor were they asked to engage in any reflection upon issues to do with masculinity or femininity. There was, in fact, no discussion of the reasons for the single-sex classes in the first place except for the explanation offered by one teacher at the start of the term: 'that this was planned so teachers would be able to respond to the needs of boys, without the distractions of the girls.'

Lookin' good?

As far as the organizing teachers were concerned, there were three significant outcomes from the project, and these were publicized widely on the school's web site, in newsletters, at the end of year speech night and even in the local paper.

First, testing conducted at the end of the year revealed that the overall gap between boys' and girls' literacy scores at the end of Year 9 had decreased to 6 per cent – a 4 per cent improvement. Second, the majority of boys within the trial programme (64 per cent) expressed the opinion that it had been a 'good experience' and asked if this model could be used in other years too. Third, there were fewer discipline problems reported in relation to the Year 9 boys during the period of the trial.

On the surface these appear to be highly satisfactory results, and the teachers who had worked on the programme felt that they had really made a difference to some of the boys involved. Plans were put in place to have similar models introduced into Year 8 and 10 classes for the following year. The staff were confident that these, too, would be a success.

A second look

Clearly there is some cause for celebration relating to this project. There are, however, further questions that need to be asked before it is possible to pronounce it a total success.

A closer look at the data, in fact, reveals several things. With regard to improved results from literacy testing, for example, there are several points that need to be made. First, boys were now being assessed in different ways from girls. It is difficult to determine, as a result, the extent to which they were reaching the same or even comparable outcomes. Second, while the overall gap between boys and girls appears to have decreased, this has not been the case for all boys. Indeed, a significant percentage of boys have actually done *worse* within this model. These are the boys who do not identify strongly with traditional or hegemonic versions of masculinity that the programme has endorsed. Particularly at risk here are boys who are regularly described by other students and even some teachers as 'feminine'. Similarly, the boys from lower socio-economic families who do not have easy home access to computer technology did not appear to fare as well as other boys.

In addition to this, individual boys within these classes reported feeling 'uncomfortable' or 'ill at ease' with the subject nature of the texts studied. One boy reported that classes were out of control; that he felt better when there were girls around. Another said that he really hadn't understood a lot of what was being discussed, because he had never heard of Harry Potter before. But he would now make sure he kept up to date with the series of books about him.

Also silent within the 'success story' outlined above are the voice of indigenous boys and those from the school's major ethnic groups – Indian, Chinese and Vietnamese children. This is an important point. We identified in earlier chapters the fundamental interconnection of gender and ethnicity as well as gender and economic status as indicators of likely literacy levels. Most recent available Australian data argue that boys from lower socio-economic backgrounds are up to 24 per cent more likely than boys from high socio-economic families to fail to meet literacy standards. Even more worrying is data which suggests that children from indigenous or non-English speaking backgrounds (NESB) are at even greater risk. In 1998, the gap between Aboriginal and Torres Strait Islander students in Australia and other students – a gap relating to the percentage of children failing to meet literacy benchmarks – was 28.5 per cent in reading and 28.7 per cent in writing (Education Queensland 2000: 22). Montague High has no evidence to suggest that the programme they implemented was able to attend to the particular needs of its students from NESB or indigenous students. Indeed, they have no way of knowing what these students made of the programme because they were not asked. All that the teachers *do* know is that there was no discernible improvement in the literacy levels of these groups.

Questions can also be asked about the claim that there was a decrease in recorded discipline problems within the English classes. Some teachers and boys expressed the opinion that behaviour didn't necessarily improve, it was just that the teachers took a more lenient approach to discipline in the absence of girls. This is difficult to prove, but it indicates the need for teachers to reflect upon their behaviour management techniques so that boys are not able to conclude that there are different kinds of behaviour suitable for male, female or mixed groups. Such an assumption works ultimately to reinforce the belief that boys and girls are inherently different, and *naturally* disposed to act and interact in different ways. This is the kind of philosophy that has been used to justify school and workplace bullying and harassment, with perpetrators regularly heard arguing that they were simply 'misunderstood' and 'meant no harm'. This is a particularly important issue to consider in light of the fact that during the course of this project Year 8 and 9 girls reported an increase in school yard harassment, which ranged in nature from name calling through to being evicted from school yard spaces by boys' domination of school spaces.

In terms of the frameworks outlined throughout this book, the response discussed here provides a clear example of the powerful effect that essentialist arguments have on any literacy reform project. This particular version of the 'valuing difference' or 'boys will be boys' mindset has led to the celebration of traditional, narrow and limiting understandings of masculinity. It is possible to argue, in fact, that the boys were introduced to even more messages than before about what it means to be a 'real boy' as a result of their exposure to books, computer programs, teachers, parents and pedagogical practices which reinforced previous messages about the 'nature' and 'roles' of boys. This is a vital point, for within the programme no opportunities were provided to help boys to question taken-for-granted assumptions about normative masculinity. As a result they did not reflect, in Chris Mclean's words, upon the extent to which the 'collective pressures of masculine culture' (Mclean 1997: 62) may have been at the root of their experiences as literacy failures in the first place. This is an important omission because if boys are:

> left to themselves they are unlikely to identify [masculinity] as the source of their problems. Faced with bullying from older boys for example, they are more likely to think about taking martial arts classes, so that they can beat up the bullies in return, than to question the ideals and practices of masculinity. More masculinity, not less, is what most boys long for.
>
> (Mclean 1997: 62)

This indifference or inattention to the cultural production of masculinity and the related consequences of this production for various boys and various girls is, ultimately, the source of our discontent with this project. We read the Montague site as an example of a project where essentialist attitudes have been uncritically endorsed. In terms of our rhizomatic metaphor, the project can be read as one which actually strengthens the bonds that anchor boys to normative masculinity. Images that occur to us in relation to this phenomenon include that of a spider web, with more and more strands being wound around the boys to tie them to hegemonic masculinity. Each strand in itself appears insubstantial, yet together they create a very strong web out of which it becomes increasingly difficult to escape. Although the spider web may give the initial appearance of flexibility or even fragility, getting outside of it isn't as easy as it looks. Throughout the Montague project boys were not given any tools to help them to unravel the web; they were not encouraged to identify the limitations of operating within the web; nor were they asked to consider the way in which Harry Potter can be seen to enact non-traditional masculine subjectivities.

In response to omissions such as these, Gilbert (1994: 27) urges educators to:

> construct language classrooms as arenas within which plurality is possible and difference is expected: where dualistic gender positions are not sanctioned, supported, or legitimated and where the textual construction of gender becomes a legitimate field of inquiry.

In the Montague situation, however, difference and plurality were neither expected nor acknowledged. Instead, the project was based on assumptions relating to the homogeneous nature of boys as a group, and the belief that a return to 'basic boyness' would solve any literacy problem.

This is in no way an atypical response. Over the past six years we have attended many forums that focused on boys. At every one of them someone, at some time, has proposed a return to 'masculine' frameworks, the adoption of pedagogical strategies suited to the 'male brain' and the use of male teachers to help boys to become men.

We are critical of this kind of unreflective essentialism because of what we see as its fundamental inability to work beyond, or outside of, the limitations of normative masculinity. At the same time, we realize that many of the strategies associated with this mindset can and do play a valuable role within education for boys. For this to be the case, however, those involved in the project need to start from a different basis from those championing the 'back to basic boyness' model. This approach is premised on the belief that things will get better for boys – in school, literacy classrooms, life – if people – teachers particularly – get better at identifying, understanding and valuing their boyness. There is, as a result, no vision or project outside masculinity associated with this framework.

In contrast to this model, an anti-essentialist, transformative or rhizomatic project has a different end point in mind. The strategies may, from time to time, appear similar, but they are employed for different reasons. We explore one such rhizomatic project in the next section.

Being and becoming: a transformative beginning

Willoughby Heights is a government funded, coeducational high school catering for a growing diverse student population. Built during the 1970s, the school has a student population of around 800, with approximately 30 per cent of students coming from households with below average income. There are only small numbers of indigenous Australian students (less than 2 per cent of the population), but there are larger groups of students from various Pacific islands.

The teachers at Willoughby – in common with other teachers throughout their area – had heard and been caught up in many of the 'what about the boys?' debates. At specially organized professional development days they had listened to many of their colleagues at other schools lament the extremes of gender reform, which have emasculated boys and caused a crisis of confidence among men generally and school boys specifically.

These teachers, however, were not reading only the popular press. They had looked into the data produced by relevant government agencies and sought to disaggregate figures that are commonly presented in a simplified fashion. In this way they had recognized that there is more than one factor impacting on literacy performance: gender, race/ethnicity and socio-economic status all appear to have connections to school literacy performance.

This didn't make the problem at Willoughby Heights any less serious, for 28 per cent of the boys were failing to achieve the literacy benchmarks set by the government. This is 11 per cent higher than the equivalent figure for girls. While conceding that it might well be the working-class boys who suffered the most, the teachers felt a strong need to be doing *something* for boys as a whole, even if the sum of the parts, as it were, never quite equals what is seen as the whole. It was not that they were averse to the possibility that there are multiple kinds of boys with multiple (and often conflicting) literacy needs. Instead they were committed to working in at least some ways to open up debates around the nature of masculinity, and to involving as many boys as possible in these discussions.

Two teachers recently had been reading critical perspectives on the link between masculinity and literacy performance and recognized that school practices may not make an association between boys and literacy appear all that easy or logical. Kate had done some research into schools and the production of masculinity and was worried. Even though she found it hard to articulate her concerns in front of all her colleagues, she was worried that the school might be helping to reproduce particular masculinities that construct limited and limiting futures for boys. It was not that the school was terribly 'blokey': there was as much emphasis on the school band as there was on any sporting team; more, in fact, for the orchestra had won titles locally and at regional level. And there was a surprisingly even balance between male and female teachers, and relatively few serious discipline issues.

There were other things that bothered her. The teachers in English tended to be women, and the teachers in technology and science were all men. Students had been given assignments to complete which use non-inclusive language, such as the essay set by the information technology coordinator titled 'Robots are the greatest boon to mankind'. Some of the students were tempted to argue that yes, robots had been great for men but really pretty awful for women, but they weren't game to risk their high marks for the sake of making their point.

Of greatest concern to Kate, however, was growing evidence that some boys were branded trouble makers or losers by students and teachers almost from the minute they walked through the door. These students appeared time after time in the principal's office, on detention and, of course, in remedial English programmes.

Kate spoke to Raul, the deputy principal, about her concerns and he agreed that boys appear to be branded 'bad kids' very quickly and given few chances to 'redeem themselves'. He was worried about the deepening divide, not just between boys and girls, but between boys and boys. He knew that one of the English coordinators – Lucy – was also concerned about a particular group of boys who continued to show up in her remedial English classes, and the teachers who were only too happy to get them out of their classrooms.

They decided to get together to pool their collective information and see if they could envisage a response. The three teachers worked through a number of key questions.

So what's your problem? Which boys? Which girls?

The teachers recognized that not all boys would be experiencing school in the same way – and not all losing – and that not all girls would be 'winning'. Accordingly, their first move had to be identifying the specific concerns they had for the school as a whole, and for any particular identifiable group.

They expressed a desire to investigate the educational experiences of boys, but to try to do so in a way that could not easily be read as a criticism of girls. This reflected the teachers' understanding that many girls in school continue to report high levels of consistent sex-based harassment. They were also aware that boys and girls who are known or thought to be gay suffer dramatically from 'bullying and vilification (defined as incitement to hatred, serious contempt or severe ridicule)'. Some research indicates that 25 per cent of gay or lesbian students leave school because of this kind of harassment (Gilbert and Gilbert 1998: 161).

The teachers recognized that any attempt to intervene with boys' literacy levels would need to articulate with a whole-school policy designed to address the multiple challenges of gender. This necessitated the acknowledgement that there would be, in fact, no 'quick fix' to capture media headlines or earn parental approval. Instead they accepted the point that their gender reform work would need to be long term, multifaceted and capable of constant renewal.

The teachers created a gender equity task force and set themselves four broad goals. To:

- work across the school to promote acceptance and inclusion of all students;

- work across the school to interrogate and problematize traditional conceptions of masculinity and femininity;
- develop strategies to respond to the needs of girls as a group and as individuals;
- develop strategies to respond to the needs of boys as a group and as individuals.

While committed to improving the educational experiences of all students, the teachers identified as their initial focus a group of 'at-risk' boys who consistently failed in English. These boys were generally working-class kids and some of them also had an indigenous Australian or Pacific island background.

Getting started: back to (gender reform) basics

In response to these objectives, the school set in place several professional development networks designed to support teachers as they worked to improve the school's overall approach to gender issues. They were provided with data relating to the school's literacy (and other) outcomes which broke student performance down, not just by gender, but also according to socio-economic status and ethnic or cultural background. This enabled teachers to recognize even more clearly that while some boys were doing badly, others were doing well.

A comprehensive 'inclusive language' booklet was developed and explained to staff, giving them the chance to discuss why it is problematic to set assignments that discuss the progress of 'mankind'. Workshops on assessment options and teaching and learning strategies were also scheduled throughout the year to provide teachers with a greater appreciation of the diverse ways in which students can and do learn. In these workshops there was a general acceptance that *some* groups of boys and *some* groups of girls tend to prefer different classroom practices. This, however, was underpinned by the recognition that these were not natural or universal truths, and that there are as many differences between girls and girls as there are between girls and boys.

The timetabling committee was encouraged to examine any of the ways in which 'masculine' subjects were timetabled in opposition to 'feminine' subjects and provided with time and resources to come up with more flexible and creative solutions. The committee ultimately recommended the 'modularization' of the Year 9 and 10 curriculum. This meant that students did *not* have to sign up for subjects titled 'Shop A' or 'Home Economics' for two whole years but instead could sign on to elective modules with names such as 'Cooking on the Run', 'Building a Coffee Table' or 'Good Buying'.

In these and other ways the task force demonstrated the importance of equal opportunity or access/equity models of gender reform (as discussed in

Chapter 2). They identified the value of removing physical barriers to students' participation and the equal importance of 'gender-inclusive' or 'neutral' language. The school newsletter was also reviewed when one teacher pointed out a recent invitation to a school fete (featuring a car and bike show) which said 'Come on Dad's [*sic*], show us your best "boys toy". Bring your car and bike and try and win a trophy.'

Teachers also made use of some of the strategies associated with a socialization mindset. They acknowledged the need to provide students with multiple images of masculinity and femininity on the teaching force, and worked consciously to avoid the stereotyping of subjects or school areas as 'masculine' or 'feminine'. Wherever possible, a man and a woman were asked jointly to lead high-profile initiatives – such as the concert band, the school production or speech night. Moreover, the school's staffing policy was reviewed to highlight the potential need for a change in recruitment practices that would foster the development of a less traditionally gendered workforce. All these initiatives were ongoing and seen by teachers not as ways to effect an immediate change, but as necessary preconditions for the kind of transformative project work that would be targeted, initially, at small groups of students and expanded ultimately to involve the entire school.

The first groups identified for participation in this transformative project work were half the students in Year 9 English classes. The teachers identified a group of ten boys within these classes who appeared to be most at risk of failing the subject English, and designed an intervention programme intended to reconnect these boys with literacy lessons. They also identified the need to run complementary programmes for Year 9 girls and boys who were *not* failing, in order to maximize the chances that the majority of students would achieve the project's outcomes.

From this point on the project took two parallel pathways; one was focused on the ten boys, the other on two classes containing a total of 35 girls and 18 boys. The teachers were conscious of their inability to deal with all of the Year 9 students, but felt that starting small would maximize the chance that they would learn something useful from the project.

In parallel (but connected) sessions the teachers responsible for the boys' group and the other mixed groups continued to ask themselves questions.

How are these students currently positioned within the school?

To begin planning ways to engage boys in literacy-related activities the teachers identified a need to be clear about the way the boys were currently positioned within the school generally. They saw a need also to be clear about the differences between boys' conceptions of their own subjectivity and the opinions about boys held by girls. To develop this understanding two teachers held discussions with the boys while other teachers worked in small group discussions with the mixed group. From the boys' group came the explicit acknowledgement of something the teachers had implicitly known: that the boys, from the early days of high school, had been branded as trouble makers by the teachers and were routinely sent out of classes. The students argued that they were bored in class; that teachers didn't listen to them when they asked questions and that everyone always assumed they would be trouble. This was borne out to one of the teachers when she walked with one of the boys to a discussion session to hear three students along the way say words along the lines of 'Look who's in trouble again.'

These were not, of course, the only 'bad boys' in the school, but the kids identified the fact that it was very hard to change teachers' opinions, and that once they were seen as bad news, then they were likely to be treated that way forever. Students in the mixed group shared this opinion. They identified a group of boys who were 'real trouble' and another group who were 'fringe dwellers': in trouble, but also picked on or persecuted by teachers who would never give them a second chance.

A slightly more surprising revelation to the teachers in relation to the group of boys was the lads' low self-esteem. All ten boys described themselves as slow, behind, not good with words and so on. They said that they wouldn't remember things; that they wanted to get jobs when they finished school, but didn't know if teachers would help them because they might damage the reputation of the school. This opinion was not reflected by the mixed group, who expressed the belief that the kind of boys who were likely to be taken into the 'remedial' English classes were generally self-centred, tough and not interested in other people. They saw them as 'too cool to worry about others' and not at all committed to school.

How is this reflected in literacy classrooms?

Not surprisingly, these kinds of opinions affected the way the kids thought about the relationship between boys and literacy lessons. For the group of boys, English lessons had become places where they were routinely labelled as failures. They admitted they had trouble learning in the way their teachers seemed to prefer, and thought that they probably would be better out of the class anyway, as they would be a disruption otherwise.

The other students shared this view. They said that while English could be really boring and of little interest to boys (or girls, as five girls insisted loudly), some of the students were prepared just to do it so they could get a good result that would help them later on. The troublesome boys, however, were seen as kids not able to concentrate or make the effort.

For the most part, discussions around English or literacy contexts and their relationship to boys emphasized boys' unsuitability and drew little attention to girls' relationship to these activities. That is to say, a lot was made of how hard it is for either 'good' or 'bad' boys to get involved with literacy activities, but little explicit attention was drawn to the possibility that girls might find this difficult too. There was, however, a group of five girls who challenged the claim that English was better for girls. They argued loudly that the books they read were irrelevant to them, that they would rather be doing any other subject (even maths) and that they wished that someone would set up special classes for them focused on *their* interests.

This reminded teachers of what they had already been thinking about: the challenge of implementing any kind of gender reform project aimed at boys without alienating or reinforcing the sense of alienation or disenchantment felt by some girls. They decided that while they *did* need to engage explicitly with boys' alienation from literacy, they also needed to ensure that the students in the mixed group were encouraged to reflect upon gender issues, gender norms and the consequences of 'doing' or contesting particular versions of masculinity and femininity.

Doing it

The teachers decided that one of their biggest challenges was to find ways to disrupt the boys–trouble–anti-literacy mindset that appeared to dominate in terms of how the boys thought about themselves and how some of the teachers thought about the boys. They decided that it would be worth trialling a small class involving only the 'failing' and 'bad' boys within which they would work on a range of literacy activities. The teachers hoped that this would give the boys a connection back into literacy lessons – and experience at interpreting themselves, not only as 'failures' or 'bad boys' but as boys who could enact, as it were, the 'multiple mes' (for discussion see Moore 2000) – or multiple subjectivities – introduced in Chapter 3.

This seemed like a laudable goal, but clearly there were problems relating to the boys' interest and motivation. The teachers decided to draw upon what they already knew about the boys' common interests – in this case, an interest in Nintendo games – as a means of drawing them together around a particular literacy task. Lucy suggested that they could also use this class as a space to try out a new computer-based web creation program that the school had wanted to introduce to the Year 9 students. She was concerned, though, that this would reinforce the rather macho image of computer studies within the school and wondered whether or not it was ever possible to use, in Audre Lorde's (1984) terms, the 'master's tools' to dismantle the master's house. This prompted some very useful discussion around the ultimate goals of the group, and the extent to which they could draw upon 'traditional' strategies to get to non-traditional spaces.

In considering this question, the teaching team recognized that getting boys involved in literacy activities by making use of Nintendo games or computer programs was not an unproblematic activity. There were, in fact, several risks involved. First, it could reinscribe the student's beliefs that they were no good at 'normal' literacy activities. Second, it could reaffirm their image of themselves as 'bad boys' by encouraging their identification with stereotypically 'macho' and aggressive heroes. Third, it could alienate them from other students. Finally, it could reinforce the masculine image of computing at the school and further alienate the girls and the 'non-techno' boys.

Nevertheless, the teachers were committed to trying something different and decided that they would risk this kind of approach if they kept in mind the 'big picture', which was ultimately to make a connection between boys, literacy and literacy competence. To minimize the risks associated with the use of these strategies the teachers in the mixed groups decided that they would also introduce students to the web page software and combine this with critical analysis of the 'masculine' or 'feminine' nature of various software, sites or technology resources. They would focus on the stereotypes associated with technological competence, and identify, particularly, the kinds of strategies that can be used to learn technological abilities, and to critique others' domination of technological resources.

The goals

With this in mind, a small group of teachers at Willoughby High designed a series of lessons for the boys with the following goals. To:

- map the boys' existing skills relating to Nintendo games and computer word processing;
- discuss with the boys their development of those skills, and how they were different from the experiences of other boys and from some girls;
- have the boys conduct on-line research relating to computer game groups, including those designed explicitly for girls;
- provide boys with an opportunity to become experts in a new Nintendo game, and to develop 'cheat sheets' for that game;
- identify these skills as literacies and to highlight their connection to other 'real world' literacies;
- ensure that the boys reflected critically upon the characters in the game – and identified the gendered roles each performed (or did not perform: in this case the boys became experts in a game where the central agent was a woman);
- encourage critical reading of all texts used;
- allow the boys to reflect upon the pedagogies they used in teaching their new skills to others (including to one of the teachers who declared himself to be a novice when it came to computer games).

In addition to this the teacher who had primary responsibility for the group – Lucy – made a commitment to attempt to:

- negotiate the objectives of each lessons with the boys;
- provide consistent positive feedback to the boys relating to their development of new skills;
- critique/problematize 'macho' behaviour and celebrate alternative displays of behaviour;
- encourage the boys to reflect upon the learning process (in oral and written reflections);
- incorporate a wide range of text types;
- advocate on the boys' behalf to other teachers, explaining the significance of their commitment to the project, and identifying their 'improved' behaviour.

The mixed group, on the other hand, was organized around a series of similar and complementary but nevertheless different objectives. These were to:

- map the classes' existing skills relating to computer technologies;
- discuss with the class their development of those skills, and how they were different to the experiences of other boys and other girls;
- reflect upon the gendered nature of technological spaces and to identify the reasons why and ways in which girls and boys can be alienated within various environments;
- identify the consequences of this kind of alienation;
- establish collaboratively principles for effective technological instruction and to publish this on the school web site at the end of the term;
- work in groups to develop competencies in using a web editing package;
- design a web site relating to the interests of *all* Year 9 students that did not reproduce gender stereotypes.

In addition to this the teacher who had primary responsibility for the mixed group – Kate – made a commitment to attempt to:

- negotiate the objectives of each lessons with the students;
- provide consistent positive feedback to the students relating to their development of new skills;
- critique/problematize either stereotypical 'macho' or stereotypical 'girly' behaviour and celebrate alternative subjectivities;
- encourage all students to reflect upon the learning process (in oral and written reflections).

Teachers working with the single-sex and the mixed groups all stated a commitment to raising critical questions regularly relating to a range of texts, cultural practices and discourses by asking students to reflect upon:

- Who and what are included? What groups of people are included or excluded? How do you know?
- What do those who are included get to do? What roles are taken by men/boys, women/girls? What evidence do you have?

- Which people and roles are valued and how is this communicated?
- Who has control? Who has access to power? Who exercises power? Who acts independently? Who initiates action?
- What are various people rewarded for and with?
- In what ways does the inclusion or exclusion reflect to your own life?
- What are the consequences of this relationship?
- What alternatives are there?

Reflections

The Willoughby project ran for ten weeks and involved two two-hour sessions and one 30-minute session each week for the boys' group and the mixed groups alike. By the end of the ten weeks Lucy, the coordinating teacher, and Raul and Kate identified five things.

First, improved operational literacies were displayed by the boys' group relating to word recognition, sentence construction and both written and oral communication. While the developments within this area were certainly not overwhelming, the boys *did* improve and, perhaps most importantly, identified the fact that they actually *were* able to learn these kinds of skills.

Second, the boys were willing to talk about and reflect upon their abilities and not just their *lack* of ability. For example, while the boys initially described themselves as 'slow', 'retards' and 'losers' when it came to school generally and English specifically, at the end of the session they claimed that they had skills relating to 'doing' the Nintendo game, but also skills in teaching others how to play.

Third, there was a shift in behaviour patterns, with the boys demonstrating an ability to display a 'literacy self' that was connected to, but not overpowered by, their 'schoolyard self'. Prior to the project these ten boys – like many others – saw literacy and 'being a boy' as oppositional positions. Similarly, they read 'being cool' or 'tough' as something that stood only in a contradictory relationship to succeeding at literacy. Throughout the projects the boys and the teachers were able to find ways to broaden students' understandings of what literacy is in the first place and also to interrogate some of the consequences of an uncritical endorsement of the 'tough guy' persona. The boys recognized their own desires to move beyond the limitations that this persona sometimes placed on them, and created, most importantly, an opportunity for them to envisage themselves as literacy successes rather than failures.

Fourth, there was an interest in and an ability to examine critically issues to do with masculinity as well as issues associated with literacy. An ability to reflect upon traditional masculine norms was illustrated by two of the students' contributions to a discussion that emerged around the Columbine High killing in the United States. While the boys were playing the Nintendo game, and teaching it to their teacher, Kate, she asked them what they thought about the idea that violent games lead to violent kids. The boys immediately made a link to the Columbine massacre that had occurred only a few weeks before. They said that it was 'stupid' to say that boys would kill other boys just because they saw it on television or on a video game. Kids, the boys argued, could tell the difference between what was allowed in the real world and what was allowed in a game. And, according to them, if others couldn't then they were psychos likely to kill people no matter what games they played. One of the boys also offered to the discussion the observation that he was sick of people looking at him like he was some kind of potential killer just because he got into a few fights.

Here the boys rejected the common argument that kids are the passive victims of their socialization and displayed an ability to identify the kinds of consequences that are attached to this kind of thinking. Kate was able to lead the conversation towards a discussion of why people interpret behaviours in particular ways, which led, in turn, to an interrogation of 'masculine' or 'macho' behaviour patterns and 'feminine' or 'sissy' behaviours. The boys identified 'typical' male behaviour within the school and highlighted its advantages and disadvantages. They built on this to discuss the overall advantages and disadvantages of being a boy and, after group discussion, recognized that these varied according to the 'type' of boy involved. They acknowledged the existence of a hierarchy of masculinities within the school and within society more generally and identified many of the difficulties of valuing *all* boys.

Following the boys' lead, Kate was able to draw upon a range of popular culture texts to add to their discussion, some that she was able to show in school and others that the boys saw in their own homes. These texts included: *Free Willy* (1993, Warner Bros), involving the story of a boy taken into a foster family who is originally regarded as a 'trouble maker'; *The Full Monty* (1997, Fox), to facilitate discussion around the pressures associated with the being a male in the workforce; and both the well known *Brassed Off* (1996, Miramax) and the Australian movie *Bootmen* (2000, Fox) to explore the ways in which traditional masculinities associated with professions such as mining or the steel industry can be combined with non-traditional interests and skills. Many of the characters in *Brassed Off* play in a brass band and one suffers intense depression (and attempts suicide) because his attempts to work as a clown to supplement his family income are mocked. In *Bootmen* (2000) the central characters are steel workers who also enjoy tap dancing, a combination which sees them subjected to significant amounts of ridicule at the beginning of the movie, where they are required to 'prove' their masculinity. Kate took the boys on a class excursion to see *Bootmen* and afterwards to McDonald's for lunch.

This opened up a very interesting discussion during which the group explored what they had liked and disliked about the movie. This discussion was followed up in subsequent lessons focused on what it means to be a male. Throughout these sessions the group were able to identify the multiple nature of subjectivity: the boys all identified their ability to be different people in different contexts, and highlighted the pleasure they got from being accepted within these various contexts and discourses and the pain associated with rejection. The boys were also encouraged by their teacher to imagine what they would like their life to be like if they could make all their own choices. Though she did not ask the boys to share their responses publicly, she noticed that several of them made reference to more creative career possibilities than they had on previous occasions.

Kate also worked with the boys to identify the kinds of behaviours that have come to be interpreted as threatening. She highlighted the multiple ways in which some boys and many girls operate constantly in 'risk assessment' mode: constantly scanning their environment for people who may be a threat to them. One particularly interesting offshoot from this discussion was the boys' admission that people were likely to assume that any girl who got attacked by a guy had asked for it in some way. This helped them to recognize why girls might be overly cautious towards boys.

Fifth, in addition to the work carried out with the group of boys, there were several outcomes associated with the mixed groups:

- students voiced an appreciation of the limits of traditional ways of being a boy or a girl, and conceded that schools needed to give students more than one chance to 'be good' and needed to respond differently to multiple misdemeanours for both boys and girls;
- the girls acknowledged that boys, like girls, could be victimized or alienated within schools, and the boys acknowledged that their behaviours *could* have an impact upon how girls felt;
- the students within the mixed group developed basic web creation competencies – a range of literacies associated with the operational and cultural dimensions of literacy – but were also able to identify the gendered nature of many technological and literacy resources.

The teachers across both groups felt generally happy with these outcomes and certainly were encouraged sufficiently to recommit to these and related projects in the following semester. They identified, however, at least three areas requiring greater attention. The first was homophobic and culturally narrow attitudes which, although often temporarily obscured, consistently reappeared and clearly influenced students' judgements of their peers. Second, they identified economic issues which were not fully explored by either group, particularly as these relate to access to various resources outside of school – books, computers, libraries and so on – and likely career paths. The third area comprised disability issues – where there had been a significant silence within discussions in both groups.

Implications

While keeping these limitations in mind, we would argue that this project – despite its small scale and the relatively 'minor' outcomes – is a good example of a project that approaches the gender/boys/literacy challenge rhizomatically. The teachers worked to forge a connection between the boys – as they were – and the boys as they could be. Thus there was an acknowledgement from the beginning that boys could operate in a state of both being and becoming: being 'basic boys' but becoming something more.

Importantly, the teachers acknowledged the important point that the longstanding cultural norms associated with gender could not be simply wished away: despite the teachers' most fervent longings, boys were not going to abandon traditional masculine subjectivities because a teacher asked them to. Instead, the project was based upon the recognition that gender norms could only be exceeded in a gradual and careful process. Rosi Braidotti (1994b) describes the process as metabolic consumption which involves 'working through . . . the stock of cumulated images, concepts and representations of woman, of female identity, such as they have been codified by the culture in which we live' (Braidotti 1994b: 169).

The principle at work here is that changed definitions of female subjectivity (and thus a fundamental challenge to patriarchal/phallocentric modes of thought, teaching and learning) can be achieved only by working through the classical forms of representation of female subjectivity so as to consume them from within. When applied to consideration of masculinity, metabolic consumption can be taken as a reminder that masculinity cannot be willed away, but must be strategically interrogated, denaturalized and imagined differently. In Braidotti's (1994b: 169) terms, 'the new is created by revisiting and burning up the old': 'Like the gradual peeling off of old skins . . . it is the metabolic consumption of the old that can engender the new. Difference is not the effect of willpower, but the result of many, of endless repetitions' (Braidotti 1994b. 182).

Importantly, the repetition and validation of new masculine subjectivities were required not just for the students, but also for their teachers and their families. The project provided alternative ways for the boys to conceptualize and enact their masculinity: links were made between their interests and such 'feminine' or 'literary' skills as research, sharing information, teaching, teamwork, negotiation/cooperation and, importantly, literacy *success*. All the boys received the highest possible grade – an A – for this unit of work and this was the first time any of them had ever received such a high grade. The teacher felt that some of her colleagues didn't believe the boys had deserved this result, and that she was just awarding them 'sympathy' marks. She worked consistently to showcase the boys' talents, not just within the traditional male area of video game playing, but in the non-traditional field of teaching and working cooperatively. In addition to this, Kate wrote letters home to the boys' families, congratulating the boys on their contribution throughout the unit and emphasizing the fact that the separate class had been an experiment designed to benefit the school. Kate's goal was to ensure that in taking part in the single-sex class the boys were seen as people making a positive contribution to a school, not as trouble makers removed from the 'normal' group.

It is this commitment to consuming and exceeding the limits of traditional masculinity – in many different sites and across many competing discourses – that distinguishes the Willoughby project from Montague's initiative. There are some superficial similarities between the Willoughby and the Montague projects. These particularly concern the way both schools made use of 'masculine' projects or activities to engage the boys and keep them interested: the key teachers at the two schools had different ideas of where they wanted to end up. While Willoughby prioritized the problematization and transformation of gender norms, Montague aspired more to the revalidation and reinscription of masculine gender norms. Willoughby was committed to a particular goal, while Montague was committed to a particular *journey* (Rowan 1998). As a result similar strategies were used in quite different ways.

On a transformative journey – or what Deleuze and Guattari (1987) might call a line of flight – we may make many moves. Some of these will appear as traditional, others as radical, but they are bound together by their pragmatic usefulness: by their ability to help us to go somewhere. In many cases, the success of any gender-based literacy reform project is fundamentally tied to the teachers' abilities to let go of fixed, one-plan-fixes-all reform plans and adopt a kind of constancy with flexibility (Rowan 1998: 22). This capitalizes on the interests, ideas and energy of a specific group, while moving inexorably towards a new location.

There is one final point we want to make about the Willoughby story. There are a number of excellent books dealing with boys, literacy and/or gender reform in schools that outline specific lessons plans that can be used by teachers to effect some kind of change in boys' interests and/or behaviours. The authors who contributed to books 1 and 2 of *Boys and Literacy: Meeting the Challenge* (Alloway *et al.* 1996) and *Boys and Literacy: Professional Development Units* and *Boys and Literacy: Teaching Units* (Alloway and Gilbert 1997) provide good examples of this kind of text. We believe the kinds of lessons and literacy units outlined in these two books are, for the most part, consistent with our own transformative agenda. Nevertheless, we have deliberately presented the key points of this chapter in a narrative, rather than 'lesson plan', format, in order to illustrate the point that gender reform is, for us, fundamentally tied to the process of telling different stories. The two narratives included in this chapter may look similar on the surface, but a closer reading reveals that they say remarkably different things about literacy, masculinity and education. Gender norms –

in their construction, normalization, contestation and transformation – are fundamentally a set of more or less powerful fictions.

Conclusions

The outcomes from the Willoughby project would not have been possible without a particular combination of literacy and gender reform mindsets. The new literacies studies framework was necessary to legitimate the conceptualization of literacy as something more than the ability to encode and decode printed texts. Similarly, 'basic' literacy frameworks do not encourage the important introduction of 'out-of-school literacies' into classroom contexts. The transformative mindset on gender reform enabled the teaching team to put traditionally masculine digital technologies to different use and encouraged, also, explicit critique of gender and gendered behaviour patterns.

We are not suggesting that this kind of approach will transform boys, schools or literacy contexts in the short term. In fact, we argue that there are no actual short-term solutions available. Nevertheless, the consistent application of the principles that underpinned the Willoughby project have the potential to connect boys to literacy activities in ways that open up the possibility for further and different connections.

The term 'possibility' is important here, for every reform project – however well intentioned, however thoughtfully designed – has the potential to work transformatively/rhizomatically or to work traditionally. An awareness of the distinction between basic essentialism and strategic essentialism can help teachers to avoid some of the more obvious traps. Making the distinction, however, is not always as easy as the examples explored here may make it seem. The image of the rhizome can help us to think about the extent to which a project is making connections from and beyond traditional masculinities. At the same time, some gender reform projects make use of multiple strategies or deal with so many issues that it is not always easy to distinguish between the transformative and the traditional.

In the two chapters that follow we explore in greater detail two of the most common strategies employed when teachers attempt to make the kind of rhizomatic connections between boys and literacy that we have argued for in this chapter. We focus on ways in which technology and popular culture (or generationally specific resources) are often used in attempts to connect boys with literate practices and thereby move them beyond the limitations of hegemonic masculinity.

In Chapter 6 we look in more detail at the strengths and weaknesses associated with the use of digital technologies in literacy classrooms, and highlight the ways in which technology can be used in transformative ways. In Chapter 7 we examine ways in which teachers attempt to engage with the generational realities of their students in the construction and design of literacy practices. We highlight the risk and possibilities associated with 'getting in touch' with students from different generational perspectives and emphasize the dangers of essentializing any group of students – on generational grounds – as inherently similar, or naturally the same. The emphasis throughout these two chapters is on the ways in which resources such as computers, popular movies or other 'kid texts' can be used either to reinforce or to challenge hegemonic masculinities, and we highlight those strategies which make links between boys and the enactment of literate masculinity.

chapter six

Exorcizing digital demons: information technology, new literacies and the de/reconstruction of gendered subjectivities

Last fall, Mattel released the Barbie PC, a pink, Barbie-themed computer for girls. But the Barbie PC comes loaded with a little more then half of the educational software found on Mattel's counterpart computer for boys, the Hot Wheels PC. Among the software titles omitted from the Barbie PC but offered on the Hot Wheels PC are Body Works, a program that teaches human anatomy and 3-dimensional visualization, and a thinking game called Logical Journey of the Zoombinis. Mattel responded to complaints by explaining that the popular Barbie programs such as Barbie Fashion Designer left less room for educational titles on the girls' computer. The other programs included on the boys' computer but not on the one designed for girls are: *The Clue Finders Math 9–12, Compton's Complete Reference Collection,* and *Kid Pix Studio.*

(Luchetta 2000: 2)

Boys, girls, computers and literacies: whose computer is it anyway?

Associations of the kind described by Luchetta that are based on the 'inherent' or 'natural' interests and capacities of boys and girls *vis-à-vis* computers might be regarded as just another instance, albeit a high-tech version, of the kinds of stereotyping and pigeonholing of boys and girls that we have described in other contexts in this book. The gender associations that give rise to 'boy computers' and 'girl computers' are commonplace in the media, in advertising as well as in the minds of some teachers. Recently, this gendered view of technology has given rise to practices in literacy classrooms in which boys are encouraged to use computers to support their classroom literacy learning. The practice has been hailed as a solution to the boys and literacy 'crisis'. On the face of it the practice seems like a logical thing to do, to exploit the well known affinity that boys have with computer technology. If, however, we adopt the stance we have in previous chapters of this book, we know to be suspicious of what are claimed to be normal or natural practices particularly about gender.

Rather than accepting computers to be something of a convenient, even magical solution to the boys and literacy crisis, this chapter examines the complex set of associations that arise when the new computing and communication technologies are added to literacy classrooms with the expressed purpose of supporting the boys. We argue that the situation is complex because there are three interrelated propositions – generally tied to essentialist mindsets associated with masculinity – that are in play. To illustrate this we have expressed the propositions in a kind of shorthand or algebra:

boys + computers = learning (1)

boys + literacy = poor literacy learning (2)

literacy + computers = literacy learning (3)

Separating these propositions in this way allow us to work through the important issues and debates relating to each, which then allows us to examine critically the validity of the proposition, that

boys + literacy + computers = literacy learning (4)

We have considered arguments and issues relating to proposition (2) in other parts of this book, where we have argued that it is not a simple matter to make generalizable associations between gender and literacy learning. In a similar manner, this chapter examines and challenges the commonly made assertions relating to gender, the new computing and communication technologies and literacy learning. In this chapter we examine propositions (1) and (3), the two propositions necessary to make proposition (4) workable.

Boys + computers = learning?

There is a large literature concerned with gender and the new computing and communication technologies. For the most part, it derives from observations of the patterns of use by boys and girls that have been reported in the mass media as well as in scholarly journals. Like other gender-based patterning we have discussed in this book, there is a tendency to see these patterns as 'natural' and as reflecting the innateness of being a boy or being a girl. When computer technology is added to this perspective it is not surprising to find that claims are made about the innate nature or essence of a computer. This section of the chapter addresses issues around gender and the new computing and communication technologies. While our focus is on classroom practice, the topic is of much wider interest and importance than that. As we will see in what follows, supporting particular stereotypes and patterns of use by boys and girls is particularly significant to companies that design, develop and market high technology gizmos for the young.

When considering the patterns of use and media representations, we see it is important to question the explanation that what we see is something that has arisen naturally, as a consequence of essential properties of being a boy, a girl or a computer. We need to ask how these things got to be the way they are. Even so, there are potential snags here. One possible consequence of thinking about computer technologies in this way is that our wish to avoid attributing natural capacities or properties to them results in us concluding that they are 'neutral'. The commonly used phrase 'just a tool' is an indicator of this way of thinking about computing or any other technology.

Arguments concerning the non-neutrality of computing and other technologies have been made over a long period (Weizenbaum 1984; Bowers 1988; Marvin 1988; Noble 1991; Kling 1996). For example, some argue that the dominance of a male-oriented business culture in software development and icon or interface naming (e.g. the 'desktop', the egocentric 'my briefcase') has worked to exclude women from participating in using and producing digital technologies. Indeed, advertising for computers, computer peripherals, such as printers and scanners, and software tends to emphasize – overtly in the early 1990s – the 'boys and their toys' domain of digital technologies (Hellman 1996; Sofia 1996; Greene 1998; Chaika 2000). As Carmen Luke (1996) puts it: 'The gendered register, style, imagery and content of on-line communications, computer software languages, CD-ROM entertainment, and the adjunct print discourse (e.g. *Wired, Mondo 2000, .net*) on cyberculture computing and net surfing gear, is decidedly male.' This was certainly brought home to us in reports of the NIIT corporation's experiment in India. This huge information technologies company, situated on the edge of a slum in New Delhi, set up a computer on the outside wall of its office complex for the locals to use (without access to expert users and suchlike). In no time at all, children had developed a language for talking about computer functions and icons that was rooted in their own everyday lives, rather than in the business world:

> They named the cursor *nci sui*, *mtr* or 'needle', because of its sharp arrow shape, and they call websites 'channels'. The hour glass is called a *nci damru* . . . the hour-glass shaped drum that the Hindu god Shiva

plays. When it appears, the children know the computer is working on something.

(Ghosh 2000: 1)

The NIIT experiment in New Delhi underscores the fact that computers need not be confined to business culture metaphors developed in the 1970s, yet these metaphors and their direct association with male-dominated business discourses and practices persist. But are these patterns of use determined by an underlying innateness in computers or in men and women? Unpacking some of these issues is not a simple matter, particularly when it comes to dealing with a technology. It is even more difficult when we have to think about computing and related technologies. A useful way of tackling the question of inherent attributes is to avoid getting mired in focusing on the innateness of humans and non-humans and, instead, to examine the relationships as they have been established in the particular pattern of use at issue. A useful question to ask in this respect is: in whose interests is it that we accept that there are particular inherent properties of humans or machines; for example, that there is a natural affinity between boys and violent computer games? In other words, it is important to distinguish between existing patterns of use and the interests that have shaped them, and any claims about the naturalness of the patterns.

The commonly held views about what girls like to do with computers have led to a perception that there is a 'gap' between boys' and girls' attitudes towards and use of digital technologies. The research literature reflects a diversity of interests and findings in this respect. Some researchers argue that their studies show no significant differences between male and female attitudes towards computers (National Science Foundation 1997; Barrier and Margavio, National School Boards Foundation, and Ory, Bullock and Burnaska, all cited in Luchetta 2000). Others contend that a lack of interest in computers – especially where girls are concerned – has to do with a disenchantment with computing cultures rather than 'anxiety or intellectual deficiency' (Luchetta 2000: 1; see also AAUW 2000a). Others again suggest that attitudes towards computers are not an effective measure of actual use (National Science Foundation 1997; Dorman 1998; Roper Starch Worldwide 1998).

The promotion of gender stereotypes is something that is now commonplace in the marketing and promotion of computer software to young people. Allucquère Stone (1996: 126–7), among many others, alerts us to ways in which female characters in early computer games were often perceived by software project managers and programmers alike. Stone recounts one 'move' in what might be called a gender-techno war in a digital games production sweatshop (Wellspring Systems). The people involved in this account are a woman from the marketing division of Electronic Arts (another company), and Memphis Smith, a programmer supervising the development of a new game called *Battle Commander*, 'which promise[d] to be the biggest seller in [the company's] history' (Stone 1996: 159).

When the pre-release version of *Battle Commander* was demonstrated at a Comdex trade show, it opened with a screen showing 'a naked young woman covered by a thin sheet, lying on an army cot', who sat up 'looking seductively at the player' when the cursor passed over her. A day or so later the woman from Electronic Arts approached Smith and asked how she might be able to influence the way women were depicted in the game. According to Stone,

> Smith looked her over as if she were a putrefying fish. He inflated his chest just a bit – something of an accomplishment, considering his already cocky attitude. 'Well, little lady,' he said in an exaggerated drawl, 'tell you what, why don't you just take it up with the artist, or better yet' – he leaned in at her, pushing his face close to hers, his voice dripping sarcasm – 'Why don't you just call my boss and get me fired?'
>
> There was a pause. 'I see,' she said, and walked away.
>
> 'The way women are depicted in the game,' Smith chuckled. 'You can always tell the ones that never get any.'
>
> (Stone 1996: 160)

Some weeks later Smith was telephoned by the president of another company which had just acquired a controlling share of Wellspring stock. The caller demanded that the opening screen/scene be changed. When informed of the demand, Smith exploded, accusing 'them damn frog women' of trying to polarize the production team. 'Frog women' referred to women not meeting Smith's criteria for 'attractiveness' – which apparently extended to 'any woman with the temerity to remark on the quality of his games' (Stone 1996: 161). Stone narrates what ensued as follows:

> Roberts calmed [Smith] down. They decided on what they believed was a compromise. The naked woman stayed. A second cot appeared in the screen, on which lay a naked man, also covered with a sheet. He did not sit up when cursored.

Accounts such as these are important in revealing the contested and negotiated space that always characterizes any technological project or innovation. Clearly, we need to attend to the values that are represented in this process and the final product. But, and this is the important point, *it might have been otherwise*. What we end up with is something that has arisen not naturally, but through a complex set of negotiations, trade-offs and compromises that is more akin to a game of Scrabble than to a reflection of fundamental attributes of men, women or machines.[1] Thus, the patterns which are commonly found in the representation of women in computer games tell us more about particular sets of interests than about anything that is innately driving such associations.

Janelle Brown (2000a: 1), for example, critiques recent game makers' claims that a new wave of game heroines has begun that will 'unseat Lara Croft with brains over bustline'. She points out that the photos accompanying the article show a 'busty sexpot' character named Joanna Dark from the game *Perfect Dark* (Rare 1999), 'in a blue catsuit so tight you'd think she was naked'. Dark is curvaceous, according to Brown, who adds, 'although whether she bulges with brains was not readily apparent'. In the article Brown critiques, Perrin Kaplan, director of corporate affairs for Nintendo explains that Joanna Dark 'is beautiful, but her figure isn't the first thing you notice. She isn't just sex and curves.' As Brown (2000a: 2) puts it, females in sexy outfits sell games: 'even the more "responsible" characters, packaged with realistic armour or unusual wit, will still boast Barbie proportions – because marketers know that boys will buy it' (see also Buchanan 2000; Chaika 2000; Morris and Veen 2000). Indeed, as the Nintendo 64 website puts it in a review of *Perfect Dark*, 'Based on her physical attributes, we're guessing that Joanna's test scores weren't the only factor leading to her flattering nickname', i.e. Perfect (Nintendo 64 2000).

On another dimension, many women, especially in the United States, have decided to act in response to the computer and video game world that values 'thrash and kill' adventure games over creative problem solving games. The former are meant to appeal deliberately to boys, while the latter have been shown by repeated research to appeal more to girls. Newspapers and magazines play directly into the masculine culture of software and video gaming. Recounts such as the following underscore the boys' toys and men-only territory of video gaming:

> Four men – though they are barely old enough to be called that – locked in mortal combat.
>
> They stare unblinking at computer screens at Wizards of the Coast in Seattle's University district. With a computer mouse, they move rock-throwing soldiers, spike-toting chariot drivers and armored elephants across ancient civilizations.
>
> In the end, a 23-year-old from Guelph, Ontario, who goes by the name Maimin' Matty, crushes the other three, building an empire and winning $2,000 and a trip to Rome.
>
> (Greene 1998: 1)

The language used by Jay Greene to describe this gaming contest speaks volumes about the culture of computer gaming, emphasized by at least one contestants' alias, 'Maimin' Matty'. In response to this gaming discourse that values violence and competition, Sharon Schuster of the American Association of University Women comments dryly, 'When it comes to computer games and software, girls want high-skill not high-kill' (quoted in AAUW 2000b: 1). Indeed, some people saw computer and video game software as being so unrelated to girls' interests that they actually applauded the release of the 'feminist nightmare' and surprisingly hugely selling software for girls, *Barbie's Fashion Designer* (Mattel Media 1996). In fact, the Barbie software was so successful that Mattel has launched since then the hot pink Barbie PC (Mattel Media 1999) that comes with Barbie adventure software (e.g. Barbie as Rapunzel, Barbie's ocean discovery dive). Many saw this software as important in challenging some of the stereotypes associated with a boys-only notion of computing by engaging girls in using computers to do 'girl things'. Others continue to lament that most software – including 'education-oriented' software – still reinforces stereotypical gender roles (AAUW 1998: 4).

It is safe to assume that the Barbie-specific software, which is not included on the Hot Wheels PC (and vice versa), sends clear messages to pre-teen children regarding what is 'right' for them to be interested in, and what is not. Without a doubt both the Barbie PC and the Hot Wheels PC can be seen as limiting for both boys and girls. This gender categorization work seems all the more ironic when we look at surveys such as that of the National Schools Board Foundation (cited in Luchetta 2000: 2). This polled 1735 households and found – among other things – that not only do girls use the Internet more than do the boys surveyed, but the girls use it more for educational purposes.

Interestingly, the 'toys for boys and for girls' debate has seen the inception of a number of companies aiming to make new technologies both accessible and interesting for girls. These include companies such as Mattel Media, Hasbro Interactive, Sega, DreamWorks Interactive, Starwave, R/GA Interactive, Broderbund and Philips media, as well as more directly girl-oriented companies such as Her Interactive, Girl Games Incorporated, Cybergrrl Incorporated and the now defunct game programming division of Purple Moon.

The Purple Moon company was in large part the outgrowth of a research project conducted by Brenda Laurel – a renowned entertainment software programmer and researcher – between 1993 and 1995 (Laurel 1995, 1999). Laurel's research was generated by growing discontent among women regarding the lack of software that interested girls (as Laurel (1999: 2) herself puts it, 'I think I got into doing games for girls because I was so tired of seeing things explode').

Laurel's research findings challenged a number of myths about girls and computers – such as 'girls don't like to fight', 'girls are too social to enjoy using computers' and 'girls don't play computer games'. According to Laurel, girls certainly do not like physical violence, but 'they seem to have no problem bopping an animated mushroom creature on the head (or any other non-human "bad guy")' (Purple Moon 2000: 2). Laurel's research also suggests that girls 'make-over' computers and suchlike to serve their own desires – such as playing single-player games collaboratively at the screen with a friend, engaging in multiplayer games at one PC or across the Internet and using email to interact with others. With regard to girls' computer game-playing, Laurel (1999: 2) asserts that girls enjoy playing

Table 6.1 How adventures for girls differ from boys' action games

Adventures for girls	*Boys' action games*
Leading characters are everyday people that girls can easily relate to, and are as real to girls as their best friends	Leading characters are fantasy-based action heroes with 'super power' abilities
Goal is to explore and have new experiences, with degrees of success and varying outcomes	Goal is to win, and the play is linear; outcome is black and white; die and start over, one 'right' solution
Play focuses on multisensory immersion, discovery and strong storylines	Speed and action are key
Feature everyday 'real-life' settings as well as new places to explore	Feature non-realistic, larger than life settings
Success comes through development of friendships	Success comes through the elimination of competitors

Source: Purple Moon (2000: 3).

computer games very much, but that 'One reason girls haven't played computer games more often is because traditionally the content has catered to boys' tastes. The few girl titles available have usually been too juvenile or have lacked the type of challenges and play experiences girls enjoy.' The Purple Moon (2000: 3) website, which is still in active existence, sums up the differences between girls' and boys' game-playing preferences in the form of a table (see Table 6.1).

The Purple Moon 'transmedia business', which produced software games for girls and which still runs a web-based 'entertainment experience', is explicitly aimed at girls (http://www.purple-moon.com). In fact, only girls are allowed to enter the various competitions or submit messages to the website's all-female cast of human characters.

Laurel's myth-busting work is certainly supported by more recent research, such as the Gallup Organization poll of US teenagers and technology. The poll was conducted in conjunction with the CNN corporation, USA Today and the US National Science Foundation (National Science Foundation 1997). The 744 children and young people surveyed across the nation were aged between 13 and 17 (no per location figures, age cohort numbers or gender breakdowns are given in the executive summary available). According to the summary of poll results,

> The survey [found] relatively small differences between girls and boys in terms of their general orientation towards technology. Boys appear to have slightly more interest than girls in science and technology sub-

jects in school, although the majority of girls as well as boys say they prefer math and science to English and social studies. Girls are just as likely as boys to believe a strong background in computers and technology will be important to their financial success in life.

Findings that suggest girls and boys – at least in the USA – share similar attitudes towards digital technology in general are supported by other large-scale studies such as a *Newsweek* poll of 508 teenagers (*Newsweek* 1997: 86) and the Roper Company's Youth Report (Roper Starch Worldwide 1998).

Another set of arguments regarding girls and their seeming absence in new technology arenas point to what some call 'the problem of linear logics' in software programming which are seen as essentially 'masculine' and ultimately exclusive to 'non-males' and others who prefer non-linear approaches to software programming. For example, Sherry Turkle (1995: 52–3) describes how one female student of hers became disenchanted with computer programming because of overt emphasises on linear rationality – a rationality most commonly associated with men (see Wertheim 1997). Lisa, an 18-year-old first year student at Harvard, preferred to approach programming in the same way as she did poetry writing – working her way from one line of code to the next, rather than carefully pre-planning the entire program according to fixed sequences of steps and stages before starting to code. And 'When she talked about the lines of code in her programs, she gestured with her hands and body in a way that showed her moving with them and among them' (Turkle 1995: 52–3). Her teachers, however, insisted that her way was the 'wrong way' and that in order to be a successful programmer, she needed to do it 'their way'. Lisa held out for two months before she found it easier to cave in to their demands – and as Turkle puts it, Lisa 'called it her "not-me strategy" and began to insist that it didn't matter because "the computer was just a tool".'

Moreover, 'being a programmer' has become connected in many people's minds with pasty-skinned, greasy-haired young men/older boys who spend their days sleeping and their nights in solitude and darkness apart from the blue light of the computer screen in front of them, the rapid clicking of keys as they develop their programs and the hum and tick of the computer through the night. Interestingly enough, these images often – especially in the 1980s – weren't all that far from the truth (Kendall 1999). Archetypal technogeeks are the mainstay of Douglas Coupland's book *Microserfs* (1995), and technogeek practices are described in full svga-colour in Fred Moody's (1995) haunting ethnography of the development of the *Explorapedia* CD-ROM at Microsoft. It is also interesting to note that the few popular culture movies that show women actively engaged with computer technology depict them as encountering danger or harassment as a result of their technology use. Sandra Bullock in *The Net* and Sigourney Weaver in *Copycat* are both victimized on account of their use of computers.

This doesn't mean, of course, that girls and women never become pro-grammers because of the 'boy culture' associated with new technologies. In the earliest days of programming, Lady Ada Byron Lovelace (Lord Byron's daughter) wrote a plan to show how Charles Babbage's analytical engine might be used to calculate Bernoulli numbers. Considered the first computer programmer, Ada Lovelace was honoured in 1979 when the US Defence Department named its software programming language after her. Six North American women mathematicians – Kay Mauchley Antonelli, Jean Bartik, Betty Holberton (also known for her work with the Cobol programming language), Marlyn Meltzer, Frances Spence and Ruth Teitelbaum – have recently been publicly recognized for their work during the Second World War. They created the programming language that ran the giant ENIAC computer (the world's first digital computer) (Brown 2000b). Eighty women were involved in the day-to-day maintenance of this new digital technology. Similarly, Ellen Ullman (1997: 14) speaks for many women when she recounts a conversation she had with two co-programmers she had contracted to work with her on a major project:

> 'We can add a parameter to the remote procedure call.'
> 'We should check the referential integrity on that.'
> 'Should the code be attached to that control or should it be in global scope.'
> 'Global, because this other object here needs to know about the condition.'
> 'No! No globals. We agreed. No more globals!'
> We have entered the code zone. Here thought is telegraphic and ex-quisitely precise. I feel no need to slow myself down. On the contrary, the faster the better.

Clearly, not all women are put off by the linearity of programming or the culture of computing. Nevertheless, and despite countless movements, or-ganizations and activities aimed at getting girls involved in using and mak-ing computers (albeit predominantly in the USA), girls' use of technology and participation in digital production and digital cultures are talked about in terms of 'crisis'. The American Association of University Women Educa-tional Foundation has long been concerned with the growing disparities between boys' and girls' participation in digital technology-centred educa-tion and professions. A recent report by this association (AAUW 2000b: 1) lists a number of statistics related to girls and technology in support of growing concerns that 'girls are alarmingly under represented in computer science and technology fields' (Schuster n.d., cited in AAUW 2000b: 1):

- Women are roughly 20 per cent of IT professionals.
- Women receive less than 28 per cent of the computer science bachelor's degrees, down from a high of 37 per cent in 1984. Computer science is

the only field in which women's participation has actually decreased over time.

- Women make up just 9 per cent of the recipients of engineering-related bachelor's degrees.

For the AAUW, involving girls in the production and use of digital technologies remains crucial in any talk about equity: 'the failure to include girls in advanced-level computer science courses threatens to make women bystanders in the technological 21st century' (AAUW 1998: 4). Concomitantly, and as with the software companies mentioned above, various support groups and committees have sprung up to get girls digital. These include the Women in Technology initiative, GirlTECH teacher training programmes and the Design Your Future internship programme.

For example, the National Coalition of Girls' Schools (cited in Walsh-Sarnecki 1998: 4) proposes the following tips to 'help close the gender gap in computer technology':

1 Tell girls about real-life places and jobs that use computers.
2 Make sure daughters have equal access to home computers.
3 Use women role models in the classroom or even as web pen pals.
4 Give girls the extra encouragement they need to sign up for electives such as computer science, physics and chemistry.
5 Don't label jobs as men's or women's work. Give girls hands-on experience.
6 Don't just get one girl involved in maths, science or computers – give her some company by getting her girl friend involved, too.

A key finding of the AAUW study *Tech-Savvy: Educating Girls in the New Computer Age* (AAUW 2000a) was that girls' reservations about participating in computer cultures were well founded. These reservations take the form of passivity in interactions where the computer is viewed as a 'tool', in response to the violence, tedium and redundancy of computer games, claims that computer culture career options are uninspiring and boring in narrow and technically focused programming classes. The report recommends that, among other things, computer labs should be done away with so that computers can more readily be 'used across the curriculum in ways that invite more girls into technology through a range of subjects that already interest them' (AAUW 2000a: 4). It also suggests that computer literacy 'needs to be redefined to include the lifelong application of relevant concepts, skills and problem-solving abilities' (*ibid.*). Another key recommendation concerns the perception of new technologies as job options: 'Make the public face of women in computing correspond to the reality rather than the stereotype. Girls tend to imagine that computer professionals live in a solitary, antisocial and sedentary world. This is an alienating – and incorrect – perception of careers that will rely heavily on computer technology and expertise in this century' (*ibid.*).

One dangerous outcome of this research into and reports about girls and computing is that boys are essentialized in particular ways. They are portrayed as lovers of violence, speed and action; only interested in linear storylines, if interested at all; attracted by the seemingly stereotyped, solitary lifestyle of computer programmer; in no way a social being interested in social interaction; and so on. As Beato (1997: 2) puts it jokingly, but with a serious point to make:

> there are girls and women who like to slaughter mutant humanoids as much as any man does, and whose only discontent with *Duke Nukem* is that the bloodbaths it facilitates are simply too tepid; on the other hand, there are boys and men who don't immediately turn into glassy-eyed alien snuff zombies when presented with the latest *Doom* level.

Locating counter examples to the dominant stereotypes is important in helping to disrupt the commonly understood associations of boys or girls and computers. Nevertheless, it is important to understand patterns of associations as things that have been negotiated and that do not reflect any essentialist attributes. Our own experiences of observing boys and young men using digital technologies in a variety of ways and for a range of purposes also put paid to claims that boys are a homogeneous group of digital technology users. Jacques, the 12-year-old Year 6 student mentioned above, is a case in point. Jacques had always struggled with literacy in school, and is a likely candidate for being the kind of boy assumed in girl-only technology talk. However, he isn't a great fan and player of video or computer games. As he puts is:

> Oh, I used to be [interested in video games]. When we first got ours: 'Oh GI's it!', 'I'm first!' Whack! (mimes fighting over the game console). That kind of thing. But now . . . I'd rather be out on my skates or something, you know, flying up the streets or something like that.

Nicholas is another young man who does not fit ardent computer user stereotypes (see Knobel 1999). He is, to be sure, an avid computer game player and computer user, and completes as much of his schoolwork as possible on the computer. In fact, as a fluent touch-typer, Nicholas finds it easier to key text in than to write it by hand. When he was 7 years old his mother used to pay him 5 cents a minute for the time spent practising touch-typing. At the same time, Nicholas openly identifies his family as his most precious thing, and has a warm and loving relationship with his parents. He and his mother enjoy a particularly close relationship and regularly read the same books for relaxation, go halves in buying music compact discs and work collaboratively on school homework and projects.

Nicholas is also a keen and regular basketball player, writes songs and music which he sometimes sings during church services, has girls as friends, is a key figure in boys' interest groups at school and is a thoroughly gregarious young man. Part of his social life includes being a member of a computer gaming network that shares popular software and gaming tips. This network shares copies of freeware downloaded from the Internet or copied from CD-ROM collections. Members of the network take turns in borrowing popular computer adventure games owned by one member, and so on. Members who travel to the United States – where game software is a fraction of the cost it is in Australia – are also enlisted as software buyers and new game scouts for the others. Nicholas's gaming network spans friends at school and church, as well as his sisters and brother and his brother's high school mates. It involves him (and the other members) in highly social practices (e.g. comparing notes on how a game is played or on graphics, cheats and so on, discussing which games to get or who has what at any given time and the like).

Similar social engagement is evident in the seemingly innumerable Internet cafes that have sprung up throughout Mexico. It is often difficult to use these facilities to receive and send e-mail messages when one is on the move. It is common to encounter small groups of young men clustered around every available computer, spending hours on Internet relay chat lines and e-mail. For them, computers are above all else *social.*

These examples and the others we could offer are not meant to detract from the important work going on around the world that aims at making new technologies much more accessible to girls. Nevertheless, we do want to broaden the argument to include boys who are often marginalized in school settings or those boys who don't fit the stereotype of a computer whiz. The important point underlying all these patterns of use and associations of humans and non-humans is that there is nothing fundamentally predetermined about them: they all could have been otherwise. To talk of positive learning outcomes when boys use computers is merely to highlight one of a very large number of patterns of use that can be discerned as these technologies are taken up by more and more of society in the over-developed countries of the world. Equally, to talk about girls being disinclined towards the new computing and communication technologies is unhelpful if the argument is based upon essentializing girls or computers.

Literacy + computers = literacy learning?

The reasons schools and teachers offer for bringing the new computing and communication technologies into schools are many and varied (Bigum 1990; Burbules and Callister 1996; Comber and Green 1999; Rowan *et al.* 2000). The basis of most rationales is an implicit association of computers with progress, typically coupled with a view that adding computers to a particular context will improve learning. Literacy learning, like other learnings organized in schools, has been a part of the broad cross-curriculum enthusiasm for using the new computing and communication technologies to improve educational outcomes. In this respect, literacy, like other areas of the curriculum, has been the subject of considerable interest *vis-à-vis* using computers to improve learning. For this reason, we will take a little space to examine the broader set of issues around the use of computers in classrooms to support learning.

There exists a large literature concerned with studying the effects of using computers to support learning. A good deal of it is based on designs that seek to remove all effects on learning other than that of the computer – no simple matter – in order to establish whether or not improvements result from using a computer. Findings from some of these studies have shown slight improvements in the efficiency of student learning. Some students do learn things a little more quickly. These studies have been popular among those seeking to demonstrate or prove the value of using computers in classrooms. They largely miss, however, the more common outcome in actual classrooms. Rather than improving outcomes, the use of new media almost always tends to *change* outcomes. In other words, students learn different things. Lee Sproull and Sara Kiesler (1991) argue more generally about the use of new communication technologies that it is useful to distinguish between two kinds of effects. They call these first order effects and second order effects respectively. First order effects are those that are used to justify the deployment of the technology by arguing for improved performance in existing practices. Second order effects are the unintended outcomes of using the technologies – those things that actually happen. Sproull and Kiesler argue that unintended outcomes are the norm. This is because 'people pay attention to different things, have contact with different people, and depend on one another differently' (Sproull and Kiesler 1991: 4).

The continuing faith in computers as a kind of generic solution to many of the learning problems found in classrooms requires careful scrutiny. Broadly, it posits that good educational outcomes derive from spending on the new information and communication technologies; that is, it is only a matter of spending more on hardware, software and teacher professional development to achieve better educational outcomes. A similar view was once held in business and industry. It was believed that investment in IT would inevitably and of itself lead to improved profitability and productivity. Analyses that have closely examined IT investment and business outcomes have shown that there is little or no association with increased profits or productivity and spending on IT (Strassmann 1997). These results have led Michael Schrage to argue that in terms of obtaining improved performances and outcomes from IT what matters is *design sensibility* (Educom Review Staff 1998). The common approach is to assume that in and of itself IT will provide good educational outcomes and improvements in schools and/or to try to make IT fit the existing mould of educational practices which make up the school. A better approach is to see IT as a still relatively poorly understood new medium that requires careful and critical experimentation. It is fair to suggest that such cautious uncertainty about the role of IT has *not* characterized the acquisition and deployment of these technologies in most schools and school systems.

We think that cautious uncertainty is an educationally sound and practical position, unlike views that naturally associate computers with improved learning in the classroom. As we have seen elsewhere in the book, it is important to question associations that embrace either an implicit or explicit argument about something being natural or inherent. New computing and communication technologies are at the base of profound changes being played out in the contemporary world. By virtue of this status they have assumed a high status in schools. It would seem 'natural' for schools to respond to the changed and changing circumstances outside schools by acquiring and using these technologies in schools. Indeed, preparing the young for a technologized world has been an important rationale for putting computers in schools for the past twenty years. To date schools have not opted to tackle the difficult but important work of helping students to make sense of the role of the new computing and communication technologies in shaping the current economic, social and cultural dimensions of their experiences. Instead, schools have tended to teach students *how* to use these technologies and have used them to support student learning. This is an important point of slippage. It is as if schools are saying, albeit implicitly, that the best and only way they can help students to respond to the new world order is to teach students how to use computers for school-related tasks.

It is important to untangle and separate claims about using computers in schools to respond to a technologized world from claims concerned with improving student learning. Having briefly considered the problems associated with the former we return to a consideration of the claims around using these technologies to promote and improve learning in the classroom, and in particular for literacy learning.

Literacy learning and computers

As we argued at the beginning of this section, the application of computing technologies to any task changes things. This means that to 'apply' computers to literacy learning is more than likely to change what is learned, and to do so in largely unpredictable ways. For this reason, it is important to examine each instance in which claims about learning and the new technologies are made. It is also better to approach the use of these technologies in classrooms more in terms of an experiment than in terms of applying a well developed and understood approach to supporting literacy learning.

That is not to suggest that things cannot be learned from what has already taken place in classrooms over a long period of time now. A difficulty lies in locating studies that have been framed in ways that do not pre-empt the kinds of associations that we have considered so far; that is, those that rely upon 'natural' capacities, tendencies or properties. For instance, in an

Australian study,[2] Lankshear *et al.* (1997) found that most computers appear to be used to develop only students' operational technological literacy skills, with little change in conventional school literacy practices apart from their being dressed up in 'technodrag'. As Larry Cuban (1986) has argued, schools tend to appropriate technologies on their terms and effectively 'school' them. That is, they use them to reproduce *existing* practices.

It may seem odd that we are describing computerized literacy practices as not much different from their non-computerized counterparts and, at the same time, arguing that when computer technology is added to an existing practice the practice changes in unpredictable ways. An approach that enables a way into this apparent contradiction is one that frames innovations or projects of the kind we are considering – those associated with adding computers to a literacy classroom – in terms of a set of negotiations and compromises between all the elements in the classroom, including the computers.[3] It is an approach which does not predetermine what role a teacher, student or computer might play, but instead understands what eventuates as something that is the outcome of a process of mutual assignment of roles by all the actors.

The negotiation of roles for classroom computers, like other technologies before them, tends to occur most efficiently by minimizing disruption to the existing networks in the classroom. Thus, for a teacher-centred classroom, technologies that can be made to align with the central role of the teacher find relatively easy passage. Examples include the overhead projector, a film projector or a single computer used to illustrate from the front of the classroom. Technologies that disrupt such patterns, however, are less likely to be able to negotiate an enduring role. An example here is a class set of computers. Even when a role is successfully negotiated between computer technologies and a literacy classroom the negotiations are rarely settled or stabilized. Work has to be done to police the roles that are assigned to all the actors. The well known fragility[4] of computer-based practices in many classrooms attests to this. These issues point to a broad set of issues and practices in classrooms all over the world.

We want here to re-emphasize the point that particular configurations of students, technology and literacy learning are always arrived at via negotiation and the mutual assigning of roles. They are not inexorably predetermined due to inherent essences in gender, computer or literacy practices. To develop this position further we draw on research in Australia which was focused on the nexus of disadvantage, literacy learning and the new computing and communication technologies (Rowan *et al.* 2000).

Tracing configurations

Marshall Primary School is a large, relatively new and rapidly growing state school situated in an expanding middle- to upper-middle-class suburb in a large city in Queensland, Australia. The school's most recent annual reports indicate that 60 per cent of school families fall within the upper middle class. The library is very well equipped with 12 nearly new Pentium II PCs on a local area network. This connects all the computers to a powerful server running Microsoft's Windows NT 4.0 for each computer. The software available on each computer is typical of primary schools – a standard word processor and simple graphics/desktop publishing packages. The server also includes a CD-ROM stack from which students are able to access databases (e.g. Microsoft's *Encarta, Dangerous Creatures, Minibeasts*). However, despite this wealth of digital technologies, student access to the computers and the Internet is extremely limited and tightly regulated. Students can only access 'pre-selected' or what the school calls 'supervised' web sites (web surfing, accessing non-vetted sites or using search engines is not allowed). Emphasis appears to be on passive browsing rather than on discovering or researching. This situation is coupled with an extremely high degree of computer and Internet access outside school that most students there have.

Caleb is a Year 6 student at Marshall Primary School. He is very articulate and poised, and his teacher describes him as a very good student academically. Caleb is familiar and at ease with computers and web-based applications. His family has had a computer at home for at least 12 years. Everyone in the family – Caleb's father, mother and older sister – uses it for various work and relaxation purposes. Indeed, Caleb reports that he first used a computer before he began school. These days, Caleb regularly e-mails his cousin Marvin, who lives down the road from him, and joins Marvin in the Yahoo chat space on the Internet most nights (http://chat.yahoo.com). Caleb also knows how to 'whisper' to someone in a MOO or chat space so that the typed message becomes private and no one in the MOO room can read it except the intended recipient. He also believes that most of the people in his class have at the very least a Hotmail e-mail account outside school.

However, despite his facility with communication applications, Caleb's use of search engines for research purposes reflects the effects of the tight surveillance and artificiality of 'web searching' at the school, and the culture of 'direct delivery' surrounding the computers there. For example, he told us how in Year 5 he once tried to use the Internet to help him complete a school project on medieval times. According to Caleb, he keyed 'www.medieval.com.au' into the 'go to' space at the top of the internet browser. But when he received the message 'your URL could not be retrieved' he gave up, claiming 'It didn't work'. Caleb says he hasn't subsequently used the home computer for school-related purposes.

Despite the resources at Marshall, Caleb's skills and understandings are largely developed by access to resources outside the school. The negotiated roles of the computers, the Internet and Caleb in the school are such that it is the existing patterns of control and surveillance which characterize the library in the school that determine the only acceptable role for the computers and Caleb in the library. Normal computer behaviour in school means working with a narrowly defined set of URLs. It is a practice that can be policed and is relatively easy to maintain. It clearly appeals to the librarian, who has reluctantly accepted housing the computers within her area. Defining a highly limited role for the computers reduces the prospect of breaking down the existing configuration. It enables the librarian to operate as she does with other resources in the library, from a position of knowing what is available and the value of each resource. Outside school Caleb has negotiated a complex and rich set of configurations that employ a range of Internet resources, defined through a different set of negotiations with hardware, software and friends. The role of Caleb's friends and relatives in his out of school networks also limit Caleb *vis-à-vis* the Internet, but they allow greater opportunity for renegotiation than is the case in school.

In this respect, schools and teachers are important actors in negotiating the roles of computers and students in literacy classrooms. In particular, we find that many teachers find it helpful to pigeon-hole students *vis-à-vis* computers. Thus students are labelled 'geeks', 'techies', 'jocks' and so on in school settings (see Lankshear and Knobel 1997a, b; Bennahum 1998). Teachers' words and actions are important in policing particular role assignments. For example, Melissa Koch's scenario set in a primary school computer lab in the USA conveys the ways in which the teacher – Ms Karlov – constructs boys as fluent computer users:

> Later, Ms. Karlov lets the students use the math software, and the boys again dominate. After several attempts to discover the reason for a program's error message, Sam shouts his frustration from across the room. Ms. Karlov answers without moving towards him, 'Try rebooting'. Marka, who is still nervous, has difficulty getting the math program launched, so Ms. Karlov reaches for the mouse and opens the program for her. The boys become very excited about scoring and try to advance to the next level. At the end of the class, Ms. Karlov rewards the three highest scorers – John, Brian, and Seth – with stickers.
>
> (Koch 1994: 1)

Koch's scenario resonates with our observations of the ways in which teachers construct students as computer users (Lankshear *et al.* 1997; Rowan *et al.* 1999). This point is made in a recent study we conducted which attempted to develop new and relevant patterns of literacy teaching and learning mediated by technology (Rowan *et al.* 2000). One of the cases reported in this study describes work with a group of four 14-year-old boys identified as having literacy problems. We discuss this study in more detail in later following sections. We draw upon it here to make the point that – as is often the case in 'remedial' English classes – each of the boys had been pigeon-holed as a 'problem' student by all his teachers and by many students.

The role assignments enjoyed by the boys, as we discovered, proved highly resilient despite strong and compelling evidence to the contrary.

Jarrod was regarded by his English teacher – Ms Mackie – and the other three boys as a 'computer whiz'. For example, in the course of the very first meeting, while one of the researchers was explaining to the boys the general gist of the project, Stuart butted in with, 'The only person who would understand this is Jarrod 'cause he's the computer whiz!' Other data we collected confirmed that this was a general feeling among the rest of the school group. For example, in the following exchange, Ben and Ms Mackie talk about their first attempt at scanning a photograph:

> *Ben:* No, well we scanned it about three or four thousand times.
> *Ms Mackie:* Yeah, it's rather complicated, isn't it?
> *Ben:* Yeah.
> *Ms Mackie:* It looks easy when Jarrod does it, but when we do it . . . boy oh boy!

And when talking to Pedro, a postgraduate education student participating in the study, Ms Mackie emphasizes Jarrod's 'computer whiz' status and assumes Ben will agree with her (which he does):

> *Pedro:* But part of that would be looking at others and saying, well instead of saying I wish I could do that, what you should be asking yourself is, 'How I could do that?'
> *Ms Mackie:* We'd go and ask Jarrod, wouldn't we Ben? [laughter]

Similarly, when Kyle asked his teacher how the session went for her that day, she willingly acknowledged Jarrod's 'superior' computer fluency:

> *Kyle:* Miss, what did you think about today's session?
> *Ms Mackie:* Well, last week, on Friday I thought I knew a little bit about the program, but I decided today I've got a lot more to learn about it and I find that when Jarrod gets on the computer, he goes so quickly that I get lost about three steps behind and I think what I need to do now is sit down and have a go with it by myself.

'Computer whiz' in the other three boys' eyes also meant someone who was acknowledged publicly within the school as such and called on to get people out of computer troubles:

> *Ben:* He [pointing at Jarrod] already gets called square every time he walks past, everyone calls him square.
> *Chris:* Why is that?
> *Stuart:* Cause he's a computer whiz. Every time he walks past, or every time we're on the computer and we're stuck, he just goes fffff ffffff [miming stabbing keys rapidly on a keyboard] and then they all get straight back into it.

Finally, Jarrod-as-computer-whiz was regarded as someone who was able to use school computers more often and play more computer games than non-computer whizzes:

> *Stuart:* Finishing early and going to play a game, 'cause we never done that. The only person who did that was Jarrod. He was the only person that finished early.

Other teachers or soon-to-be-teachers involved in the project picked up on the 'computer whiz' identity of Jarrod, as in this exchange between Pedro and Kyle:

> *Pedro:* Kyle, have you done links yet?
> *Kyle:* Hyper-links?
> *Pedro:* Yeah.
> *Kyle:* I haven't done it.
> *Pedro:* You want to have a run through doing it and Jarrod, do you want to help him out doing that? Let him do it [Jarrod], you just guide him as to how to do hyperlinks.

Exchanges such as the following are couched in terms of who was perceived as being able to 'share' the computer during paired sessions:

> *Leonie:* So Kyle's talking about how it's hard to share this kind of stuff, how did you guys find [turning to Jarrod and Ben], was that difficult?
> *Jarrod:* No, not really.
> *Ben:* No, it was pretty easy with Jarrod.

This was an interesting comment from Ben, considering that he spent the entire session watching Jarrod work the mouse and program on which they were working. Jarrod, on the other hand, made it quite clear right from the start that he was indeed a computer whiz, such as shown in this exchange with Pedro, a student teacher participating in the study, during the first day of the study:

> *Pedro:* Jarrod, did you learn anything from Ben today?
> *Jarrod:* Nope.
> *Pedro:* Did you learn anything from Jarrod today?
> *Ben:* Tonnes.

'Computer whiz' translates not only into someone who 'shares' in the eyes of Jarrod's peers, but also into someone who would make a good teacher:

> *Leonie:* And last week you said you didn't learn much, was that different today?
> *Stuart:* Yeah.
> *Leonie:* How come?

Stuart: 'Cause I actually listened to Jarrod.

Leonie: Is Jarrod a good teacher?

Stuart: Yep. If he goes on to study to be a teacher, he would most probably be one. He'd most probably get a job, being a teacher.

During our first session with the group, Jarrod took pains to explain that he had done a short course on Basic computer language programming when he lived in Brisbane two years before. Indeed, Jarrod almost fits the archetype of a 'computer nerd' with his lanky body, stringy blond hair and pale complexion. He certainly didn't cultivate as 'tough' an image as did Stuart and Ben. The interesting thing, of course, was that as the project progressed the more it became obvious to us that Jarrod didn't actually know as much about computing as he and the others seemed to credit him with. For example, when trouble-shooting what turned out to be faulty speaker connections on one computer, Jarrod concluded authoritatively that it was a 'software problem'.

Finally, Ms Mackie's construction of Jarrod as a computer whiz seemed to be fixed firmly in her head. Even when it was clear that Stuart, Ben and Kyle had moved past Jarrod in terms of being able to create web pages and navigating computer files, programs and functions, she continued to refer only to Jarrod as a computer whiz:

> *Ms Mackie:* Why would I do that, was Jarrod away or down at the library, and someone came and helped us and got us started? One of the things that we were thinking about, [turning to the researchers] can I put it to these guys now? Was with these computer experts here, I mean these people know much more about them than I do, and Jarrod and Pedro, yes he's a bit of a whiz apparently too, how would you people [pointing at Stuart, Kyle and Ben] feel about gaining some expertise on, you know, some games maybe or how to use a digital camera or something, and then some time in next semester, when say Mrs Moresby goes to teach this Tools of Technology [class] to her class, you guys go in as teacher's assistants and help.

Intriguingly, Ms Mackie applied traditional masculinity/technology associations to Jarrod but not to the three other boys participating in the study. She referred to the principal researchers as computer 'experts' and singled out Jarrod from the group of four boys for special mention. She also suggested that the other three boys might like to 'gain some expertise' in relation to computer or video games and using digital cameras (despite all four boys being keen gamers outside school, and their facility with setting up various research equipment throughout the semester). In these ways Ms Mackie continued to construct Stuart, Ben and Kyle as 'digital novices', despite the 'computer whiz' behaviour they displayed in the second half of the project.

We conclude this chapter with a more detailed account of the project in which Jarrod, Stuart, Ben, Kyle and Ms Mackie participated. The study brings together our position with respect to proposition (4): 'boys + literacy + computers = literacy learning'. We want to show that such glib assertions mask the bringing together of three highly problematic associations:

boys + computers = learning (1)

boys + literacy = poor literacy learning (2)

literacy + computers = literacy learning (3)

Our aim is to trace some of the problematic dimensions of these propositions and illustrate how it is possible to move beyond essentialist positions by disrupting key parts of a network of which the four boys with whom we worked were part.

Transforming technologies: a case study

The overarching goal of the following study[5] was to plan and implement an intervention that would develop 'new' or revamped pedagogical approaches to using digital technologies in literacy education. At the same time it was designed to identify and counteract as far as possible traditional markers (and experiences) of disadvantage in these contexts (Rowan *et al.* 2000). We were particularly interested in working to dismantle the subject positions associated with disadvantage and gender by linking them to other subjectivities.

The project itself had emerged from our unease with what we saw happening in many schools with respect to the use of new technologies in literacy education (Lankshear and Bigum 1999). This unease was prompted in part by examples of what *could* be done with young people and digital technologies. We had encountered interesting examples in other research, notably those provided by the work of Michael and Ludmila Doneman. The Donemans worked mainly in non-formal community settings as cultural animateurs. In their work with socially disadvantaged young people they employed a cultural apprenticeship approach pedagogy, in conjunction with artistic activities, operational computing skills, cross-generational and cross-cultural interactions and considerable energy and imagination. The projects we witnessed involved an array of *new literacies* which yielded websites, community archives, digital shows projected via powerboxes, video walls and such like (MWK 2000). The project we envisaged hoped to build on insights obtained for such work.

The project comprised four networks – three in a large city and one in a rural area approximately 500 km away. Each network involved a small group of students, a teacher, at least one researcher and a cultural worker or

Aboriginal Elder. The particular network discussed in the previous section was made up of the four secondary school boys and their English teacher, Ms Mackie, along with a postgraduate education student (Pedro), a research assistant (Lynn) and two researchers (Leonie and Chris). Not all participated in every session, but all played an important part in what took place.

The aims and shape of the project were explained to participants prior to the first session. These included the idea of teachers wanting to learn from students how to teach computing effectively to *their* students. The researchers provided each student with a Walkman-type tape-recorder for recording their thoughts about the project task and about the study in general. The students would keep the recorders at the end of the project. Data were collected during 20 hours of observation over 14 weeks during a school semester. The project meshed with a request from Ms Mackie that all four boys help her run a Year 9 subject called 'Tools and Technology' in the following semester.

The study results are far from generalizable. On the other hand, the school is a quite 'typical' Queensland regional high school, and the four boys would be familiar to every teacher working in such a setting. Stuart, Kyle, Ben and Jarrod provide us with a *telling* (as distinct from *typical*) case that can be used to investigate gender constructions from a particular theoretical stance (Bloome *et al.* 1993; Knobel 1999). We aim to describe what went on in ways that will spark a validating 'click of recognition', a 'yes, of course' (Lather 1991: 69), in terms of many readers' own experiences of boys, literacy and technology.

The lads

Stuart is chatty and friendly, which often belies his deliberately cultivated 'tough' look – his blond hair is shoulder-length, and shaved close to his scalp high above his ears (for those in the know, a 'radical mullet' style). He is also given to wearing oversized, slightly tatty shirts and shorts, or casually worn school uniform. Unsurprisingly, from a new literacies studies perspective, Stuart has little trouble with literacy outside school contexts. At home, he is able to strip down his motorbike and put it back together again correctly. He told us he learned to do this by first watching his dad work on his bike, then from being left to his own devices to figure out a problem, or to tune the engine, or to rebuild it once his father had taken it apart. When we asked what he does when he encounters a problem when working on his bike, he replied without hesitation, 'I read the manual when I get stuck.'

Kyle has an olive complexion and long dark hair that he usually wears tied back in a ponytail. Like Stuart, Kyle has a 'tough' look to him and, while he is not particularly tall, it is easy to imagine that (unlike Stuart) he would be the winner in a fist fight with peers. He usually wore shorts and a muscle shirt to the sessions and we got the feeling this was his usual school apparel in summer. Kyle had the most careworn or 'world weary' look about him of all the boys, but this disappeared when he began talking about things that interested him, and he would become articulate and entertaining when describing things that mattered to him (e.g. the merits of a four-stroke over a two-stroke motorcycle engine).

Ben lives outside town on a farm of about 200 hectares. His family run a herd of cows on their farm and Ben uses his motorbike to help round them up for his parents. He too can strip his motorbike and put it back together in working order. Ben is what is often described as a fresh faced kid – with a kind of Tom Sawyer impishness in his general demeanour. He smiles readily but seems slow to look people in the eye, and when we first met him he would belittle himself and his abilities at every opportunity. Despite giving himself a hard time in relation to his literacy and computing abilities, Ben seems an affable lad who would avoid hurting anyone if he could. Ben also has a dry sense of humour, and a range of lines that regularly drew laughs from the others in the group. For example, when Stuart was being somewhat slow in moving about the different control icons of Microsoft's *3D Moviemaker* (1995), Ben commented with friendly impatience, 'C'mon Stu. You move like my grandmother. And she's in a home!'

Jarrod is blond and tall. Interestingly enough, his 'computer whiz' status in the group/school seems to generate a mix of admiration and resentment in the other three boys, and this may help to explain a strange mix of tentativeness and arrogance Jarrod himself displays during each project session. Interestingly, although quick to talk about any computer or technology-related subject, Jarrod is slow to offer his opinions on other issues. He seemed to find it hard, at least during the first few sessions of the project, to relate easily to the other three boys, despite having collaborated with them previously on a number of school-based projects. In addition, Jarrod is adamant that he prefers hands-on subjects at school, such as woodwork, metalwork, art and physical education, because 'you're learning trades'.

Disassembling dominant cultural understandings of teachers and students

Given what we were told about the four boys prior to the study – that they were English 'failures', often in trouble, difficult to control but more interested in being part of a 'special' English programme than in being excluded from classes – we felt it was important to work consciously and overtly in an 'anti-essentialist' manner with the boys once the project had started. To begin with, we actively unpicked the seams of traditional teacher–student pedagogy models within each session. Right from the start, and with very little prompting, the young men made it clear that for them the role of a teacher is a normative and unappetizing one. For example, in response to Ms Mackie's suggestion at the start of the project that they act as 'teachers' during the Tools and Technology classes (suggested perhaps as a 'reward' for mastering a range of web building skills), Stuart snorted, 'No way!', claiming, 'Then I'll get called a square by all my friends!' The other three boys insisted that they not be called 'teachers' or 'experts', perhaps out of fear of making a fool of themselves in front of their peers. For example:

Chris: What could we do that wouldn't make you a square?
Ben: Don't tell them that [we're 'teachers' or 'experts'], you know.
Ms Mackie: Well, you'd be a lot of help in the classroom, wouldn't you? [laughter]
Ben: I just know a bit of this, you know.

During a later session, they showed clearly their deep understanding of the relationships between themselves and the various teachers they had – explaining in large part why the last thing they wanted to be called was 'teacher'. For example:

Leonie: What do you think teachers think is a good class? What do you think teachers like?
Stuart: A class that doesn't play up all year long, and like now, the first thing when they get to class – everyone's yelling and doing anything they want, sort of my English class now. That's why we're not in it, I think.

Later, when Leonie asked them, 'What do you reckon would make a teacher feel good?', they responded in turn:

Kyle: Being quiet.
Jarrod: Doing what she says.
Ben: Make yourself look like you're doing work.

The boys also discussed how reading, writing, speaking and even listening in class is not conducted on an equal, or even collaborative, basis. The teacher dictates when they will read, write, listen and speak, and when they won't – actions that do not comply with the teacher's expectations are seen as 'trouble making' and the like. Kyle provided a short anecdote for the researchers to help to explain why he often loses the desire to write in class:

Kyle: Well, I think the thing that gets you is, like, you'd be sitting there all ready to fire away, and the maths teacher just goes 'Ra, ra, ra. Do this up to page *x*' and you're just sitting there and sitting there.

Or, the observation that:

Ben: Mr Young . . . just tells me to sit there and do nothing if I don't know how to do it. So I just sit there and get my Walkman [out].

Towards the end of the project sessions, when the boys had become fluent in a range of web page building skills and understandings, they agreed readily to the labels 'coordinator' and 'editor'.

In response to the lads' early comments, and with the support of Ms Mackie, we worked throughout the study actively to disturb traditional relationships between the teachers at the school and these four students. In doing so, we were ever mindful of Barbara Rogoff's conception of 'cultural apprenticeship', which involves learners and experts working together on a *real* task in ways where each learns from the other. To begin with, learners and experts work closely together on a task until the learners are able to complete the task or elements of the task themselves with only some support from the experts. Later, following sufficient guided practice, the learners become proficient at the task and budding experts themselves (see Rogoff 1995, 1996). What is particularly appealing about this theory of learning and teaching is that it breaks down orthodox master–student binaries of traditional apprenticeships and puts in their place something very close to how people learn to do things everyday.

In relation to the four lads' web page building project, we began by having the boys explore the functions of Microsoft's *3D MovieMaker* (1995) in order to establish a common base of computer know-how. This was followed by an exploration of *FrontPage* to support the construction of web pages by the lads. Once the boys had a basic familiarity with the workings of the software, the days were based around working on tasks related to designing, trying out and testing their web pages. The style of work was based upon mutual support and sharing in which young and old, experienced and inexperienced worked together to solve problems that arose from the building of the four sets of web pages, one for each student.

The decision to create a set of web pages devoted to motorbikes grew out of an initiative already in place. The English coordinator, Ms Mackie – a devoted teacher – had volunteered her own non-teaching time to work with this group of four boys, during their regular scheduled English lessons. They had already completed a number of projects together, and at the time of the project they were producing a magazine based on a passion shared by the lads – motorbikes. The magazine project had involved them in collecting information from the Internet and elsewhere, as well as a session spent interviewing motorbike mechanics and enthusiasts about the various qualities of different motorbikes (e.g. evaluating the difference between two-stroke and four-stroke engines). The boys wrote their interview questions before the excursion, and Ms Mackie drove them to a large town about 40 km away for their fact-finding mission.

We therefore decided to build on the gains made by Ms Mackie, and on the interests of the boys, by helping them to become fluent in useful information technology skills by means of constructing a web page version of their magazine. The researchers were particularly keen that the project the group worked on had links to 'authentic' literacy practices and resonated with the real world in which all four students lived, and embodied 'authentic' uses of computers and web page building. Indeed, the four boys are able to articulate accurate evaluations of the meaninglessness of inauthentic practices. For example (in the following exchange, Lynn is the research assistant):

> *Stuart:* [talking about computer keyboarding classes] Every time that started up we used to get kicked out of class.
> *Lynn:* What for? What did you do to get kicked out of class?
> *Stuart:* 'Cause I never used to do it.
> *Jarrod:* What *didn't* he do to get kicked out of class! [laughter]
> *Lynn:* Okay, why did you try all those party tricks to get kicked out of class?
> *Stuart:* 'Cause all we done for about an hour and a half was just sit there, going tap tap tap. I went to sleep one day.
> *Lynn:* So if you're going to do some typing to make a web site in a magazine is that going to be a little bit better, you can handle doing that?
> *Stuart:* It's just I can't sit there for an hour and a half just going tap tap tap.

We hoped that channelling their passion for motorbikes into the project, making use of information and images they had collected already and providing a context for them to acquire new skills in actively *using* digital technologies would engage them in a task they would find as meaningful as possible within a school setting. The project enjoyed some success in this respect. The boys all worked willingly on their web pages. After the first few sessions they even seemed to be hanging around waiting beforehand for everyone to arrive. By the end of the project they had produced 16 interlinked pages between them, three or four pages each, varying in style and emphasis. This was an interesting outcome from a group of boys who were judged to have serious problems in reading and writing.

We taught the students a range of skills used in successful web page construction by means of demonstration, modelling and scaffolding. We also provided the four boys with teaching approaches that they could use to instruct other students. In many ways, this strategy explicitly positioned the students as soon-to-be-experts. This inverted their usual roles as 'trouble makers' to one of potential experts. In our opinion this aspect has the greatest potential for allowing the boys themselves, and others in the school, to recognize that their positions as 'failures' were not fixed, permanent and natural. Rather, they were positions that could be challenged, disrupted and rejected.

In creating a kind of cultural apprenticeship within the context of the project sessions, the make-up of the group itself contributed greatly to blurring the edges between learners and experts. One important element was Ms Mackie's active participation in a number of the project sessions. The boys watched their teacher struggle with and learn the same skills and processes that they were learning. They were positioned from time to time as *her* teacher. This provided a concrete basis from which all four boys could readily understand that operational skills like those needed to operate a computer and code hypertext markup language (HTML) are *learned*, not innate. They are learned in the same kind of way that the skills associated with tuning, repairing and modifying their motorbikes are learned.

Teacher and student roles were further blurred by the participation of Leonie (researcher) and Lynn (researcher assistant), neither of whom was very familiar with the functioning of PCs. Moreover, none of the participants – including the adults – was experienced with the particular web page construction software used in the school. Hence, the process of collaboratively building the boys' motorbike web site provided a genuine learning experience for everyone involved. Pedro also contributed to the blurring of roles. In previous years he had coached two of the boys in soccer. His wife had taught a third in primary school and Pedro knew him quite well. This helped to make for less 'teacher-like talk' and more coach-like talk between Pedro and the four boys (see positive coaching metaphors as reform models in Mahiri 1998; see also Heath and Langman 1994). After the project had finished, Pedro spoke of what he had learned in terms of unlearning the kinds of authoritarian approaches to teaching that he remembered best from his own schooling and had encountered in his pre-service teacher education experience.

The 'unschool-like' character of the project sessions was underscored by the regular presence of Holly, Pedro's 6-month-old daughter. The initial reason for bringing her to sessions was that Pedro had encountered trouble in finding a babysitter to cover the hours he was working on the project with the group. However, it didn't take long to agree that having the baby in each session might work to 'disrupt' traditional notions of classrooms and authority, as well as to unmake traditional childcare roles in the community. We were none the less surprised at the extent to which these tough, trouble making boys welcomed Holly into the group. Every session they would stop by her pram first thing and hold her hand, pull funny faces, speak in gentle, baby-like voices and generally show that they liked her and were glad she was there.

Chris, the other participating researcher, has a long history of working with young people and computers, and contributed much to the relaxed atmosphere and fun of each session. We also found that, among other things, giving over the responsibility of setting up the video-recording and audio-taping equipment to the boys also helped to minimize a 'researcher–subject' relationship forming between the adults and boys. After the first few sessions we found that we had very little to do in terms of setting up tape recorders, cameras and other bits of equipment. The boys had taken it all over and had become quite proficient in their use. Finally, inviting the boys to use the adult participants' first names also helped to reposition normative roles of experts and learners by removing social markers of authority.

Disrupting dominant cultural understandings of 'being a boy'

In addition to the refiguring of teacher–learner roles within the project, underpinning our work with these four students was a commitment to intervening in the ways in which these boys, as well as their teachers and other students in the school spoke about them(selves) as 'boys'. This necessitated, in the first instance, acknowledging that the four boys came to our network activities with long histories of being students of a particular type in their school.

To us, all four boys appeared to conform – albeit in varying degrees – to models of masculinity widely pervasive in Australian society (Macpherson 1983; Walker 1988; Moore 1998). In general, hegemonic masculinity in Australian state schools sees boys rewarded for being 'tough', independent, aggressive and practical, rather than intellectual. For example, the four boys who participated in this project are known in the school as 'problem students'. They are often among the first to be hauled off to the principal's office as suspects in graffiti attacks, or told not to attend various lessons and to sit outside the classroom instead. They also performed a range of hegemonic masculinities. For example, they engaged in mock (and not so mock) punch-ups during network meetings. On one occasion they spent almost an entire session searching the Internet for pictures of 'babes' on motorbikes to add to the web pages. During the excursion to the university Stuart hurt his knee, but insisted emphatically, 'Don't touch me', to ward off people who were trying to help him.

However, what is more important here than listing fairly predictable displays of normative masculinity is the extent to which these instances are just that, *displays* or *performances*, rather than necessarily natural or biologically determined sets of behaviours. Accepting that these performances are learned and negotiated socially challenges educators to look for ways of disrupting them. Thus the activities undertaken throughout the network sessions were designed to interrupt the boys' (and their teachers') unproblematic endorsement of hegemonic masculinities. This involved three strategies:

- providing the boys with opportunities, choices and 'power' not routinely ascribed to boys with a history of trouble making;
- providing the boys with consistent and clearly articulated feedback concerning their abilities to display those skills – in literacy and technology – which they are routinely expected *not* to possess;

- demonstrating a way of thinking about and responding to 'boys in schools' that saw them in positive rather than negative, productive rather than disruptive and transformative rather than stereotypical ways.

This was based on an acknowledgment that while boys + technology does not automatically equal learning, nor does it automatically *not* equal learning: the point is, there is a need for boys and technology and literacy to be combined in ways that move all the categories beyond the stereotypes or limitations associated with each. In other words, we need to be working outside of the associated norms to create what we have described throughout the book as rhizomatic connections or assemblages.

Within this framework the four boys were allowed a greater amount of autonomy than they were used to at school. They made decisions about what skills and techniques they would learn and when they would do it. Typically they consulted with one another and members of the research team about layout and design, colour, choice of content and so on. They were free to wander around the project room as they liked, to seek help as they needed it, to 'work' the video camera set up in the room and to train it on anyone or any group they liked. They were able to audio-record whatever they wanted using the handheld tape recorders we gave them, and so on.

The researchers also actively endorsed the achievements of each boy. This necessitated more than simply giving positive reinforcement. It required encouraging the students to question *why* they would speak about themselves negatively with regard to literacy and technology, and helping them to recognize the achievements they made. The boys' self-defeating comments were evident in the first few sessions of the project, and manifested themselves at various points throughout. The students regularly criticized themselves, their abilities and their propensity to make 'mistakes', and the researchers just as regularly negated or diverted their self-criticisms. For example:

> *Ben:* Then I went to that picture [pointing to an icon on the screen], then I went to that Word Art.
> *Leonie:* Excellent. Now you pick another one.
> *Ben:* That one [he clicks on a Word Art icon, but it doesn't open]. Oh, I'm so stupid.
> *Leonie:* It's not stupid.

Or the boys would despair of their ability to 'get it right' the first time round. For example, and commenting on their concerns about recording their audio-taped journals, Jarrod and Ben make the following points:

> *Jarrod:* It's got ours and Ms Mackie [on it]. I hate doing that. You're sitting there talking and you muck it up, so you have to tape over it.
> *Leonie:* But why? How do you muck something up?
> *Ben:* You forget what to say.

Jarrod: You talk in to it . . .
Leonie: But that's okay. We don't expect you to be talking as though you've done a big speech.

Or they would comment hopelessly on their abilities in general. In this example, Kyle refuses to acknowledge that he is beginning to master the process of inserting hyperlinks between web pages:

Leonie: You were getting pretty good.
Kyle: Ohhh, I don't know. Probably not.
Leonie: Why not?
Kyle: I'm not good enough.

Stuart's comments during the second session echo those made by Kyle and Ben:

Stuart: I don't really get what we're doing so far 'cause I'm a slow learner, but I'll catch up.

In addition, this seemingly shared mindset of 'not being good enough' or of 'being stupid' or of 'mucking things up' carried over into their actions, and their expectations of what others – especially adults at school – thought of them. A telling example of this occurred one day when Leonie just happened to look at Stuart during the course of one session for longer than a glance, and Stuart guiltily snatched his cap from his head as though he was in the wrong to be wearing it inside. At some time during a later session, Stuart was getting a drink from the sink in the staffroom and Leonie simply looked over to see that he was OK, to which he responded hastily, 'It's my own cup!' Stuart's responses suggest that he, and no doubt the others as well, had come to know a 'gaze' or a 'look' as always signifying something done wrong, with no possibility, it seemed, that it could be otherwise.

Interestingly, further along in the sessions – and with perseverance on the part of the researchers to assure the four students they were doing well – the boys appeared to reassess their abilities, and began undertaking activities with more confidence and with less self-flagellation. In fact, they all seemed to assume – in stark contrast to when the project started – that they *would* be able to achieve the result they desired. For instance,

Leonie: Do you want to save your page?
Ben: Yep. I got my little thing-a-ma-jig in there, so I can save on that, can't I.

And later:

Ben: I wonder if I can do that again. And now I need another picture.
Leonie: Well, we know how to do it now.
Ben: Yep, and I'm going to do it.

In working to introduce these four boys to a range of literacy and technology practices, the researchers were conscious of the need to be aware of and responsive to the investment these particular boys had in 'acting like (real) boys'. This involved identifying the relationship between the kind of masculinity the boys identified with and their literacy achievements in and out of school. In school, the boys each enacted a 'real boys don't read or write unless forced to' persona, although they are also able to *read* accurately the culture of the school and their (constructed) place within it. Outside school was a different story – at the very least, they regularly read motorbike magazines, motorbike manuals to troubleshoot a maintenance problem, labels on various oils and greases for their motorbikes and notes from Mum, as well as write down motorbike details or motocross results, and so on. We also have every reason to believe they hold deep understandings of the social nature of language and literacy.

For example, Kyle provided us with an articulate account of the importance of context in written and verbal interactions. Leonie had asked Kyle if he could help her to decipher a note left by a teacher. Kyle looked at the note and remarked:

> *Kyle:* Just like my mum, no detail.
> *Leonie:* Yeah, not very helpful.
> *Kyle:* My mum never gives enough detail. She'll say, 'Buy some sugar.' And I'll say, 'What kind?' And she'll say, 'Just sugar', and I'll go and there'll be all these kinds of sugar. Not enough detail.

Nevertheless, we had little evidence that the four boys' language and literacy understandings and abilities were ever put to good use in any of their school subjects – other than the projects they worked on with Ms Mackie. Of course, the disjunction between these boys' literacy practices in school and their much richer language and literacy uses out of school is not fresh news (Heath 1983; Delgado-Gaitan 1991; Gee 1996; Mahiri 1998; Knobel 1999; McCarthy 2000). This particular study re-inforces how little influence the recommendations of previous studies appear to have had in changing the literacy practices valued in schools. If anything, many schools and certainly most governments have moved in a different direction and embraced standardized testing, benchmarks and 'old basics' approaches to literacy education. Boys like the four involved in this project continue to be constructed as being in need of 'remedial' or 'special' literacy classes, and continue to convince themselves as well that they are 'no good' at literacy or at anything valued by teachers or schools.

Disrupting remedial literacy lessons

Over the course of the project, all four boys clearly demonstrated that they were building a solid base of (operational) technological literacy understandings and fluencies. These included being able to: create image and HTML files, save them to a directory structure on the computer's hard drive, as well as on removable 3.5 inch disks, and retrieve these files at another time to continue working on them; insert images into HTML pages; create eye catching titles in a word processing program, convert them to image files and then insert them at the top of an HTML file; and create logical connections between files by means of hyperlinks on words or images.

We believe the four boys also displayed understandings of a cultural dimension of technological literacies. Right from the start of the project they were already able to talk about copyright laws and what can and cannot be taken from other people's websites. They demonstrated an understanding of the relationship between motorbike enthusiasts and the Internet by suggesting a link between their pages and motorbike companies already advertising on the Internet to help to give cachet or authoritativeness to their own website. They paid attention to design and colours that would, as they put it, 'catch people's eyes'. They were also able to discuss the 'power' or cultural effects of Internet domain names and the practice of one company riding on the back of a domain name. An example Jarrod gave us was of a porn company that uses the domain name http://www.whitehouse.com to capture visitors who have mistakenly entered that URL in their attempt to reach the US government site at http://www.whitehouse.gov

In terms of more conventional literacy use, the boys willingly keyed in information about motorbikes in general. They also produced short descriptive passages about their own motorbikes and their motorbike riding, and brief reviews of motorbike models and engine types. For at least one of the boys this was a 'first' since reaching high school. By constructing a website on a topic in which they all had a vested interest, all four boys 'rewrote' – even if only temporarily – their roles as poor English students, as they crafted texts that clearly were meaningful for them. Indeed, the web page project made these boys visible as learners and students, rather than merely as 'trouble makers'. As Ben put it:

> *Ben:* Yep. There's like teachers here [in the project] that listen to you, not like the ones in class. 'Miss, Miss', 'Yeah I'll be there in a minute.' Half an hour later . . . nothing. Here you just have to call out a name and they come.

Of course, the project situation was atypical. In some respects it was close to ideal, with an average ratio of one adult to each student – hardly a replication of classroom situations. However, the scope of our project was deliberately small and we never intended it to become a generic pedagogical model. We wanted to examine, illustrate and disrupt the patterns and associations of disadvantage, literacy and new technologies. Besides, teachers already are well aware that one-to-one teaching and small class sizes are the most effective responses to literacy learning troubles, a situation constructed regularly by Ms Mackie. We deliberately worked to provide an environment within which the boys could conceptualize a *different* role for themselves. This was a necessary but not sufficient condition for any transformative literacy/technology activity.

We believe the project contributed in a modest way to making a difference to the ways in which the boys thought about themselves as competent computer and literacy users, as well as to transforming the ways in which they were perceived in the school. The boys were not construed as 'remedial' and were not dumbed down or stupidified (Macedo 1993) by the project on which they elected to work. In this way, we saw some of the effects our commitment to a transformative model of difference had – a model within which disadvantage and normative masculinities are understood as culturally produced and thus capable of reconstruction.

Boys in the reconstruction business

We are not claiming in any sense that the simple combination of strategies we used created a major or even necessarily a sustainable long-term shift in the boys' and Ms Mackie's (and others') thinking. There were, nevertheless, several outcomes that indicated how the boys' perceptions of themselves as boys, as English students and as technology users changed noticeably – if not dramatically – over the course of the project.

First, the boys commenced the project with an outward commitment to displaying all the stereotypical markers of hegemonic schoolyard masculinity. By the end of the project, however, they moved easily between the traditionally masculine activities of computer work and motorbike discussion, and the traditionally feminine pastimes of discussing their families, interacting with babies and producing colourful, attractive titles for documents. They also gave spontaneous and articulate 'thank you' speeches at the close of the project and in other 'social' occasions that occurred during the life of the project.

Second, over the course of 14 weeks, these four boys expressed an interest in poetry, drama and the music of Harry Belafonte. These are all interests that could be seen as rather surprising or contradictory for this 'hardened' and 'tough' group of boys. Yet the boys talked about them openly and with a candour that suggested they trusted the adult participants. Furthermore, their manner suggested that the project had possibly contributed to 'undoing' some of the consequences of being the kind of boys their teachers seemed to expect them to be (i.e. independent, unresponsive, always in trouble, anti-authoritarian, non-academic, failures at school literacy and so on).

Third, by the end of project, all four boys had become sufficiently skilled at web page construction to contemplate working as assistants in the Tools and Technology classes in the following term. When Ms Mackie saw that all four boys were now, in her terms, computer whizzes, she asked the boys again in the final session if they would help with the Tools and Technology unit. Instead of groans and exclamations of 'No way!' they answered 'Sure', and 'Easy!' Ms Mackie asked how the classes could be managed in terms of computers, tutors, groups of students, time, activities and so on. As the discussion progressed, the boys gently wrested control of the conversation from Ms Mackie and among themselves worked out a logical and effective rotational plan at a pace that left Ms Mackie gasping for air and asking them to slow down and go over it again for her.

We do not want to claim that by the end of the study any of the boys had become a high literacy achiever in the normal context of their schooling. We do, however, argue that the disruptions and repositionings that were effected during the course of the project had ongoing effects and contributed to positive transformations within the school in relation to these four boys. We know, through our ongoing contact with Ms Mackie, that she has continued to see these boys in a different light since the close of the project, and they all contributed to the teaching of the Tools and Technology class in the following term. Interestingly, in discussions after the project the boys expressed dismay at the prospect of teaching repeat classes. One quipped, 'Teaching must be so boring.'

Conclusions

Techno-pushes from governments, educators and parents alike link the new computing and communication technologies with progress. This facile association ignores the complex and heterogeneous nature of any technological project. We cannot simply consider a piece of technology in isolation: it is always part of a much larger set of relationships, relationships that have been negotiated and around which there are likely to have been all kinds of compromises. So what we 'see' in any setting in which computers are deployed needs to be read as peculiar, odd, something that is not 'natural'. This then allows us to ask how things got to be the way they are and how a particular set of associations might have been made otherwise.

Thus, what matters for us concerns what students and teachers *do* with computers, what associations are made and what is made to appear normal or natural. Efforts to 'get boys reading and writing' by plonking them down in front of computers propagate a popular (mis)connection between boys, new technologies and remediation. They also maintain ultimately disadvantaging cultural models that expect all boys to have a 'natural' affinity with computers (whereas, by default, girls will not), or assume that using computers with boys who struggle with school literacy will automatically solve their literacy problems. Initiatives aimed at addressing social misconceptions concerning girls and digital technologies (e.g. that they are afraid of computers, that they don't like playing computer games, that they just don't understand the logic of computers) now abound. These various programmes, clubs, women's groups and the like appear to be having some success in providing girls with alternative computer cultures. They do this by diverse means. Some use purpose-designed computer games that refuse to succumb to the 'kill and thrill' themes and action of boy-targeted games. Others create Internet spaces for 'girls only', where girls do not run the risk of being put down by boys who are fluent computer users. School-based events that bring in female scientists, computer programmers and so on to speak with girls and encourage them to take up careers in science and technology fields are further examples.

Brenda Laurel once commented in relation to designing computer games that appeal to boys that 'we need to come up with some *representation of personal agency* other than violence' (Laurel 1999: n.p.). Her observation about personal agency is a useful benchmark for working with both boys *and* girls in the context of learning to use digital technologies. We like to think that Stuart, Ben, Kyle and Jarrod obtained a sense of personal agency through participating in the study. Stuart's comments are indicative:

> *Stuart:* I don't mind getting called 'square' now that I'm a computer whiz. I know the codes. When I put my pages on [the Internet] it's like when I was looking up motocross [on the Internet] for our magazine, and there was one page in there where it had like all these little pictures but they were all circles, not square, and you clicked on them and they were all movies. Everyone can see them and they'll see my pages too.

For Stuart to get to this point in a public self-assessment speaks to the extent to which the project was successful in disrupting the networks in the school that had positioned him as a trouble maker with poor literacy skills. Disrupting networks of these kinds is not a simple matter. In Stuart's case they were robust and resilient and required much more than the evidence of change in Stuart to interrupt them. Dismantling these networks took a lot of time and effort and was often frustrating, as others in the school refused to acknowledge the shifts and changes that arose from Stuart's participation in the project. What was striking to us was just how durable Stuart's role in the school was. The durability of networks is not achieved accidentally: a lot of effort had to go into making sure that roles and relationships are policed over time and are able to resist disruptions. These school attributions just cannot be wished away. What was required was self-conscious and self-reflective dismantling moves directed at performances of normative masculinity, trouble making and poor literacy.

We began this chapter with an examination of the proposition that giving boys access to computers will improve their literacy learning. We used a set of equations to represent a simpler set of precursor propositions that linked boys, technology and literacy. Examining each in turn, we showed that each of the propositions like *boys + computers = learning* unnecessarily trivializes what are complex and important educational issues and reinforces and enhances the performance of normative masculinity. In tracing the way in which particular attributions are made to technologies, genders and their specific associations, we emphasized the importance of not taking any of these for granted, of challenging so-called natural affinities and predispositions. Linking culturally valorized technologies like computers with normative masculinity will clearly strengthen the traditions that separate some boys from literacy learning. What is important, therefore, is to make connections between boys, literacy and the new computing and communication technologies in rhizomatic ways, working against positions that posit innate, gender-specific roles for girls or boys in respect of using computers for literacy learning.

To return to propositional form, we would argue that:

boys + literacy *can* equal learning;

and

boys + technology *can* equal learning;

and, more importantly, boys + literacy + technology *can* equal new learning about *gender, masculinity and technology*, provided they are all informed by a new literacies mindset that is predisposed towards transformative, rhizomatic pedagogy.

Notes

1 For a detailed account of negotiations and trade-offs around the development of a technology see Latour's (1996) account of the failed electrical vehicle system in France.

2 The report can be accessed at http://www.business.cowan.edu.au/rhetorics/

3 This approach derives from actor–network theory, a sociology concerned with the study of technologies and innovations.

4 Fragility in the sense that computer-based practices have proven difficult to make routine. Dependence upon a particular teacher and the well known instability of the technology make the long-term reproduction of particular practices difficult.

5 Details are available at http://www.edca.cqu.edu.au/cdile

From Pacman to Pokemon: Cross-generational perspectives on gender and reform in a 'post-feminist' age

We have emphasized the need for an approach to gender-based reform that works to dismantle the language systems and social practices that construct women and men, boys and girls, masculinity and femininity in binary relationships with one another. We have argued the need to create and circulate alternative and multiple figurations of masculinity and femininity, and to celebrate these consistently and publicly. Indeed, this goal underpins all our arguments. We assess the validity, workability, sustainability and desirability of various responses to the boys/literacy challenge in terms of whether and how they can facilitate this production and circulation of multiple ways of being and becoming a boy or a girl.

This important task can be operationalized in two broad ways. First, it involves working to make explicit the assumptions that underpin many seemingly natural or normal gender practices and to draw attention to the consequences of these practices. Second, it involves working to dismantle the subject positions associated with these gender norms by linking them to other subjectivities. This is the rhizomatic project of weaving connections from where one starts to other less regulated and less policed subject positions. We have highlighted the power attached to normative or hegemonic masculinity and the ways 'masculine' contexts like sporting fields, mathematics classrooms or technology labs tend to legitimate only particular performances of masculinity, particular subjectivities. We have acknowledged too the role that so-called 'feminine' spaces like English classrooms can play in shoring up the distinction between male and female. It is less easy, however, to regulate, monitor or stereotype the boy who accesses multiple subject positions. Against the criteria associated with normative masculinity, the football player who excels at maths may be easily valued; and the dancer who excels at English may be easily devalued. But what is to be made of more hybrid subject positions? For example, the football player who enjoys English and the school band? Or the computer whiz who reads poetry? the blonde haired, blue eyed girl who plays the drums and hates mathematics? Each of these subject positions works outside of the boundaries of normative masculinity and femininity and can blur what often appears to be a rigid distinction between male and female, between normal and deviant.

Multiple figurations of masculinity and femininity – no matter how dramatically or partially they differ from the mythical norms sustaining particular gender regimes – have the potential to unsettle fixed understandings of what it means to 'act like a man' or to 'be a good girl'. This potential is tied to his or her ability to show the viability and sustainability of alternative subjectivities. As we argued in Chapter 5, it is not possible simply to 'wish away' hundreds of years of gender normativity. Boys will not like literacy just because we tell them to, or because we argue that it's good for them, or put up posters that say 'Boys can read too'. The most powerful approaches work to make connections between and beyond 'traditional' boys so that they can imagine and experience the performance of less highly regulated subject positions.

Chapters 5 and 6 explored some of the ways in which this attempt to move towards multiple figurations of masculinity can be actualized. We have distinguished between those strategies that ultimately work to reinscribe traditional or normative understandings of 'man' and 'woman' and strategies that open up new ways of conceptualizing these positions. These chapters focused on some ways in which teachers can construct literacy and technology-based programmes or interventions that work rhizomatically to overcome the limitations of gender norms associated with masculinity and femininity. In particular, we have stressed the importance of creating connections between boys and a range of literacy practices, so that the kind of logic which associates literacy with femininity can be broken down.

This chapter builds on preceding arguments by exploring a common strategy used to engage boys (and girls) in school-based literacy lessons: namely, adopting 'generationally specific' resources and teaching strategies. The chapter addresses one of the most challenging dimensions of contemporary education. This is the difference that exists respectively between the 'world views', life experiences and conceptual frameworks of teachers and their students. Conscious of the fact that introducing generationally relevant teaching processes is far from a simple task, our broad goal in this chapter is to map some of the common generational mindsets held by educators and to identify ways in which they animate particular (and different) literacy practices. We distinguish between practices that provide limiting, stereotypical or tokenistic engagements with the 'real lives' of students, and practices that acknowledge the diversity of the student group, and attend to their diversity as much as to their generational specificities.

The chapter is organized in three sections. The first identifies some of the common discourses used to discuss the 'nature' of contemporary kids and the 'loss' of their 'childhood innocence'. The second explores ways in which relationships between teachers and students are further complicated by the diverse range of attitudes within each group relating to the nature, purpose and outcomes of any gender reform project. The third provides examples of ways in which particular combinations of these mindsets result in more or less transformative literacy practices.

Aliens or alienated: adult perspectives on contemporary youth

Generation X, Generation Y, Generation Next. MTV kids, couch kids, slouch kids. Children of the (technological) revolution and members of the Nintendo generation. These and numerous other labels have been used over the past twenty years to try to sum up widespread feelings about the nature of contemporary youth. Each label works to distinguish the current 'generation' not just from those of the 1950s and 1960s, but also from those that are separated by only a few years, rather than decades. This use of the term 'generation', as it is often applied to cohorts of kids, is strongly tied to technological discourses within which – as Bill Green and Chris Bigum (1993: 135) note – generation is 'a convenient shorthand way of referring to major changes in the architecture and design of hardware and software (used in their most generic media sense).' To speak of Generation X or Generation Y, therefore, is to distinguish one cohort of kids from another in terms of their access to digital technologies more so than in terms of birth dates. Within this kind of framework, it seems to be a long way from the days of Pacman to the reign of the Pokemon.

Mapping generational differences has become very common in recent decades. During this period it began with the identification of post-war children as baby boomers (and sometimes veterans). Now, however, it has become an industry associated with mapping what are seen largely as *technologically* produced or mediated generational differences. This reflects, among other things, a growing feeling (at least among some 'adults' in over-developed countries) that 'childhood' – as it is romantically and nostalgically conceived – is no more, and that rampant technological developments are at least partly responsible for this change. Indeed, comparing the youth of 'now' with the youth of 'then' has become a new and popular 'adult' hobby. The lament is widespread and easily recognized: where once kids roamed the streets as happy innocents, now they are kept under lock and key. Where once they entertained themselves, now they are ferried between home and organized recreation. Where once they were active, now they are passive. Where once kids grew into teenagers, now they morph into screenagers (Rushkoff 1997: 3).

We are especially concerned with two strands to this kind of argument. First, a large section of literature is organized around the central notion that childhood – and its attendant 'natural innocence' – has been eroded; and the differences (real or imagined) between contemporary kids and earlier generations are conceptualized negatively – as though today's kids have 'lost' or are 'missing' inherently valuable abilities or skills. Second, an equally significant body of work sees contemporary kids as, indeed, fundamentally different from the kids of earlier years, but equipped – perhaps in compensation? – with new and valuable skills or literacies. Thus they are seen not as much as *lost* but, as always, as potentially alienated from adults who seemingly cannot understand their particular life experiences. In this mindset being 'different' does not carry the same negative or pejorative connotations and refers, in a more matter-of-fact style, to the inevitable differences between parent and child; between adult and youth. These two mindsets – in their various manifestations – have different things to say about the role and nature of school generally and literacy lessons specifically. They are worth exploring in more detail here.

The death of childhood and other tragedies

In his popular book *The Disappearance of Childhood*, Neil Postman claims that childhood is an 'endangered species' (Postman 1994: 4). He acknowledges that childhood was a culturally produced 'social artifice, not a biological necessity' (Postman 1994: 143) but laments the way in which the line between child and adult has increasingly eroded. He argues that the distinction between adult and child has blurred. This is a result of an increasingly technologized world in which there are no secrets, no distinction between the public and the private and no 'adult' policing of childhood knowledge. This blurring process has led to the 'decline of childhood' and the 'diminution' of the 'character of adulthood' (Postman 1994: 134).

Postman is by no means a lone voice here. As David Buckingham (2000: 1) observes in *After the Death of Childhood: Growing up in the Age of Electronic Media*,

> the claim that childhood has been lost has been one of the most popular laments of the closing years of the twentieth century. It is a lament that has echoed across a whole range of social domains – in the family, in the school, in politics, and perhaps above all in the media.

This lament takes various forms. Some commentators argue that an overexposure to mass media has helped to erode the fundamentally 'innocent' nature of childhood. For example, Phillip Adams, writing in an Australian newspaper, argues that children's (over)exposure to a mediated world is accelerating a maturation process that presumably decreases kids' potential 'innocence':

> Secrets made childhood possible. Secrets protected childhood. Remove those secrets – and the new technologies have blown them to smithereens – and children are accelerated into adulthood so rapidly, so ruthlessly, that they become tiny adults by the age of five or six.
>
> (Adams 2000)

Adams continues:

> Instead of taking children slowly, carefully, from the world of once-upon-a-time and happy-ever-after, we plonk them in front of the telly, or the computer screen, where they learn about man's inhumanity to man, parents' inhumanity to children, at a time when they're still needing, wanting to believe in Father Christmas, the Easter Bunny and the Tooth Fairy.

Adams, like many others, represents 'innocence' as a childhood right. The consequences of children's 'over exposure' to mass media do not end simply with losing this right. Other consequences are seen to relate to cognitive and social abilities. Much has been made, for example, of the belief that television requires different (and lesser) skills from print media. Harold Innis, Marshall McLuhan and Neil Postman all argue that 'print is essentially symbolic and linear, and hence cultivates abstraction and logical thinking', while television is represented as a visual medium that requires no special mental abilities (quoted in D. Buckingham 2000: 26–7). Postman (1994: 78) claims that television 'requires perception, not conception', and that the strategies required to make sense of TV are of a different – and lesser – order to those associated with reading. He writes:

> Television offers a fairly primitive but irresistible alternative to the linear and sequential logic of the printed word and tends to make the rigors of a literate education irrelevant. There are no ABC's for pictures. In learning to interpret the meaning of images, we do not require lessons in grammar or spelling or logic or vocabulary. We require no analogue to the McGuffey Reader, no preparation, no prerequisite training. Watching television not only requires no skills but develops no skills.
>
> (Postman 1994: 78–9)

This concern that children are now losing particular interpretive and thinking skills is echoed by commentators who warn that kids are increasingly less able to entertain themselves, and to think and express themselves. These claims that kids are losing (or failing to develop) what are represented as valuable 'cognitive' and social skills are often legitimated via their attachment to discussions about the amount of time children spend with electronic media and speculations concerning the dangers of this kind of media use/abuse. For example, media commentators have increasingly drawn attention to the amount of time that kids spend consuming various media products, including shows available on both free to air and pay TV as well as videos. One recent Australian estimate argued that children have typically watched 5000 hours of television by the time they start kindergarten at the age of 4 (Adams 2000: 32). A large study conducted by the Kaiser Family Foundation in the United States found that the 'typical American child spends an average of more than 38 hours a week – nearly five and a half hours a day (5:29) – consuming media outside of school' (http://www.kff.org/content/1999/1535/). Interestingly, the study also revealed that children's use of electronic media involves far greater use of TVs than computers.

> Nearly seven in ten kids (69 per cent) have a computer at home and nearly half (45 per cent) have Internet access from home. Among kids eight and older, one in five (21 per cent) has a computer in their bedroom. But despite this widespread access to computers, kids still spend a comparatively small amount of time with computers, averaging less than half an hour a day (:21) using a computer for fun, compared to two and three quarters hours a day (2:46) watching TV.

The distinction made between television use and entertainment technologies has been blurred by the phenomenal success of home video game systems. Although early systems such as Atari and games played on the Apple II computers appeared to lose out to the video arcade games, the introduction of Nintendo in the mid-1980s marked a dramatic change in the market. Gene Provenzo (1991: 8) informs us that

> Nintendo first introduced its hardware system in 1986. By June of 1988 it had sold 11 million units. In 1990 there were 7.2 million Nintendo entertainment systems sold, and total sales for the Nintendo Corporation amounted to $3.4 million.

In the ten years between 1980 and 1990, sales figures for the video game industry went from US $446 million dollars to four *billion* dollars (Provenzo 1991: 10). The industry has continued to grow, earning an estimated seven billion dollars in 1997, and in one study, children were found to spend at least 4.2 hours a week playing video games (Dorman 1997).

Information about the amount of time children spend with televisions, computers and video games is regularly coupled with speculation about the effect these associations are having on their health. This demonstrates the fact that evidence of technologically mediated entertainment is not read by adults as merely time spent on a particular hobby – like skateboarding or stamp collecting. Instead it is read, within a particular 'loss of childhood' discourse, as time that is at best lost or wasted and, at worst, contributing to the breakdown of traditional understandings of childhood.

Within this discourse, much attention is drawn to data that describe kids as 'less active, less fit and . . . less likely to use sports equipment' (Agoglia 1999). Agoglia's article (published, interestingly, in a journal called *Sporting Goods Business*) quotes statistics to show that the 'staples' of youth activities have tumbled. He claims that 'bicycle riding has dropped a whopping 21.2 per cent between 1990 and 1998' and that during the same period skateboarding, which he describes as an activity 'long associated with the carefree play of youth' has fallen by 23 per cent (Agoglia 1999: 34).

Agoglia is self-consciously concerned about the effect that this apparent change to kids' leisure activity will have on the sporting goods business. Others with less obviously financial orientations argue that the levels of inactivity associated with media use are actually not normal. For example, Tommy Thompson, Chair of the Health Physical Education and Recreation Department at the University of North Carolina, writes:

> In today's society, a typical American child can watch four to five hours of television per day, sit at his or her computer for another three to four hours per day, play a couple of hours of Nintendo, and still be told that he or she is leading a 'normal' life. This is nonsense. It is not 'normal' for a child to refrain from physical movement. It is unnatural for human youth not to run, jump and play.
>
> (Thompson 2000: 189)

Other authors emphasize what are seen as health and welfare risks of inactivity. A recent report from the non-profit US research organization Child Trends speaks of the 'new morbidities' that have taken the place of diseases such as polio and argues that children in the twenty-first century now negotiate morbid threats to their health, including 'obesity, premature sexual activity, drug use, and gun violence' (cited in Wagner 2000). Concern about the rise of the overweight 'couch kids' or 'telly tubbies' (Corboy 2000) is expressed in many academic and popular texts. These often make an unproblematized assumption that kids are increasingly overweight because of time spent in front of televisions and PCs. As one author writes, 'Overeating and underactivity during infancy and early adolescence make children particularly vulnerable to excessive weight gain. Both of these elements appear to go hand in hand with television watching' (Corboy 2000: 30). It is for these kinds of reasons that Generation X also has been referred to as Generation XXL (Cowley 2000).

The link between media use/abuse (or consumption) and the incidence of obesity relates not only to decreased levels of activity, but also to the messages kids receive about food. A recent study of food advertisements on television aimed directly at children found that 'food ads targeted at children generally reflect the dietary pattern associated with an increased risk of obesity and dental caries in childhood; and cardiovascular disease, diabetes and cancers in adulthood' (Wilson *et al.* 1999: 647).

Another study completed in the UK found a parallel between what are widely defined as poor dietary habits and the incidence of childhood asthma (cited on ABC Radio 2000). Thus a chain of association is drawn between kids' inactivity, their use of TV and entertainment technologies, their poor dietary habits and their increasingly poor (or declining) health.

This angle on the generational debate emphasizes the 'costs' to children of contemporary lifestyles. Attention is drawn to what kids have lost, what they now lack, and there is an associated pressure placed on teachers to try to rectify this situation. This pressure is intensified within discourses that emphasize not just the 'lost generation' (Agoglia 1999) but also the rise of troubled and 'bad' kids.

From sad kids to bad kids

One step on from the concerns expressed about the *welfare* of children is the worry that they are becoming desensitized and less *civilized*. Some commentators have argued that the extensive nature of kids' contact with mass media (and particularly the kind of 'real life TV' that began with the telecast of the Vietnam War) has caused a loss of feeling. One humorous example of this belief is provided by an extract from the animated TV show *The Simpsons*. In one episode, Homer – the working-class and famously inactive, overweight and TV addicted dad – is worried about having to tell his kids that he is going to have a triple by-pass operation. The kids assure him that nothing he has to tell them could be traumatic:

Bart: Nothing you say can upset us. We're the MTV generation.

Lisa: We feel neither highs or lows.

Homer: Really? What's it like?

Lisa: Ehh. [shrugs]

In many cases this perceived loss of sensitivity – of the ability to care about the feelings and experiences of others – is seen also to have resulted in a loss of manners or civility. Postman's voice is once again prominent here, arguing that schools and families need to insist on a return to the 'rigorous standards of *civilite*' (cited in D. Buckingham 2000: 27).

Postman's point is echoed by many others who argue that besides losing the innocence of childhood we are breeding new, uncontrolled and uncontrollable children involved in increasing displays of aggression and violence. At its most extreme, this lament about the emergence of a new 'wild child' sees kids not simply as innocent victims of inadequate supervision, but as a new and frightening 'breed' unto themselves. These are kids who torment and harass other kids and, increasingly, adults (especially the elderly); kids who are active in violence; kids who commit mass murder; kids who bash or kill their parents; kids who know no remorse.

In this vein, a PBS Frontline special called *Little Criminals* which screened in the USA contained the subheading: 'A six year old California boy nearly beats a baby to death. What makes a child so violent? How do we deal with him?' (http://www.pbs.org/wgbh/pages/frontline/shows/little/). A burgeoning fear of youth violence – linked unproblematically to male children – is made explicit in the ensuing on-line discussion, which provides other links to 'troubled kids' sites, most of which emphasize the inclination towards criminality of young boys.

Similarly, Jennifer Buckingham (2000) begins her exploration of 'boy troubles' with a review of juvenile crime. She cites Australian data to argue that 'rates of property crime have doubled in the period from 1973/4 to 1994/5, and that rates of violent crime were five times higher at the end of the period than at the beginning' (Buckingham 2000: 2). She also argues that in the most recent available data, boys made up 80 per cent of juvenile arrests for violent crimes.

Reports like this highlight the search for an explanation that makes sense of rising youth crime, particularly crime perpetrated by boys. This search inevitably identifies a broad-based desensitization of youth (associated, among other things, with the kinds of TV/video game practices described earlier) as a major factor. The furore that emerged after 2-year-old James Bulger was kidnapped and murdered in England by 10-year-old boys who had supposedly just watched a violent movie provides a good example. The discussions about the effect of TV and video movie violence that preceded both the Port Arthur killings in Tasmania, Australia, and the Columbine High killings in the USA provide others. These debates reflect high levels of anxiety – largely on the part of adults – that televisions, computers (particularly computer games) and various electronic games are corrupting children so that they miss out on the benefits of a 'normal' or 'traditional' childhood and are also potentially in conflict with society itself. Thus bad boys are seen as one further product of technologically dominated and inadequately monitored contemporary culture.

Within this strand of the loss of childhood discourse teachers are placed under a different set of pressures. Their role is increasingly seen as one that necessitates the close regulation of television and other entertainment technologies and, wherever possible, the introduction of critical perspectives relating to media texts so that kids, too, might learn to view them with suspicion and perhaps distaste. It is in schools, the argument goes, that kids can learn to validate literacies associated with print-based text, and to distance themselves from mass mediated communication forms. Postman (1994: 152) argues that 'as a creation of literacy, the school will not easily join in the assault on its parentage. In one form or another, no matter how diluted the effort, the school will stand as the last defense against the disappearance of childhood.'

Within this kind of mindset, introducing popular culture and other media resources into classrooms is largely tied to making them objects of (adult) critique. It can be argued that this merely serves to reinscribe the gulf between adult and child. We are not against introducing kids to critical literacy strategies that can be usefully applied to the analysis of popular culture and media texts. Rather, we are suggesting that an abrupt and incautious approach to this kind of critical strategy does little to foster links between student and teacher. Indeed, it has the potential to redraw the lines that already stand between 'them' and 'us' in the classroom.

An alternative approach to describing contemporary kids emphasizes not what is *wrong* with kids, but rather what might be *different* about kids, and it is to this discourse that we now turn.

The children are dead: long live the kids!

The literature we have discussed to this point has tended to emphasize the costs to children specifically and society more generally of kids' over-exposure to various forms of electronic media. Clearly there are some real and legitimate issues to be dealt with in this literature (including, for example, the parallel that seems to exist between kids' activity levels now and their subsequent adult heath and welfare). This, however, is not the only story that can be told about contemporary childhood. Discussions around the youth of today can emphasize not the loss of childhood, but the emergence of new figurations of childhood – new ways of being a kid that come with new skills, abilities and resources. In this discourse, the emphasis shifts from conceptualizing contemporary kids in either a deficit model (where they are seen to lack 'old fashioned' and inherently valuable skills and interests and behaviours) or a deviant model (where kids who have stepped outside of the bounds of normal and socially acceptable behaviour). It moves instead to a difference model in which they are seen not as bad, or as deviants when measured against some pre-existing 'norm'. Rather, they are seen as different, where difference can be represented in positive terms.

Working to acknowledge the specificity of kids' experiences necessitates several moves. First, it is important to recognize that contemporary 'Western' children are part of a technological revolution. There are kids among us who have never known anything other than a world where cash is dispensed from automatic teller machines rather than over bank counters; where groceries are rung up via scanners; where videos are checked out to a customer's bar code; where our video recorders and TVs come with remote controls and timers to turn them on and off; and where microwaves are as common as toasters.

This recognition that the landscape which kids now negotiate is funda-mentally different from the landscape of the 1960s and 1970s is captured well by John Perry Barlow's distinction between those in Western society who have been born into an existing technological state and those who have seen the changes happen around them. Barlow uses the terms 'immigrant' and 'native' to differentiate between those who have never known any other world, and those who have had to adapt. As we have written elsewhere, this distinction – which we prefer to refer to as one between 'insiders' and 'outsiders' – relates to those who have been born into and have grown up in the context of cyberspace, on the one hand, and those who come to this new world from the standpoint of a life-long socialisation in physical space, on the other (Rowan *et al.* 2000). This distinction marks off those who understand the Internet, virtual concepts and the IT world generally from those who do not. Within Barlow's framework, newcomers to cyberspace don't have the inherent experiences, history and resources available to them that insiders have. And so, to that extent, they cannot understand this space in the ways that insiders do. Barlow believes that this distinction falls very much along age lines. He says that, generally speaking, people over the age of 25 are outsider-newcomers. Conversely, 'if you're under 25 you're closer to being an [insider], in terms of understanding what it [i.e. the Internet, virtual concepts and the information technology world generally] is and having a real basic sense of it' (Barlow, in Tunbridge 1995). Douglas Rushkoff (1997: 2) echoes Barlow's point when he argues that 'We are all immigrants to a new territory. Our world is changing so rapidly that we can hardly track the differences, much less cope with them.' He goes on to say that 'Without having migrated an inch, we have, nonetheless, travelled further than any generation in history' (Rushkoff 1997: 3).

Rushkoff refines his argument to acknowledge that there are significant differences in terms of the relative abilities of the last three generations of humans to cope with and respond to the contemporaneous constancy of change:

> The degree of change experienced by the past three generations rivals that of a species in mutation. Today's 'screenager' – the child born into a culture mediated by the television and computer – is interacting with his [*sic*] world in at least as dramatically altered a fashion from his grandfather as the first sighted creature did from his blind ancestors, or a winged one from his earthbound forebears . . . what we need to adapt to, more than any particular change, is the fact that we are changing so rapidly. We must learn to accept change as a constant. Novelty is the new status quo.
>
> (Rushkoff 1997: 3)

In contrast to those authors cited above who read this change as damaging for society generally and children specifically, both Barlow and Rushkoff seek to acknowledge the reality of technologically mediated change, and point to the skills of children as vital for the human race's ability to adapt to and cope with this change:

> Rather than focusing on how we, as adults, should inform our children's activities with educational tidbits for their better development, let's

appreciate the natural adaptive skills demonstrated by our kids and look to them for answers to some of our own problems adapting to postmodernity. Kids are our test sample – our advance scouts. They are, already, the thing that we must become.

(Rushkoff 1997: 13)

Far from being at risk or 'lost' in the contemporary world, therefore, this discourse reads kids as people with *new* sets of skills – including media-related literacies. These literacies make kids better equipped for the current media context than are the adults who are meant to be protecting them. For example, Rushkoff rejects the notion that TV – particularly MTV styles of television that make use of rapid shot changes – are reducing kids' attention span. Instead, he argues that it takes greater intelligence to process rapidly changing images than to process the more traditional – and slower – imagery (Rushkoff 1997: 50). He argues as well that remote control kids have a broad attention range, and an ability to process visual imagery extremely quickly. These are literacies, he claims, that will be highly valued in future workplaces.

The perspective that kids are actually better equipped than adults to cope with the world which adults regularly seek to regulate in order to protect children (as witnessed by the rise of 'net nanny' censorship programmes) is also found elsewhere. It underlies Bill Green and Chris Bigum's influential paper 'Aliens in the classroom' (1993). Green and Bigum speak of the emergence of the 'postmodern student-subject' and argue that the children of contemporary classrooms possess fundamentally different life experiences, interests and skills from those of kids of earlier years.

Such work challenges us to make explicit the assumptions we bring with us about kids, when we shape up educational programmes designed to respond to 'their' needs. It is also interesting to reflect here upon the ways in which adults are regularly positioned in powerful relationships with kids, and are thus more likely than not to take themselves as 'the norm' and read the kids as the 'aliens'. During recent years we have increasingly come to the opinion that while there are aliens in the classroom, they are, in fact, adults.

Real/good literacy lessons

A perspective that conceives students not as fundamentally deviant or dys-functional but as individuals who may well have experienced feelings of alienation within school systems that appear seriously removed from their own 'real' worlds raises different challenges for teachers from those we explored within the 'death of childhood' discourse. Specifically, teachers are challenged to identify ways in which they make links between what might be read as traditional school knowledge and that which students may describe as their own, real world knowledge.

This necessitates getting to know more about the 'real world' of kids, and then adapting, modifying or fundamentally transforming classroom and schooling practices in response to this knowledge. A key strategy here is finding ways to acknowledge and respond to the vast range of 'everyday literacies' displayed by students, and the absence of these literacies within schools. While not every teacher has the time to research each student and develop a detailed map of who they are and what kinds of literacies they *do* display, important insights can be drawn from existing work.

The data already cited – within both the alarmist and pragmatic discourses associated with childhood – affirm the significance of TVs, computers, electronic games and all their associated characters and discourses within the lives of many kids. This is a 'reality' that needs acknowledgement. Lankshear identifies research concluding that today's students from developed countries are generally more likely to engage with literacy practices in classrooms if the texts that are used are *meaningful* to them. He argues that there are two levels to meaningfulness. One relates to an individual's ability to make sense of what texts actually say. The other is a larger sense of meaningfulness which relates to an individual's understanding of where the texts are at, or what practices they are about (Lankshear 1997: 121).

Taken together, these ideas suggest that educators need to find ways to identify students' 'real worlds' and to encourage the creation of links between school, home and other sites. This position is in stark contrast to the stand commonly taken up within the 'death of childhood' discourse, where commentators are more likely to call for an increased distinction between home and school, so that traditional school literacies can be reinstated and revalued. Schools are commonly regarded as sites where kids' popular interests need to be policed. While students may be encouraged to present show-and-tell type activities on things relating to their home or their hobbies, many of the things they enjoy most are actually banned from schools.

Ray Misson (1998: 55) highlights the tensions associated with making use of popular culture texts in the classroom:

> In dealing with popular texts, teachers often walk a tightrope, not wishing to set themselves against students' judgements, but at the same time wanting students to see the possibly damaging limitations of the texts they are consuming. If a teacher points out the limitations of Home and Away, she or he can be cast as staidly negative; if the text is allowed simply to do its ideological work unnoticed, then the teacher is scarcely taking on the responsibilities of an effective critical literacy teacher in making students aware of what the text is asking them to believe.

The kind of classroom practices enabled by acknowledging that kids possess a range of literacies not routinely acknowledged in literacy classrooms have not resulted simply in 'feel good' strategies. In many cases researchers are driven by a basic belief that incorporating 'kid' texts into the curriculum has the potential to open up valuable learning opportunities. As Carmen Luke and Keith Roe (1993: 118) note, 'To suggest that children's and adolescent popular culture has nothing to offer but crass commercialism is to ignore the kinds of potentially empowering lessons that the young construct from media texts and invest in cultural practices.' The recognition that kids can develop a range of valuable skills through their engagement with various forms of entertainment and information technology contrasts markedly with the mindset that sees technology and mass media as responsible for the *loss* of skills and abilities.

The 'real world' of contemporary kids presents challenges and opportunities to teachers. We are not, however, naively arguing for the unreflective wholesale adoption or incorporation of popular culture and kid-centred activities in classrooms. Such responses actually skirt taking responsibility for teaching students to be critical consumers *and* producers of social discourses and practices. Many of the popular resources created for children, for example, contain highly gendered meanings. As we argue in Chapter 6, technologically mediated entertainment is particularly steeped in narrow representations of masculinity and femininity, and we have no wish to see teachers endorsing such images.

It is also important to remain aware – as we argue in Chapter 5 – that access to computing and gaming technologies follows gendered pathways. Girls generally have less time or space to use home-based digital technologies and are less likely to define themselves as experts relating to any computer activity (National Science Foundation 1997; Roper Starch Worldwide 1998). Equally important, however, is the awareness that not all boys are interested in these resources either. Not all boys play *Star Craft*, negotiate the mazes of *Golden Eye* or hunt nocturnal Pokemon in increasingly specialised Game Boy games.

A further complication emerges from the economic status of children in schools. Despite widespread beliefs, not every kid in First World countries has access to a home computer, Nintendo console or Game Boy. Recent studies document the relationship between economic status and regional location and the likelihood of a household having access to computers and/or the Internet. Teachers cannot simply assume that kids can access or participate in even the most culturally legitimated technologically based activities (National Science Foundation, 1997).

Taken together, these perspectives on the contemporary nature of kids pose important challenges for teachers. Yet it is precisely this kind of discussion that is often missing from debates about current schooling practices. During a research project conducted in the latter months of 2000, we worked with young people in an Australian secondary school to identify what they saw as strengths and weaknesses of schooling. Part of the study involved asking the kids to think about the extent to which school was connected to their lives – to their 'multiple mes'. Students in Years 8, 9 and 10 insisted that there was little connection between their outside selves and their school selves. They acknowledged that they played many roles – child (son/daughter), sports player, babysitter, worker, shopper, reader, viewer and so on – but argued that school was only interested in their 'school personality'. In addition to this, the kids argued that they were never consulted about school issues, that their teachers had 'no interest' in what their life was like outside of school and that 'no allowance at all' was made for kids' paid work outside school – or other – commitments. According to these young people, all that mattered to teachers was *school* work.

During the same period (in October 2000) we conducted a workshop with a group of primary school teachers focusing on ways in which to engage children in discussions of cultural diversity. Participants spoke long and articulately about the value of popular culture texts for helping kids to think about difference and diversity. They gave numerous examples of movies that provide alternative and positive images of masculinity and femininity, of racial difference and of disabilities. When the facilitator asked how often they actually made use of these kinds of resources in their classroom the teachers – almost as one – said, 'Oh never, we just don't have time to watch a whole movie. There's too much else to do.'

This example highlights the difficulties teachers have in legitimating the use of popular culture or other 'real world' activities within their teaching practice. It is this difficulty as much as anything else that illustrates the space standing between many teachers and many students. How, then, is it possible to bridge this gap?

Bridging the gap

Our approach to generational challenges, as with the other issues we have raised, reflects three desires:

- to get to know more about where students actually *are* at (and, by extension, to rely less upon our stereotyped understandings of what kids are 'really' like);
- to reflect upon what this tells us about kids' understandings of themselves as gendered subjects;
- to build on this knowledge to problematize rigid understandings of masculinity and femininity and to introduce, circulate and legitimate alternative and multiple figurations of 'boy' and 'girl'.

Within this framework, popular culture texts and the 'real world' experiences of kids become central. There is little point bemoaning the rise of TV and technology and refusing to engage with it in class. There is no point in sneering at or deriding Pokemons and Nintendos or *Neighbours* and *Friends* and hoping this will effect some kind of attitude shift among kids. Likewise, nothing useful is served by denying the powerful role that these popular culture texts play in confirming and policing gendered patterns of behaviour. For the teacher working to effect some kind of transformation in the way kids conceptualize and enact masculinity and femininity, these resources are important. What needs to be determined, however, is the extent to which they become battlegrounds, which further inscribe the differences between kid and adult, or accepted territories within which diverse opinions, perspectives and ideas can be shared and built upon.

The new literacies studies and rhizomatic framework we have developed throughout the book espouse a clear preference for the second option. We believe that teachers and students will benefit from the ability to weave links between kid worlds and school worlds, and that these links can play a vital role in engaging kids in traditional and contemporary literacy practices.

We have framed several principles that we believe can facilitate this process.

First principle. It is necessary to get to know more about kids *as they are* and not as we would wish them to be. Obviously, there are limits to possibilities here. Not every teacher can research every child. None the less, useful resources highlight the kinds of experiences kids are likely to encounter. Furthermore, many teachers make good use of questionnaires or group interviews with students in order to get broad pictures of the kinds of things they like and choose to engage in beyond school. It is important for teachers to know what kids do outside of school, and to have some familiarity with the entertainment technologies (computer-mediated or otherwise) that kids find pleasurable.

Second principle. Teachers need to develop a clear understanding of how popular culture texts can reinforce or challenge gender norms. The greatest weapons against the stereotyping associated with some popular texts are the transformative images in others. Disney's *Mulan* (1998) and *Pocahontas* (1995) tell different stories to *Beauty and the Beast* (1991) or *The Jungle Book* (1967). *Ever After* (1999) is a dramatically different tale from the traditional versions of *Cinderella*. *Stuart Little* (1999) and *Babe* (1995) have very different things to say about families from movies like *Home Alone* (1990).

Third principle. Teachers need to recognize that there will be significant differences within any group of students, in terms of their relationship with and attitude towards various popular resources. As we have argued before, not all kids get pleasure from computers. Not all boys are technogurus. Neither are all girls digitally homeless. Teachers should be alert to important potential differences between themselves and their students, between student and student, and within the students themselves. Kids change too.

Fourth principle. Teachers need to be sensitive to the pleasure that many children draw from popular resources and tread softly when attempting to engage kids in their critique. Teachers walk a fine line when attempting to integrate popular culture or generationally relevant resources into the classes. To quote Ray Misson (1998: 55),

> in dealing with popular texts, teachers often walk a tightrope, not wishing to set themselves against students' judgments, but at the same time wanting students to see the possibly damaging limitations of the texts they are consuming.

Fifth principle. Teachers need to differentiate between the positive and negative inclusion of cultural resources. By extension they need to be aware of the differences between inclusion and exclusion, between tokenism and centrality, between stereotyping and illustrating diversity, between valuing and devaluing activities, people and practices.

Taken together, these perspectives maximize the ability of teachers to identify the relationship between gender and literacy, and, by extension, dramatically improve their ability to generate links between boys and girls and alternative conceptions of masculinity and femininity. In the third section of this chapter we offer some examples of the specific ways in which the kinds of sensitivities we are advocating here can be used to shape classroom literacy activities. Before we move to this, however, it is necessary for us to acknowledge one further complicating issue that teachers working to effect the kind of gender-aware analysis and reform we have been advocating must negotiate: the challenges of engaging in any kind of gender based project in a 'post-feminist' age.

'Don't call me baby': gender reform in a 'post-feminist' age

All attempts to engage with gender in an educational setting require those involved to negotiate a complex terrain that surrounds and penetrates the classroom environment. This terrain reflects the kinds of generational differences identified in the previous section, and one particularly powerful dimension of these differences is tied to the fundamental theme of this book: attitudes towards gender.

To begin, we have no wish to stereotype all teachers as either pro-feminism or anti-feminism or as pro- or anti-gender reform. Nor do we want to argue that all children are 'over' that 'feminism thing'. If, however, we limit our discussion to teachers who are working on some gender-based reform project and kids who are participating in them, it is possible to identify two recurrent themes. First, there are at least some differences between the ways in which teachers and students evaluate, prioritize or appreciate gender reform work. Second, there are at least some tensions between male and female kids who take part in these projects.

In attempting to design a reform project focused on boys and literacy, therefore, teachers need to respond not only to the generational issues outlined in the previous section but also to different opinions concerning the point, purpose and politics of the project in the first place. There are several specific challenges we want to table here.

Feminism has gone too far . . .

First, there is no getting away from the fact that many kids in many countries have been exposed to – and are well aware of – the whole 'what about the boys?' debate. Boys and girls have been exposed to the 'war against' boys' discourse explored in Chapter 1. They have often encountered attempts to position boys as the 'victims' of unscrupulous and over-zealous feminists; the victims, in fact, of girls. In recent years this kind of claim has become more common and, indeed, more emotional and inflammatory. A recent magazine article by Australian icon Ita Buttrose provides a good example. Buttrose (2000: 78) writes:

> Improving educational opportunities for boys should not be seen as a slap in the face for all that girls have achieved. But all the evidence suggests boys are getting a raw deal. It's time we told those meddling gender equity experts to keep their hands off them.

We are concerned here with the extent to which teachers and students in schools are aware of and shaped by these anti-feminist, or anti-reform, discourses. This is not a question we raise lightly. From the post-structuralist perspective informing this book, individuals negotiate their sense of themselves – their subjectivity – at the intersection of multiple and competing discourses. For this reason we must be aware of the discourses around masculinity currently circulating within schooling and other cultural contexts.

As we have observed, overt debates concerning the victimization of men and boys have the potential to reinscribe traditional perspectives of normative masculinity. At the same time they can make it very difficult for teachers to open up debates about the social construction of masculinity without being positioned as anti-male or, ironically, anti-feminist. Of course, schools themselves can also buy into this discourse by encouraging students to debate the pros and cons of gender reform. This strategy – and its side effects – was well illustrated for us by an episode of the popular Australian current affairs show *Four Corners*, screened in the mid-1990s. This particular episode, focused on boys' educational outcomes, featured a debate between students at a high school with the title 'Has feminism gone too far?' The boys were asked to argue that yes, it had. The girls, predictably enough, were arguing that no, it had not. Pitting girls and boys against each other in these kinds of ways helps to reinforce the idea that there are a finite set of positive schooling outcomes which must be fought for, and that boys are fighting on the opposite team to the girl. This does little to encourage ongoing gender work in schools.

Haven't we finished with that gender thing yet? Or can't you just get over it?

It is not just boys – or boys who buy into the 'boys as victim' discourse – who pose challenges to teachers. Many students – girls and boys – adopt a suspicious attitude towards gender reform of any kind, regardless of whether it is focused on boys *or* girls. Many teachers in a workforce with a steadily ageing population have lived through the second wave of feminism. Some participated actively in the pursuit of equal pay for equal work. Others have campaigned to be allowed to keep their permanent positions in the teaching workforce after marriage or pregnancy. Still others have negotiated myriad sexist policies and procedures, ranging from their right to wear trousers to work through to their right to be considered (on merit) for promotions. And many of them have had the benefit of tertiary education to provide them with opportunities to reflect upon the consequences of traditional gender norms. A recent survey of teacher education students at an Australian university saw students nominate the study of gender as one of the most challenging and transformative activities undertaken during their degree. A recurring theme throughout the survey was that being given dedicated space to explore gender issues allowed students to think of things they had never really thought about before. One student claimed that the course 'was excellent for me as a future teacher as it opened my eyes'. Another wrote, 'I liked it because it was an interesting subject that explored ideas I wouldn't have explored otherwise.' Such sentiments echo throughout literally hundreds of evaluations collected over the past five years.

The opportunity to think about the wide range of issues associated with gender is more commonly made available to adults than to children. For this and other reasons, in supported and supportive environments, teachers and students (as well as teachers and other teachers) often have vastly different things to say about the gendered nature of classroom practices and the ways in which these practices can be transformed. Many boys and girls in education systems at the dawn of the twenty-first century are growing up in societies that tell them that all the gender issues of the 1960s and 1970s have now been solved. (It is important to note that it is mainly adults who are circulating this perspective; hence, 'teachers' are not a homogeneous group either.) They live in an era when feminists who want to push things 'too far' have regularly been demonized, and find themselves in a space which reasserts the equal opportunity model of the early twentieth century. According to this model, if women and men have the same rights and, if the women are good enough, they'll have the lives they desire. This poses a real dilemma for the teacher who wishes to investigate or respond to the gendered nature of classroom or educational practice. How is it possible to raise questions about gender roles, gender norms, gendered classroom and social behaviours without being dismissed by kids who have at hand a wide range of anti-feminist propaganda? Is it, in fact, possible to do this at all if other staff advise them to 'just get over it': advice that was also recently given to us?

I'm not a feminist but . . .

An interesting variation on the 'just get over it' discourse explored above is the 'I'm not a feminist but . . .' stance. Within this stance girls will articulate their commitment to equal rights – and express strong views relating to their own rights – without wanting to attach themselves to labels such as 'feminism'. This relates to the positioning of the current generation of boys and girls within a period that is sometimes known as 'post-feminism'. While one cartoonist claimed 'I'll be post-feminist in post-patriarchy', many other commentators have noted that the time for feminism has passed and that what we need now are not feminists but 'equalists' (http://people.delphi.com/pdsippel/equal.htm).

At one popular website for women – Pleiades – young girls conducted a discussion around whether or not they saw themselves as feminists. This involved most of the contributors saying yes, if being a feminist means believing in equal rights, but one girl responded to the question, 'Do you consider yourself a feminist?' With the answer 'Not really, maybe an equalist' (http://www.pleiades-net.com/voices/girl55/24_18.html).

This is in no way to imply that all girls are reluctant to align themselves with the work of feminists, or to suggest that girls are backing away from the 'girl power' discourse that has emerged over the past ten years (a discourse we will return to in a moment). It *does*, however, point to the fact that, unlike the case with culturally authorized subject positions like 'cheerleader' and 'girlfriend' or even 'scientist' and 'teacher', for a girl to align herself with the subject position 'feminist' generally requires some conscious choice to resist the stereotyping of feminism and feminists. On the other hand, while girls (and boys) may look suspiciously at concepts explicitly related to feminism or 'gender reform', it is important to note that many girls have taken up various 'girl power' or 'power chick' discourses that have emerged in popular culture texts over the past decade.

Girl power

Through music videos, television, movies and on endless pieces of clothing and other merchandise, girls and boys of recent years have been increasingly exposed to a new kind of female subjectivity: one associated with independence, aggression, courage, risk taking and technological competence, as well as beauty, 'femininity' and heterosexuality. Independent, active and gorgeous heroines designed for teen audiences, such as Xena: Warrior

Princess, Buffy the Vampire Slayer and the trio of witch sisters – Prue, Piper and Phoebe – from *Charmed*, have gained cult followings. So, too, have the action heroines aimed at slightly older audiences: women including Ripley from the *Aliens* series, Sarah Connor from *The Terminator* (1984) and *Terminator 2 – Judgment Day*, and both sides of Geena Davis's split personality – Charlie and Sam – from *The Long Kiss Goodnight* (1996).

Similarly powerful images are to be found in the popular music scene. Over the past ten years Alanis Morriset, Sinead O'Connor, Toni Childs, Lisa Loeb and many, many others have vocalized women's right to respect, independence and self-determination. While young girls may reject the words in Helen Reddy's anthem, 'I Am Woman,' the Spice Girls' 'girl power' albums became instant hits. Thousands of pre-teen girls danced around houses singing, 'If you wanna be my lover, you gotta get with my friends; Make it last forever, friendship never ends. If you wanna be my lover, you have got to give. Taking is too easy, but that's the way it is' (Spice Girls 1998). More recently audiences have eagerly embraced the sentiments of Shania Twain, who sings about the joys of coming home to a well cooked meal, and the gutsiness of Madison Avenue, who reminds a would-be suitor, 'I belong to me, so don't call me baby'.

This power chick discourse poses two real challenges to the work of gender reform. First, it can work to obscure the ongoing nature of the gender-based discrimination still experienced by many girls – particularly those who don't have the same hard-edged glamour of many of the popular power chicks. Second, it can work to alienate the boys who are on the receiving end of the strange mix of assertiveness and aggressiveness that it often produces. This is a point worth exploring in more detail.

Angry young men

While many girls feel themselves empowered by the kinds of power chick discourse explored above, there are fewer such discourses made available to boys. This is not to say that new figurations of masculinity are not to be found in popular culture. Certainly there are. The male stars within 'chick shows' such as *Sabrina* or *Charmed* or even *Neighbours* and *Friends* are routinely positioned as more sensitive guys than those associated with the television era that brought us *Magnum*, *The Mary Tyler Moore Show* or *Married with Children*. This is not to say that gender stereotypes are broken down, because the guys depicted and valued are still uniformly attractive and more, rather than less, 'macho'. None the less, there is much more variety within these positions. Michael J. Fox in *Spin City* is a powerful, popular and sensitive character. Harvey in *Sabrina* respects Sabrina's independence, and is regularly shown in a caring relationship with his mum and younger brother. Harrison Ford's portrayal of the US President in *Airforce One* (1997) is combined with an equally strong performance by Glenn Close as the vice-president. Both the male and the female roles are valued (although it is the president, of course, who rescues the hijacked plane and saves the lives of his family).

Popular music provides slightly more scope for multiple masculinities. Apart from the 'bad boy' bands, there have always been interesting alternative masculinities making their way in the music world. For example, the 'gender-bending' Ziggy Stardusts of the early 1970s gave way in the 1980s to 'glamour boy' rock bands wearing big hair and dresses and gender-neutral technomusic bands. Currently, there is a range of 'nice boy' groups in popular circulation. Many of these are marketed explicitly at female audiences. Among them are some like the internationally successful singer/ dancer Ricky Martin (a kind of Tom Jones for the twenty-first century). Martin consistently refuses to answer questions about his sex life (unlike Jones!), insisting that he is a singer, and his sexuality is irrelevant.

This is not the only kind of story. Many other popular culture bands continue to perpetuate bad boy masculinities and some have become notorious for their out of control behaviour. Television shows continue to serve up images of traditionally male characters, many of whom explicitly devalue the initiatives of women. And the recent spate of disaster movies such as *Deep Impact* (1998), *End of Days* (1999), *Armageddon* (1998) and *Independence Day* (1996) all give central, privileged and heroic positions to the male characters.

Meredith Brooks topped the charts with her hit single 'Bitch', where she celebrates the multiple dimensions of her character with a chorus that runs: 'I'm a bitch, I'm a lover, I'm a child, I'm a mother, I'm a sinner, I'm a saint, I do not feel ashamed, I'm your hell, I'm your dream, I'm nothing in between, You know you wouldn't want it any other way.' In contrast, an Australian male spoof of this song, 'Bloke', contains the lines: 'I'm a bloke, I'm an ocker; and I really love your knockers; I'm a labourer by day, I piss up all me pay; Watching footy on TV; Just feed me more VB; Just pour my beer and get my smokes and go away.'

Our point here is that many girls can draw on positive alternative images of femininity which stand against traditional gender norms, such as images that resist, for example, the consistent positioning of women as passive, weak or emotional. In contrast, it is more difficult to find images of masculinity that do not continue to draw upon traditional masculine norms and ask heroes to demonstrate courage, fearlessness, independence and heterosexuality. The images *are* there. But they are in no way as overt or 'out there' as those of the kick-butt girls.

Risky business

Teachers seeking to implement any kind of gender-based reform in their schools or classes must, then, be prepared to negotiate a diverse range of perspectives associated with popular images of girls' and boys' respective power and rights. They also need to accept that there may be a significant gap between girls' (and boys') beliefs about the 'equalist' nature of schooling and the day-to-day realities of that space. This means that any commitment to opening up debate around gender norms will not occur in neutral territory. Classroom contexts are made complex and dangerous not only because of the generational differences between staff and students, but also because of the gendered nature of these differences and the different interpretations likely to be made of boys, girls and schools.

Taken together, the 'post-feminism' discourses and the various generational perspectives outlined above create an extremely challenging environment for teachers in which to undertake the kind of gender-based literacy reform we advocate in this book. On the one hand, it is easy to argue that teachers need to make connections with where students are at. On the other, we recognize that these starting points (and the literacies associated with them) also need to be interrogated, so that schools do not simply reinscribe traditional gender norms (see Chapter 5). Although it is pedagogically useful to incorporate kids' 'real life' or 'everyday' literacies within the classroom, this must always be done with an eye to where teachers want their classes to end up.

In short, any kind of popular text and any kind of 'kid literacy' has the potential to contribute to transformative literacy practice, but *only if* teachers are able to negotiate the complexities associated with their use. This involves acknowledging both the pleasure that students may get from a range of popular texts or everyday literacies *and* the need to use this pleasure as a basis for connecting students – in rhizomatic fashion – to the kind of critical thinking strategies employed with the new literacies studies.

This is indeed a risky business, and as a broad strategy it asks a lot of teachers. The five principles advanced in the previous section can be reframed here as six challenges:

- How can teachers go about the process of identifying kids' 'real' interests and existing literacies?
- How can teachers link these existing student interests to their own literacy strategies?
- How can they make use of a wide range of texts while remaining alert to the ways in which they might reinscribe traditional understandings of masculinity and femininity?
- How can these traditional and limited understandings of being a 'girl' or a 'boy' be usefully challenged without further alienating students from schools and teachers?

- How can they best acknowledge the differences within and among students?
- How can we respond to this diversity without taking part in essentializing, stereotyping or tokenizing behaviour?

Underlying these challenges is a question about whether teachers can make links between teachers (and their gendered realities), students (and their gendered realities) and the kinds of literacy practices that open up and lead to new realities, without leaving behind elements of the present that afford pleasure, comfort and security. In the following section we suggest some strategies for responding to these generational challenges in efforts to create literacy classrooms that work to transform dominant understandings of masculinity and femininity and strive accordingly to improve literacy experiences for girls *and* boys.

Living on the edge: cross-generational teaching strategies for transformative literacy education

The contexts described in this chapter are clearly challenging for teachers. We believe, however, that the risks – dangers – associated with attempting to teach across generations and with popular culture texts are worth it. They offer pathways into new ways of interacting with students, and can help us to circulate new understandings of masculinity. In this section we explore more closely the five principles we think can inform usefully cross-generational teaching in transformative literacy classrooms. The discussion emphasizes ways in which a particular application of each principle supports the interrogation of limited/limiting gender norms and the circulation of new figurations of masculinity and femininity.

Getting to know you

Our first recommendation for teaching across generations in transformative literacy classrooms is an obvious one. Teachers need to get to know more about their students. This is particularly important when we consider that students spend comparatively little of their time actually *in* school. Caryn Meyers (2000) puts forward some basic principles in her 'mind the gap' checklist designed to facilitate communication across/within generations, and she advises baby boomers and Generation Xers to:

- take time to play;
- get over it (their cynicism);
- pick up your cyber-smarts.

Within this framework, teachers are challenged to engage with kids outside the confines of dominant academic or school discourses. To this end, teachers clearly need as much information as possible about the life circumstances of a student. This includes information relating to where they live, the kind of household/family structure they are part of, their religious beliefs and their own hobbies and interests. Importantly, we are referring here to information relating to real kids in real classes, and not the kind of child we often read about in educational policies or curriculum documents. There is no real short cut when it comes to getting to know about individual kids. There are, however, some very obvious ways in which teachers can try to make a connection between themselves and their students.

Some information can be gleaned tacitly, during the course of casual conversation, or through information picked up at school dances, fetes or camps. Other information will only emerge if the teacher makes a deliberate habit of inviting the kids' lives into the classroom. This can be done in diverse ways. These include regular 'about me' sessions, where students talk in small groups about something they enjoy. Alternatively, information gathering can be used as a means of facilitating student-centred assignments, where they pick a topic they are interested in as a focus for a research project. Similarly, students can be asked directly to express an opinion on what they would like to study. When this occurs, however, it is important that the teacher is willing and able to follow through. In the case of one school we visited recently, the junior English class voted unanimously to study Steven King's *The Green Mile*, only to have the choice vetoed by the principal.

Similar but different: avoiding stereotypes and valuing difference

Kids' engagement with media and entertainment technologies is problematized in diverse ways by commentators, researchers, parents and teachers. In this discourse, schools (and teachers) are challenged to find ways to 'protect' kids from the deleterious effects of their hobbies; to educate them about the dangers of their pastimes. This places educators in a precarious position, a position where they can be easily read as 'out of touch' with the interests of 'real kids'. In addition to this, reading kids as 'innocents' in need of 'protection' raises the possibility that kids will be read as a homogeneous group: that all kids will be seen as potentially at risk; that all kids will be seen as potential criminals; that all kids will be seen as technologically obsessed. Running alongside a need to get to know more about students is an associated need to avoid stereotyping individuals or groups on the basis of their gender or race or age, and actively to value the differences between students and teachers. As we have seen, it is common for teachers to ascribe to children skills, interests and abilities which, they believe, are 'different' from those of kids of earlier times. This can lead to situations where teachers actively devalue 'new literacies' or, alternatively, to a tendency to assume that all kids now display the kinds of skills that are conjured up by labels such as Generation X or Generation Y.

For example, a common strategy identified by teachers for valuing students' existing literacies within the classroom is to position kids as the experts within particular technology-based (read: computer) activities. This has the worthy potential to acknowledge kids' experience and to break down the distinction between teacher as expert and student as novice. If uncritically adopted, however, this kind of strategy can work to marginalize or alienate those students who do not have the kind of expert knowledge the teacher is looking for. Given the gendered patterns of access to computer time at home (and school) reviewed in Chapter 6, one of the greatest risks here is that these lessons will reinscribe the masculine/feminine divide by associating boys with technological competence and activity, and girls with technological ignorance and passivity. Anyone sitting at a desk working on a computer who has had the need to ask for assistance and then has experienced a male leaning over them, commandeering the mouse, the chair and, ultimately, the computer itself will recognize the dangers here. The likelihood of this occurring is intensified by the greater time boys generally spend using computers as entertainment technologies outside of schools. As James Funk and Debra Buchman (1996) remind us:

> Since the introduction of the simple but hypnotic 'Pong' nearly 25 years ago, consistent gender differences have been found in children's time commitment to electronic game playing . . . Males are found to spend significantly more time playing than females, across locations (home and arcade) and across age groups. In our 1990s surveys of 900 fourth through eighth graders, proportionate gender differences persisted across the grade levels examined.

But this pattern does not relate to all boys. Factors like economic status and ethnicity impact powerfully on the technological, oral and written literacies developed by boys. Teachers must, therefore, walk a fine line between acknowledging the realities of kids' worlds and alienating some students further from classrooms by ascribing to them experiences, interests or abilities that they do not have.

This is not the only risk. As we have argued, boys are not a homogeneous group. Not all boys understand all there is to know about computers. Some feel the technology to be alien or boring and are uncomfortable within discourses that try to position them as experts: this kind of strategy can make boys feel 'unnatural' or 'failures' because they do not meet an implied masculine benchmark. At the other extreme, it is possible for these kinds of activities to encourage boys to claim greater levels of competence than they actually have; to overestimate their abilities (consciously or otherwise) in order to satisfy the assumed demands of the teacher and their peers. There is a risk that attempts to engage with generational specificity may result in stereotyping students in ways that can reinscribe gender norms (a risk illustrated in the early days of the research project discussed in the previous chapter, where Jarrod, in particular, appeared to 'fake' a high degree of familiarity with computer technology).

To take another example of the dangers of stereotyping, Mike Males argues that the evils assigned to contemporary kids are largely the invention of the media. Males argues that baby boom youth:

> suffered death rates from drugs such as heroin and barbituates double to triple that of today's youth . . . And they continue to use, abuse and die from drugs and alcohol at much higher rates than the so-called reckless teen 'wastoids.' Adolescent health and behavior are improving, not declining, and . . . if there's a new trend, it's a tendency to be surprisingly 'mild in the streets'.
>
> (Cited in Johnson 2000)

Buying into these kinds of stereotyping clearly has the potential to impact upon the risks that teachers will or will not take with their classes.

As we have argued throughout, to avoid dangers associated with stereotyping, homogenizing or essentializing particular individuals and groups of students, teachers need to be alert to multiple ways of 'being a boy' and 'being a girl'. This involves multiple conceptions of 'expertise' and 'knowledge' rather than more tokenistic gestures towards 'kid knowledge'. Teachers need to be always on the look out for areas of student competence and constantly encouraging kids to display out-of-school literacies. This may sound straightforward. In fact it is not. For example, one student we have worked with was disciplined by his teacher for refusing to produce a third rough draft of an assignment on paper, before proceeding to the computer. He argued that he always wrote straight on to the screen at home, and that he was better at this form of composition. The teacher disciplined the boy and actually tried to have him suspended for 'resisting his authority'.

In a different study a student teacher who was trying to get a group of Year 9 boys to conceptualize and design a web page using pencils and butcher's paper was completely unable to interest the boys in this task. They simply tuned out of the lesson and waited until they were allowed to get on to the computers before they began to think about the design, sequencing or content of their pages. This example highlights a significant generational difference between the student teacher and the students with respect to procedure. This was a difference the student teacher could not recognize. His generational mindset was at odds with the mindset of the students. He privileged a particular 'teacherly' approach to learning. The students found nothing within this approach that was relevant to them. When the student teacher was able to acknowledge that the kids may have had different, but still valid, techniques for approaching their task, the lesson proceeded much more smoothly.

Besides getting to know their students, and learning to recognize the skills that they bring to the classroom, teachers need also to acknowledge that students bring to any educational environment an array of existing (and gendered) skills. If these skills are valued then there is a stronger chance that teachers will create the kind of link necessary to facilitate the critique of the origins (and gendered nature) of these skills and understandings. This is important because we are not arguing for teacher–student bonding that simply exists at the 'feel good' level. Instead, we believe that in addition to working in multiple ways to value student knowledge, teachers need also to link these attempts to an overall project associated with identifying and critiquing the production of gendered patterns of knowledge. This leads to our third recommendation.

Gender mapping

To effect any kind of challenge to the way literacy, masculinity and schooling are conceptualized, teachers and students alike need to develop a clear understanding of how gender norms are constructed and how they impact upon individuals' lives. This means that the kind of new literacies studies framework explored in Chapters 4 and 5 must routinely be put to use to help students to identify gendered patterns of behaviour both within their classroom and in broader social contexts. This applies to both 'natural seeming' technologies – computers, Game Boys, dishwashers and so on – and popular culture texts. Of course, asking kids to look critically at entertainment technologies or other technological objects that have a 'natural' status in their lives is a challenge akin to asking kids in the 1980s to look critically at their vacuum cleaner or electric oven. This is not to say that this kind of critique isn't necessary or possible. Indeed, the interrogation of patterns of behaviour associated with any kind of household technology (or appliance) is a vital component of gender reform. What we are acknowledging, however, is that it is often necessary to work with kids to facilitate their identification of behaviours as learned, and competencies as developed, rather than as *naturally* masculine or *naturally* feminine.

An effective way to do this is to have students regularly identify areas of their own expertise, and have them trace the ways they developed these skills and understandings. Within this kind of framework students will regularly identify the ways in which they learned to be good at karate, or Nintendo, or skipping, or swimming, and will usually point to the influences of their environment, their friends and their families. This strategy enables students to identify that knowledge which often appears to be gendered – and biologically inherited – is actually learned and acquired. This is not to deny, of course, the influence of 'natural' ability: some kids are 'naturally' better swimmers than others, for example, but in most cases kids will be able to identify how they learnt to do, or get better at doing, a particular task or activity.

Students are also very capable of building upon this kind of activity to identify some of their own literacies, and to consider ways these could be taught to others (an example of which we discussed in detail in Chapter 6). This is a practical and effective way for teachers at once to acknowledge the literacies/skills of their diverse student group, and to denaturalize assumptions relating to the gendered nature of knowledge. Showing the processes through which knowledge is learned – and often gendered – opens up possibilities for students to imagine their relationship to particular bodies of knowledge in new ways.

To complement these kinds of activities, it is important for teachers to make conscious efforts to incorporate transformative texts within any teaching activity: to make active use of 'counternarratives'.

Countering gender narratives

In earlier chapters we have stressed the point that gender norms are produced by the kinds of stories that are told (and retold) about what it is to be a boy or a girl. These stories are more or less powerful depending upon how often they are told, which institutions participate in their circulation and the extent to which they appear to resonate with the 'real lives' of kids. Attempts to engage boys in literacy classrooms are fundamentally about getting the kids to 'buy' different stories about masculinity. That is to say, we are conscious of the importance of connecting boys to new and non-traditional practices of skills so that they can see (and help to create) alternative stories about masculinity.

These alternative stories can be described as 'counternarratives': stories that move beyond the limitations of gender norms and illustrate multiple ways of being a boy (see Chapter 3 above). The counternarrative relates not only to the stories that are produced within schools and classrooms, but also to stories circulated within these sites. That is to say, in their day-to-day teaching, teachers make use of a wide range of texts and each topic that they cover, each genre that they use, has particular gender patterns. Texts on the same topic, or in the same genre, that contest those gender norms are counternarratives.

Fairy tales provide a case in point. It is relatively common for teachers to make use of non-traditional fairy tales in their classrooms. *The Paper Bag Princess* (Munsch 1989) and *Princess Smartypants* (Cole 1986) are regularly given as examples of the genre which challenge gender norms; in other words, they can be read as counternarratives. Every genre, every topic, has its own traditional narratives and counternarratives relating to gender. Identifying them requires teachers (and students) to learn to map the gendered spaces, patterns and behaviours within these texts (a strategy we advocated above). In addition to these overt discussions of how gender norms are produced, naturalized and reinforced, it is valuable for teachers to incorporate counternarratives in a day-to-day, matter of fact way. Here again, the key principle is multiplicity. If different picture books containing a range of different gender norms (and not just gender role reversals) are continually introduced and given a key and central place in the classroom (alongside more traditional and familiar resources) then there is a greater chance that kids will see them as legitimate texts.

This highlights the important distinction between tokenistic inclusion of a transformative text, and centralization of a transformative text. It is quite common for teachers at some time or other during the year to make an effort to incorporate feminist fairy tales or posters of boys reading into their literacy classrooms. There is a big difference, however, between occasional 'token' inclusions and strategies whereby alternative stories are given a central role in learning programmes and valued in the same kind of way traditional texts have long been valued. This suggests a further key strategy. For teachers to work cross-generationally they need to demonstrate a willingness to include and value texts that are popular with the kids. This is a risky strategy we need to explore in more detail.

Perilously popular

In an earlier section we mentioned the gendered nature of many popular culture texts and technologies, and the associated risks of inviting them uncritically into school and literacy classrooms. We have no wish to advocate the uncritical incorporation of popular texts or technologies – any more than we would advocate the uncritical adoption of any of the strategies we have explored. We do, however, want to offer some suggestions about how this risky business can be managed.

For a start, it is necessary to be clear about why one would invite popular texts into the classroom. As far as we are concerned, the goal is to help to make connections between kids and teachers. These are connections that can be used to facilitate the kinds of critical thinking associated with the new literacies studies and the kinds of creative imagining associated with rhizomatic approaches to masculinity. To move students away from traditional gender norms, teachers need first to demonstrate a connection with the students themselves; otherwise it is all too easy for their work to be dismissed as that of 'old fashioned' or 'out of touch' feminist losers. Making connections with older students is often a simpler process, for similarities in life experiences associated with the workforce, families and so on can create points of connection. Working with kids requires teachers to find some points of connection other than those that rest upon 'teacher authority' and 'school knowledge', and it seems to us that popular culture texts have much to offer in this respect.

Second, it is necessary to remain aware that not all texts are popular with all kids. *South Park* has a cult following among some kids; others prefer *The*

Simpsons; some are deeply fascinated by all forms of popular sport; and others would rather watch the Discovery channel on cable TV. Once again, therefore, it is necessary for teachers to acknowledge the multiplicity within what often appears to be a homogeneous generation, and to make use of more than one kind of 'real world' text in the course of a school term or year.

With these two points in mind, it is crucial to recall that one cannot incorporate a popular text into lessons solely to critique it. One cannot simply disconnect students from the kinds of gendered practices that they feel comfortable with, or the everyday texts they draw pleasure from. To mess with the texts or artefacts central to a children's world is to mess with their sense of self or their subjectivity. Teachers may develop more sensitivity to this issue by reflecting upon the extent to which their own sense of self is tied up with what they do and the objects or texts with which they interact. Misson (1998: 54) provides a useful reminder to teachers when he points out that the

> child who desperately wants a Barbie campervan or a Sony PlayStation or a Tamagotchi for his or her birthday is essentially no different from the adult who wants an electronic organiser or the *Boogie Nights* sound-track or a copper-base frying pan. In all these cases, the thing is wanted not only for the use that can be got out of it, but because the person sees themselves as the kind of person who owns a Barbie campervan, a copper-base frying pan, or whatever. In other words, the objects we desire are a statement to the world, and even more potently to our-selves, about how we see ourselves and how we want to be seen.

When working to critique popular culture texts, therefore, it is important that teachers not only work with texts that they believe are limited or limiting in what they have to say about gender, but also give central spaces and valued places to popular texts that *are* transformative.

In the various research projects concerning boys, schools and literacy we have conducted since 1995, the most transformative classrooms have been those where the teachers were able to find texts that resonated with kids' interests *and* could be read as counternarratives to traditional gender norms. For the boys in the project discussed in Chapter 6, the movie *Dangerous Minds* (1995) was an effective text. It portrayed a female teacher willing to listen to and work with working-class kids; kids who, in the film, explicitly critiqued the relevance of novels such as *My Darling, My Hamburger* but engaged more enthusiastically with the poetry of Bob Dylan and Dylan Thomas. This text allowed the boys to articulate their own sense of disasso-ciation with traditional curriculum, and to appreciate the opportunities they were given to explore their own interests within English lessons. Significantly, on the final day of the project one of the boys presented the research team with a taped version of *Gangster's Paradise*, the theme song from *Dangerous Minds*.

In another of our projects, conducted at a high school in a metropolitan working- and under-class area, students were given opportunities to construct web pages based upon their favourite hobbies. One girl – an indigenous Australian and a designated literacy and digital technology failure – created two pages: one dedicated to Winnie the Pooh, the other to the 'bad boy' singer Tupac Shakur. This combination allowed the researchers to discuss with this student, Sheba, the multiple ways in which kids express themselves and the ways in which they negotiate these various selves in school spaces. This subsequently opened up a valuable group discussion around 'multiple mes' and the possibility that people can have a complex network of interests.

Thus, popular culture is neither inherently useful nor inherently irrelevant to literacy teachers. Its value is fundamentally tied to the objectives of the teacher, and the teacher's ability to capitalize on small departures from gender norms that can often be found in these resources. Two further brief examples are worth noting.

What a Babe

In *Babe* (1995), the movie about a young pig who decided to become a 'sheep pig', the stoic, unemotional farmer Hoggett adheres to traditional gender norms throughout the movie until one of the final scenes. When Babe learns that people actually *eat* pigs he becomes so distraught that he runs away, gets caught in the rain, catches a cold and – even when brought home – lacks the will to eat or drink. Concerned that his pig might actually die, Farmer Hoggett takes Babe on to his lap, holds a baby bottle to his lips and sings a song. 'If I had words to make a day for you, I'd give you a morning golden and true; I would make this day last for all time, and fill the night deep in moonshine' (original lyrics by J. Hodge 1978, cited in *Babe* 1995). Farmer Hoggett becomes so involved in his singing that he dances an extraordinarily funny and decidedly unmasculine jig around the room. This in turn motivates Babe to get up, drink and go back to being a sheep pig.

The transformative potential of this movie is tied to three things. First, it is extraordinarily popular with children and, indeed, with adults. Second, it follows many traditional gender norms, particularly those associated with Farmer Hoggett and his wife and Babe's other surrogate parents – Rex and Fly, the sheep dogs. Third, it shows regular and valued departures from gender norms. For example, Farmer Hoggett sings and dances and his pig lives (and wins the sheep dog trials). Rex relaxes his authoritarian stance and is rewarded with the love of Fly. Babe himself rejects traditional sheep dog norms of aggression. He uses good manners to persuade sheep through the various hurdles of the sheep dog trial course. He is rewarded for his success with the happiness of the farmer.

In terms of the rhizome image that underpins our book, *Babe* works to make connections between traditional masculine qualities and alternative behaviours and interests. This connection is acknowledged, validated and rewarded by the characters in the movie.

Not just a pretty face

A different example is provided by the popular Hollywood film *Ever After*. The story is based on the European fairy tale Cinderella. *Ever After* stars human actors, and features Drew Barrymore as the very independent Danielle. The film conforms in many ways with the fairy tale genre. It provides a handsome, able bodied, white and financially secure prince and a similarly beautiful, white, able bodied (though impoverished) potential princess. A wicked stepmother is added to the mix, together with royal traditions pressing the prince to marry and numerous obstacles standing between the prince and Danielle. The film challenges gender norms, however. It represents Danielle as strong, confident and heroic, and the prince as a man who (ultimately) learns to value these qualities in a partner, and who also acquires an appreciation of books, justice and compassion. Near the end of the story the prince, realizing at last his true love for Danielle, rushes to rescue her from the slavery into which she has been sold. By the time he arrives, however, Danielle has won her freedom by stealing a sword, convincing her captor that she knows how to use it (by slashing his cheek) and forcing him to unchain her. Like *Babe*, then, *Ever After* is able to give non-traditional characters a central role, and to value and reward them for their departure from these traditions. Once again, the departure is neither so radical nor so abrupt as to risk alienating the audience. Yet there is an unmistakable difference between Danielle's relationship with her prince and the more traditional relationship between Cinderella and Prince Charming.

Implications

We have tried in this chapter to identify some of the key challenges associated with cross-generational teaching, including those relating to the potential differences between the ways in which students and teachers might think about gender reform, literacy, technology and popular culture. We have also attempted to identify equally diverse ways in which teachers and schools have responded to these potential differences. In some schools, for example, kids' literacies, interests and 'real lives' are explicitly excluded, whereas in others they are not merely included, but given a central and valued place. In some schools, assumptions about generational differences lead to stereotyping (of kids and students), whereas in others thoughtful reflection upon the particular experiences of kids and teachers can lead to an acknowledgment and valuing of diversity. In still other instances, teachers may make token efforts to value the generational realities of their students while their colleagues elsewhere make more substantial efforts to incorporate and validate students' multiple selves.

Once again, this points to the power of mindsets in all school practice. Those who see TV and technology as dangerous and read kids as alienated from 'real' values and desirable behaviour may seek to edit it out of kids' lives (or at the very least ensure that they are able to control their usage and to critique its content). Within this mindset, schools become places for reinstating 'old values', a process that involves, among other things, prioritizing books and other traditional knowledge sources over on line resources. In addition, schools work to develop in kids a distrust of technology, and seek to keep technology use 'in perspective': as simply one part of a well rounded education and childhood.

Within this framework, kids are not only represented as being at odds with an education system that ostensibly exists to meet their needs but, in addition, their existing skills, understandings and abilities are seldom recognized and their interests are seldom appreciated. In terms of the nexus between literacy, masculinity and schooling that is the subject of this book, this is indeed a dangerous situation. The danger exists at two levels. First, if teachers work to restate traditional skills or values, they may easily fall into the trap of making use of the kinds of traditional texts, teaching styles and classroom practices that have helped to drive a wedge between boys and literacy in the first place. Second, by keeping the popular and 'real' world of kids outside of the classroom, they miss valuable opportunities to draw kids' attention to the diverse ways in which social realities and gender norms are constructed and mediated. This, in turn, allows limited and limiting versions of masculinity to go unchallenged.

Alternatively, the teacher who is willing to risk introducing popular culture and 'kid knowledge' into his or her classroom has immediate access to a much wider range of resources to use when seeking either to make a tenuous connection between boys and literacy or to open up debate about what it means to be a boy in the first place. Our focus has been on the need for educational strategies that are able to make connections with the 'real worlds' of boys and girls, in order to construct literacy lessons that move them beyond the limitations imposed by culturally constructed versions of masculinity and femininity. Not surprisingly, our preference is for the mindset that acknowledges and values the real world of classroom kids.

This is, in fact, our bottom line.

Dominant models of masculinity and femininity construct boys and girls in generally oppositional relationships. They rest upon limited and limiting conceptualizations of what it means to be a 'boy' or a 'girl' and associate particular skills, abilities and interests with sex-categorized bodies. Schools have long contributed to the circulation and naturalization of these patriarchal gender norms. Consequently, they have become sites where the apparent oppositions between male/female, active/passive, science/literacy have been reinscribed and naturalized. This environment has produced tensions between boys and literacy and between girls and boys. It has also constructed and reinforced hierarchies of masculinity, and celebrated some ways of being a boy, while persecuting others.

Any response to the current educational challenges faced by boys and girls, therefore, will only succeed if it is tied to a broad-based, wide-reaching project of cultural transformation. This transformation is based upon the desire to unravel the bonds of masculinity and femininity that work to constrain and limit both girls and boys, and to create new and supple articulations between 'masculine' and 'feminine' characteristics. In this process, traditional understandings of what it means to be a 'good boy' or a 'normal girl' are brought into question, as new, multiple and changing figurations of masculinity and femininity are produced, validated and celebrated.

We have relied on the image of the rhizome to illustrate the kind of thinking that produces these new figurations of male and female subjectivity. By moving laterally, and beyond 'official' spaces, the rhizome has the potential to make connections with people, places and ideas that are often kept apart. Its strength lies in its ability to make multiple connections, some of which may be long lasting, others of which will be fleeting. In relation to boys, literacy, technology, popular culture and schooling – the subjects at the heart of this book – rhizomatic thinking alerts us to the need to examine our practices and assess how far they work to reinscribe the fixed, arboreal logic that produce masculinity's uneasy relationship with schooling or, alternatively, to move us in new directions.

Moving beyond normative masculinity (and femininity) – making the rhizomatic journey – asks several things of those involved:

- first, the ability to identify the operation and power of existing gender norms;
- second, the willingness to explore the origins of these norms, and to highlight ways in which our existing school practices may reinforce them;
- third, a recognition of the diverse ways in which individual boys and girls are positioned within and by these normative understandings of gender and the varying consequences of these positionings;
- fourth, an appreciation of the need for these multiple consequences to be responded to in equally multiple ways;
- fifth, a commitment to acknowledging the multiple subjectivities of the student group, and an associated willingness to work with the 'real life' interests and existing skills of kids;
- sixth, a preparedness to make use of a diverse range of strategies and resources in seeking to exceed the limitations of dominant understandings of masculinity or femininity;

- seventh, a desire to interrogate continually where each strategy is leading, so as to ensure, as much as possible, that the limitations of gender norms are exceeded and to evaluate learning outcomes once strategies have been applied;
- eighth, and finally, a concern to ensure that kids are not 'cut adrift' from familiar and comforting subjectivities, but are instead carefully supported as they make connections between themselves and new or multiple subject positions.

Taken together, these characteristics constitute what is fundamentally the transformative mindset on which this book is based. While they offer a framework for thinking through any proposed literacy programme, they do not offer guaranteed reform. Indeed, any such guarantee would not be worth the paper it is written on. This is because:

- Each site where literacy reform is conceptualized and enacted is fundamentally different from others.
- There are so many combinations of masculinities and femininities within any school.
- There are so many differences among and between particular groups of boys and girls.
- Individual students and teachers have different skills, interests and resources at their disposal. Hence, it is impossible to put forward a formulaic framework for gender-based literacy reform.

The principles outlined here – and throughout earlier chapters – provide, instead, the kinds of navigational devices we believe have most to offer those seeking to negotiate complex gender terrains.

As mentioned in the introduction, we have aligned ourselves with a kind of nomadic subjectivity. This is a subjectivity defined by a commitment to the act of going. We acknowledge, also, the point well made by Lucy Suchman (1987) when she distinguishes between the kind of journey characterized by an adherence to a particular *voyage*, and the kind of journey organized around a desired *destination*. If, as Suchman urges, we are able to stay focused upon *where* (rather than *how*) we are going, then we will be much better positioned to make situated decisions about the best course to follow, the best path to pursue at any given moment. If, however, we begin with too rigid an understanding of how we will progress, then there is a very real danger that the plan will impede our progress.

With regard to the boys/gender/literacy/school debate, we believe that the two most powerful resources available to educators are the ability to imagine things differently – to think beyond the limitations of normative masculinity – and the associated ability to act in situated and strategic ways in the day-to-day process of moving towards a different future.

Conclusion

Introduction

The key idea we have tried to elaborate in this book is that a transformative approach based on an anti-essentialist perspective has the most to offer educators who want to address issues associated with boys, literacy and schooling. As we understand them here, essentialist mindsets assign natural characteristics and potentials to particular groups of people or things. From essentialist perspectives, phenomena like literacy, masculinity/femininity, technology and so on are seen as having some kind of inherent or fixed essence that defines who or what they are, how they will, can and should behave and operate, and how they are best responded to or interacted with by others.

As we have seen, essentialist accounts of boys, masculinity and literacy abound in educational literature. These encourage us to believe that there is some best way to teach literacy to boys based on the nature of literacy and the nature of boys, and that to make advances in this area is a matter of pursuing ever closer approximations to the final solution. The fact that different views of the right approach or solution exist does not undermine underlying essentialist beliefs and assumptions. It merely shows that people can be mistaken about *how* things really are, yet correct in assuming that they really are *some* way, and that there *is* a way to solve a given problem. In this context it is worth noting that essentialist positions are associated with 'solutions' of the 'easy', 'quick fix', 'off-the-shelf' and 'one size fits all' variety. As we have shown in previous chapters, most essentialist positions enable simple causal relationships to be made which either justify inaction or support simple reactions.

In contrast to essentialist positions, anti-essentialist perspectives emphasize the contingency of all socio-technical patterns and formations.

Anti-essentialist perspectives acknowledge the *appearance* of *natural* behaviours or properties, but see these as things to be explained rather than as explanations in and of themselves. They seek to 'denaturalize' taken-for-granted assumptions about the way things are, and insist on looking at how characteristics, behaviours and potentials are *produced* and *made* to appear natural. With respect to our topic, an anti-essentialist perspective impacts on each component of the boys–masculinity–literacy–technology problematic. It rejects biologically based and other 'innatist' explanations (e.g. from male psychology, from physiological science) for identified behaviours and dispositions and, instead, emphasizes the cultural production and naturalization of tendencies that become associated with sex-specific bodies.

An anti-essentialist perspective also opens to question – in ways that are precluded by essentialist mindsets – many other contexts besides masculinity that are often tied to debates around boys and/or literacy. For example, when we work from an anti-essentialist perspective we reject assumptions that computers are inherently and automatically – essentially – learning technologies, or that contemporary kids are naturally technologically competent. In relation to the boys and literacy challenge, then, we have been distinguishing between those mindsets that aim to define and solve 'the current challenge' by getting to know more about 'real boys' and then teaching them in appropriate 'masculinized' ways, and mindsets that try to move beyond traditions of normative masculinity. Moreover, the latter perspectives refuse to reduce 'the current challenge' to a single homogeneous problem that takes the same form in all cases and can be solved by a single strategy.

Finally, by way of recapitulation, essentialist mindsets interpret behaviours, dispositions, contexts and the like as 'givens' and, to that extent, as things we have to negotiate and work around. Conversely, anti-essentialist mindsets approach all socio-technical patterns and formations as *possibilities* – possible, but not inevitable, 'worlds' – to be transformed, precisely because they are contingent constructions that can be disassembled and changed. Not only *can* we transform them, but we *should* work to transform them in the interests of better ways of living and being.

By way of concluding our argument we want to make three final points that seem to us important. We discuss these points below under the following headings:

- Now you see it, now you don't – the devil is in the detail.
- The hard yards.
- Yes, it's political.

These points can be usefully contextualized and anticipated by means of a metaphor that comes directly from the territory we have been exploring. This is a metaphor of computer(ized) games and their supporting gaming systems (e.g. Nintendo, PlayStation, Dreamcaster).

What you see and what you (might) get: three 'moments' of Nintendo

While we will not want to push the metaphor too far here, we think there are some useful parallels between taking up (or 'buying into') a position on boys and literacy and taking up a game for Nintendo (or almost any computing program, for that matter). We can think of taking up the game in terms of what we call three 'moments' (in a sense close to that used by dialecticians). Each 'moment' can be thought of as a qualitatively different 'state' within the potential transformation or evolution of a process or phenomenon, rather than in the more literal temporal sense of 'moment'.

The first 'moment' can be equated with buying and playing the standard off-the-shelf Nintendo game. As such the game comprises the gaming system, software, instructions on how to play the game and so on. In this moment the game is construed and approached at face value. Players learn to 'drive' the game within official or conventional parameters. They follow the instructions provided, master the controls, work on coordinating eye and brain and so on.

The second moment may be seen in terms of an 'extension pack' where people get *more* out of the game than is originally there, either through the common practice of adding in new gaming components or by using the game more creatively. They do this by getting beneath the surface features, taking a closer look to see what the software permits and/or obtaining 'unofficial' expert or specialized information on how to make one's game more efficient (e.g. 'cheats' gleaned from magazines, on-line discussion groups or websites). For adults watching kids make complex and creative uses of a gaming system, it may appear that a Nintendo, Dreamcaster or PlayStation can be made to do just about anything, or made to perform at just about any level when used (manipulated, controlled) by a kid who has mastered 'cheats' and shortcuts, who has discovered and follows hidden pathways and so on. The player who locates 'cheats' for the game on the Internet or via peers is likely to play a more refined and successful game than the player who stays close to the instructions and information of the standard package. The same is true of the player who experiments with the software, trying to unravel from the outside (since you cannot get into the code) what was put into it by the programmer. Such a player might be able to best guess or subvert the programmer's logic and achieve outstanding or even aberrant performance. Using, for example, the A and B keys in a certain way on his Nintendo game console while a particular warrior in *StreetFighter Alpha 3* (Capcom 1999) has a large sword in his hand, he is able to make the warrior's head spin around at high velocity – a 'trick' never mentioned in the game book or cheat sites, and which never fails to send all watchers into paroxysms of laughter.

Alternatively, an 'extension expert' – someone who has cracked the logic of additional tricks and functions programmed into the game, or who is able to build on existing moves to create new ones by means of 'combo moves' – might mess with the rules of the game and creatively appropriate its capacity to introduce an effect into the game rather than simply play to win. For example, in the popular Nintendo game *Legend of Zelda: Majora's Mask* (Nintendo 2000) players often abandon the goal of saving Clock Town from being squashed by the moon, preferring instead to track down the 24 different masks the main character – Link – can wear and to experiment with the different effects each has (e.g. the fairy masks can show when fairies that need to be captured are near, the Goron mask turns him into a giant capable of crashing through huge iceblocks and rock).

Within this second moment the game is not what it seems on the surface. It is not *essentially defined* or delimited by its standard off-the-shelf form. Hidden, or at least less overt, aspects emerge by accident or design. The game can become problematic or challenging on unanticipated levels. Its components can be made to work in different ways. There is always more to the standard game than meets the eye, although not all players discover or are alerted to these things.

No matter how sophisticated the performance and inventiveness – 'techspertise' – of an expert player seems, it leaves unexamined a host of broader issues associated with the game. There is a third kind of response, or way of taking up the game. This corresponds to a third 'moment' that can be construed as 'the new game'. In this moment the game as a whole is taken as something to be explained rather than negotiated, or as something to be critiqued rather than mastered, or as something to be transformed rather than completed. This kind of orientation to the game is intimated by an example provided by Sherry Turkle (1995), and might easily be imagined for cases like the artefacts developed and produced at the Wellspring Systems outfit described by Allucquère Stone and mentioned in Chapter 6.

It is not a mode of engagement with video games that is either common or much spoken about. It is directed at the assumptions and models employed by the designers and developers. It is a mode beyond the level of theorizing of the game that produces rules like 'if you punch the mushroom then the ghost appears'. It seeks to understand and map the conditions which allow mushrooms and produce ghosts. It takes the relationship between mushrooms and ghosts and other interactive objects as things to be explained.

Turkle's example concerns the nature and role of underlying assumptions of simulation games and how players are positioned in relation to these assumptions. While sim games may encourage players to 'think in an active way about complex phenomena [whether real life or not] as dynamic, evolving systems . . . they also encourage people to get used to manipulating a system whose assumptions they do not see and which may or may not be "true" ' (Turkle 1995: 70). Specifically, Turkle refers to an account by a sociologist, Paul Starr, of playing *SimCity 2000* with his 11-year-old daughter. In the course of the game Starr commented critically that he thought the game had an inbuilt bias against 'mixed-use development'. His daughter replied impatiently that this was 'just the way the game works'. Starr found her words familiar and recalled a colleague saying much the same thing to him some months previously when they had been working at the White House.

> We were discussing the simulation model likely to be used by the Congressional Budget Office (CBO) to score proposals for health care reform. When I criticized one assumption, a colleague said to me, 'Don't waste your breath,' warning that it was hopeless to try to get CBO to change. Policy would have to adjust.
>
> (Turkle 1995: 70–1)

Turkle comments that while we might easily criticize sim games for the assumptions built opaquely into them, and debate whose authority we accept and to whose opacity we surrender, it is important to ponder how far art actually imitates life in such cases. Social and economic policy deals with 'complex systems that we seek to understand through computer models'. These models have assumptions built into them, and the models themselves are used to shape policy and action in the real world. Real-world policy making is strikingly like playing a simulation game whose in-built assumptions remain opaque to the vast majority of people impacted by them. 'Policy-making, says Starr, "inevitably rel[ies] on imperfect models and simplifying assumptions that the media, the public, and even policymakers themselves generally do not understand . . . We shall be working and thinking in SimCity for a long time" ' (Turkle 1995: 71).

We have contextualized the third moment – the new game – at length because the idea is central to the position we have adopted in this book. From an anti-essentialist transformative perspective, 'essences' that function as hidden assumptions are to be uncovered. Simulation games whose assumptions are biased against, say, mixed-use development parallel real-world programs for boys' literacy education whose curricular and pedagogical approaches assume normative masculinity and, to that extent, are biased against alternative forms of being a boy/male. Our position here is that real-life 'games' (like off-the-shelf literacy education approaches or *programs/packages*) that draw us in and incorporate us – even if we can operate within them as highly skilled unorthodox players – are not to be taken as givens to be negotiated (even skilfully). Rather, they are to be explained, critiqued, engaged and transformed. In the end we may become what we assume, or what others assume on our behalf.

To be essentialized is to be named, constructed, reduced and constrained to just one of any number of viable possibilities for doing and being –

unless and until we can escape it. To embrace an anti-essentialist trans-formative perspective is to accept the importance of keeping options open, in the name of human development and informed choice – core democratic values – and to recognize that we 'make the road by walking' (Horton and Freire 1990), that the road is really many *roads* and that these roads are not predefined and inscribed on a single map of life. To buy (into) essences and assumptions like normative masculinity is to foreclose on human potential, which is a potential to *be* in all sorts of ways. The only given is that to be at all is, necessarily, to be something or other, someone or other, some subjectivity or other, from moment to moment. To be sure, this is com-patible with a predetermined, given, naturalized script. It is also, however, compatible with scripts that we write and rewrite for ourselves as beings in process – where we guide our way by testing the possibilities we entertain in the light of having critiqued options to hand.

With this background in place we want to conclude by making three final comments about our commitment to an anti-essentialist mindset and a transformative approach to literacy education and gender reform.

End notes, or and, in the end . . .

Now you see it, now you don't: the devil is in the detail

It is no easy matter to distinguish between essentialist and anti-essentialist mindsets. Often it may be one thing to align oneself with an anti-essentialist perspective – to feel committed to it – and another thing altogether to be able to operate on it effectively in an informed way in daily practice. This was brought home to us concretely and graphically during a professional development activity we ran with a group of experienced secondary school teachers on the theme of boys, school and literacy. We began the session with an overview of some claims commonly made in popular media about boys and literacy. This became a basis for distinguishing between claims based on biological or other essentialist grounds and claims that read gen-der or gendered behaviour as culturally produced phenomena. In ensuing discussions participants readily concurred that many of the arguments they had encountered on the topic were based on a deterministic biological model. They identified, equally readily, important limitations in this model. Within a half-hour they arrived at a consensus that possibly an anti-essentialist perspective had more to offer their work than an essentialist perspective.

The facilitator proceeded to describe some strategies used by her research team to attempt a literacy intervention with boys based on anti-essentialist understandings of gender reform. She summarized the strategies on a trans-parency as a series of points (brief points designed to fit on to a single trans-parency), and described how the researchers had aimed in practice to:

- provide students with choice;
- encourage their diversity;
- build upon where they were at;
- use positive reinforcement;
- set achievable goals;
- reward student effort.

After observing the list for some minutes one of the participants said in mild anxiety, 'But . . . that's what we're already doing, isn't it? How is this any different?'

This question seemed to resonate with other members of the group, who began to say that yes, in their day-to-day teaching practice they certainly did work to provide students with positive reinforcement or negotiated learning opportunities and so on. More than anything else throughout the workshop, this moment captured for us the challenge of moving into a critical, anti-essentialist space. None of the strategies listed on the abbreviated transparency were in themselves *automatically* anti-essentialist; none of them were guaranteed pathways to gender transformation. As the popular saying goes, the devil is in the detail.

It is easy enough to provide most kids with positive reinforcement (with some, of course, extra effort is required). But it is much more difficult to recognize and reinforce moments of gender 'transgression' – deviation from inscribed normativity. Similarly, it is one thing to give learners in a group the opportunity to negotiate their assessed work. It is another, however, to recognize, understand and support the kind of negotiation that may lead beyond conventional, normalized masculine or feminine spaces. The anxiety expressed by teachers at the workshop seemed to illustrate very clearly the difference between endorsing anti-essentialist perspectives *in principle*, and an *in practice* understanding of how to use these perspectives in day-to-day reflective assessment of pedagogical work and how to transform it in accordance with a commitment to gender reform.

The key point here is that to participate in transformative literacy practices, educators need *both* a working knowledge of a range of anti-essentialist perspectives (including in areas other than gender reform alone) *and* a kind of battle-hardened appreciation of how a good idea translates into practice. This is the difference, for example, between being able to write a recipe for a perfect soufflé and being able actually to *make* one that doesn't deflate. To given an educational example, it is one thing to provide positive reinforcement to the girl working quietly on her English homework. It is another thing altogether to provide positive reinforcement to the boy writing poetry about butterflies, if all his friends are criticizing or making fun of him. Strategies are only transformative when they are used in a particular context, in response to particular gender performances. The teachers in this workshop struggled to use their intellectual acknowledgement of the values of an anti-essentialist perspective to talk about how they might practically develop a transformative agenda in their classrooms.

In the next section we look at some aspects of what is involved in acquiring both the working knowledge and the battle-hardened application. Meanwhile, it is useful to consider some of the immediate everyday empirical reasons why it is often so hard to distinguish essentialist and anti-essentialist perspectives and to denaturalize what appears to be natural.

A major reason why this is so complex and demanding is that teachers simply do not live or work or seek to respond to literacy issues within a vacuum. Every teacher concerned with literacy education, gender reform and learning outcomes is challenged on a daily basis to negotiate an array of complex and often contradictory forces. These include the various needs and demands of students, parents and community members, policy predilections and curriculum frameworks of government, accountability requirements of education administrations and a barrage of 'solutions' advanced by 'experts' of different stripes in the fields of literacy, gender reform, learning technology, curriculum and programme development and so on.

Within such contexts teachers are often obliged or otherwise inclined to look for 'off-the-shelf', quick solutions to pressing problems, and to implement them in class in the hope that they will live up to their promises. Many such solutions take the form of research-driven packages or generic programmes officially sanctioned and monitored by education departments. Moving beyond an 'off-the-shelf' or 'quick fix' response to the teaching and learning challenges of classrooms is hard work. Even where proffered solutions are not made more or less compulsory by education administrations, the solutions themselves are often cleverly and persuasively packaged and attached to powerful mainstream or media-generated hype.

There are parallels here with the lure of off-the shelf gaming systems like Nintendos or PlayStations. These and other games have been extraordinarily popular, partly because they promise so much in such a small and self-contained package. And while certainly they are expensive, they also appear to promise endless solutions to the longstanding problem of how to entertain kids. This image, however, is at least partly an illusion, for as anyone who has lived with a child and a video game set will probably realize, buying a set is just the beginning of the story. The console needs controllers, the controllers need rumble packs and every game seems to have a second and third and fourth version.

In the case of packaged solutions to the challenge of boys, literacy and gender reform, successive versions, alternative variants and the like further reinforce our incorporation into the ruling logic. This tends to be a logic of *reliance* on procedures, techniques and resources built on essentialist foundations – since it is usually only by essentializing something or other (e.g. literacy, 'boyness', masculinity) that generic packages and programmes can be designed as solutions in the first place. Underlying essentialist assumptions are not always evident, however – any more than we are aware of operating assumptions in other key areas of life, such as the example reported by Turkle that we quoted above. Because of their seeming natural-ness, these assumptions function to produce the kind of arboreal models we introduced early in the book: adding one more layer to the tree like structure of normative masculinity.

Of course, off-the-shelf solutions made available to teachers often come with an expectation that teachers – being professionals – will adapt and customize them to their own local requirements. While some teachers – in-cluding teachers with genuine concerns about boys' literacy and gender reform – may take off-the-shelf solutions and try to implement formula-driven strategies unreflectively in order to address their concerns, others will not. Among the latter will be some who begin with the off-the-shelf solution but who quickly realize that, like all such solutions, this one contains 'bugs' and challenges, and will need to be *made* to work optimally. Others again will expect from the outset that they will have to adapt the solution to the contingencies of their class. This, however, is where real difficulties can arise for distinguishing essentialist and non-essentialist perspectives.

On the one hand, the difficulty may be a function of trying to graft anti-essentialist notions of gender on to a pedagogical 'tool' that has been designed to operate with normative masculinity or femininity. On the other hand, the difficulty may involve a clash of 'paradigms' that are contradictory: for example, trying to use a formulaic approach for transformative purposes (a painting by numbers approach to transformation!). Either way, the solution is not conducive to distinguishing essentialist and anti-essentialist perspect-ives, or even to being aware the distinction exists. The more that teacher education, professional development, research-driven pedagogical 'solutions' and the like move down a technicist, pre-packaged, formulaic line, the more difficult it will be for educators to think and practise in anti-essentialist ways.

Once again, although we do not want to push it too far, the Nintendo metaphor is useful here. We can imagine teachers who align themselves with an anti-essentialist approach to gender reform and transformative values seeking sophisticated and skilful ways of trying to make a 'boys and literacy education solution' work. They may discover hidden 'snags' or potentially fruitful confusions or ambiguities in the package, and try to build on these, or somehow to subvert them. In this they may parallel the skilled Nintendo player who achieves high performance against the conventional measure of winning, or who may even discover some special hidden effects or moves along the way. In the end, however, to stay within the parameters of the game itself is to miss the point that it may well be the game – the 'solution' package or approach – that has to become the object of critique and to be transformed.

Over time, some teachers may independently reach this conclusion as a result of their efforts to make a solution work and to understand why it does not. In other cases – and this may have been the situation for some of the teachers in the professional development workshop mentioned above – teachers may reach this conclusion by being offered a chance to consider it as a possible frame for interpreting their own experiences. However they arrive at a sense of wanting to align themselves with an anti-essentialist mindset and a transformative approach to boys' literacy and gender reform, two things seem certain. One is that getting there will have involved a considerable struggle against the hegemony of essentializing and technicist mindsets that pervade education systems. The other is that the most difficult work probably lies ahead.

The hard yards

We are strongly committed to the values and potentials of an anti-essentialist mindset. We do *not*, however, want to give an impression that 'doing' it in a classroom is easy, or that pursuing an anti-essentialist position is a sure route to successful transformative pedagogy at the intersection of (boys') literacy and gender reform. On the contrary, gender reform – within literacy education or any other domain of social life – is nothing less than very hard work. As we have mentioned, it is work that often meets with opposition, derision, vindictiveness and a sense of defeat. In addition, it is work that usually must proceed on several fronts. With respect to the boys/literacy challenge, a transformative approach requires willingness to denatural-ize not only assumptions associated with boys (What is a boy?), but also assumptions and dispositions associated with essentialist views of literacy (What is literacy?), technology and popular culture.

We insist on distancing ourselves from any notion that anything less than hard work is involved. Often, books advocating reform of one kind or another present themselves as having answers, or as providing a sufficient basis for readers to 'go forth' with confidence of success. This is rarely warranted, of course, and it is certainly not true for this book. We are not in the business of claiming to provide answers and guarantees here. On the contrary. We offer this book more as a statement of encouragement, support and solidarity for like minds and potential like minds. We are saying that we believe the broad position we advance is better than essentialist positions. We want to invite others who have not already done so to consider this option. And we most definitely want to lend our voice of support and encouragement to others who have already decided on this option. A large part of the task involved in gender reform is, of course, building commun-ities of tolerance, support and solidarity.

To appreciate something of the kind or quality of hard work that is involved, and what makes it hard, it may be helpful to consider a roughly parallel example of mindset change from a completely different field of endeavour: prototyping within design and manufacture.

In his book *Serious Play* (2000), Michael Schrage observes that successful innovative companies have turned conventional approaches to prototyping on their heads. According to Schrage, the usual approach to prototyping involves getting as much as possible of the problem solving and final design worked out in advance and only then to build the prototype. Against this, Schrage invites readers to consider prototyping as a form of serious play. Rather than extensive and careful planning prior to the prototype activity, Schrage advocates starting the prototyping with the bare minimum decided in advance and letting the prototyping be the medium of design development rather than its penultimate outcome. Schrage suggests that when talented innovators innovate, the audience bothers not about the specifications they quote but about the models they have created.

This is nothing less than inviting people in high-pressure, high-stakes fields to start seeing their roles, practices, theory etc. in precisely the opposite way to which they are accustomed. The risks are high. The temptation is to stay with what one knows, because to err could mean to go bust. The approach is radically uncertain. It is to begin and *then* move out, rather than first covering the ground and then moving in. 'A prototype', writes Schrage (2000: 208), 'should be an invitation to play.' But to play *seriously*. Moreover, this will be a form of play in which having the ability to say 'This is not working' is absolutely crucial. Anyone engaging in prototyping as serious play must be very tough about the outcomes of the moment-by-moment process and judge them rigorously and honestly.

In a parallel way, adopting an anti-essentialist transformative mindset within literacy and gender reform requires an unceasing and tough-minded commitment to questioning the taken for granted in the search for productive new possibilities. And it requires an equally tough-minded and unceasing commitment to questioning the success of our outcomes from using a trans-formative approach based on anti-essentialist premises. It involves pursuing reform – change for the better – without a safety net. Some transformations may not work at all. We need to acknowledge and learn from this. As Schrage (2000: 205) argues, fail early and fail often. Some may work in one context but not others. The practice is fundamentally experimental. It is risky but playful in the same sense of 'playful' that Schrage employs. *Seriously* playful. Perhaps the practice we are advocating is better described as *risqué*, but where we are ever mindful that human subjectivities are implicated in what we do (and omit) in our pedagogy. To be *risqué* is *not* to be reckless or rash. Educators never have the right to be so. Equally, to take no risks is to accept – and reinforce – the status quo.

The hard work extends to putting our own gender subjectivities under scrutiny and keeping them open to critique, experimentation and transfor-mation, as a corollary of adopting an anti-essentialist perspective on, and commitment to, gender reform. This is hard work in at least three senses. It is *existentially* hard work because it means risking subjectivities we may be comfortable with. It is *emotionally* hard work, because we fail and are defeated often, and we may encounter intense and bitter opposition from those who prefer people like us the way we were. It is also *intellectually* hard work, because successful and productive experimentation is rarely if ever blind, and is almost always well informed. In many cases it is also physically hard work, as it is often necessary to do a lot of work to produce the kinds of resources that will support transformative practices. In working on our *selves* as well as on our pedagogy, there is no substitute for exploring what others have done and seeking out exemplars of the possible. The best way to have an appropriate strategy or response that we can employ (seemingly) 'on the fly' to a fresh situation is to have available a wide repertoire of options – theoretical, practical, existential – to draw upon. These do not simply materialize out of thin air. They become available by actively pursuing exemplars and experiences, and remaining open to them when they arise.

In the end, the point we reach in this book is not a set of answers or failsafe procedures. Instead, it is the beginning of a journey to be taken with a compass more than a map, and in the knowledge that it will be a long haul because there is no final destination. More than getting there, the journey is about learning how to travel in ways that add value to being gendered subjects rather than being complicit in a zero-sum game. This is a game where for some boys to realize their essence is for other boys to fail at being what they 'should be', and for girls at large always to experience their worth as being indexical to normative masculinity.

As with those who pursue transformation in other domains of social practice against currents of normativity, actualizing an anti-essentialist mindset at the meeting points of literacy education and gender reform call us to:

- learn from unexpected connections;
- be alive to fruitful examples and experiences;
- be alert to gaps, contradictions, tensions and openings that can be turned into opportunities for experimenting, exploring diversity, etc.;
- fail early and fail often;
- practise and practise;
- resist final closures on the big issues and keep moving;
- understand that every change changes the context and calls for new strategies;
- play, take risks;
- remember that the devil is always in the detail.

We are, then, lending support to a disposition. We are saying we believe it is appropriate for educators working in literacy with a commitment to gender reform to experiment, take informed risks, think outside the range of the normal – as long as we are rigorous in assessing outcomes. Literacy education in a context of gender reform is not about experiment for experiment's sake. It is always accountable to producing demonstrably better outcomes. These are outcomes that *work* for people in the world. And they will always involve much more than literacy basics and, indeed, literacy outcomes alone.

Yes, it's political

Essentialist mindsets are outgrowths of particular kinds of networks and relationships in and through which we live our lives. They ultimately work to reinscribe those same networks and relationships. These networks and relationships have material effects. They shape social life and the distribution of social goods (from wealth and success to self-esteem) within the practices that build up around them. Anti-essentialist mindsets are also outgrowths of particular kinds of networks and relationships in and through which (other) people live their lives. The networks and relationships attaching to anti-essentialist mindsets, however, are in radical tension with those attaching to essentialist mindsets. They are also in tension with the kinds of distributions or allocations of social goods associated with essentialist networks and relationships and the practices they support.

Consequently, to adopt and seek to enact an anti-essentialist mindset is to take up a position against certain kinds of networks and relationships, and to seek to build competing ones with a view, ultimately, to displacing their essentialist counterparts. To adopt an anti-essentialist mindset is not, then, something one merely does in the head or by reading books or listening to people. It is a way of living that is made real, and that is refined and made more efficient, in the practice of everyday life. It is, then, a political choice, and acting on it is to engage in political work. It is to work to try to build and shore up networks and relationships of one kind rather than another and, in so doing, actively to seek to disassemble other kinds of networks and relationships.

To engage wittingly, wittily and productively in this work requires a *praxis* comprising both analytic-theoretical-critical work and practical network building, assembling, disassembling, detaching and 'policing' work. We need to pursue the best understanding we can of the 'nuts and bolts' of social practices that sustain essentialist ways of thinking and acting and the forms of normativity they beget: within gender relations, literacy, concepts and practices of technology and so on. Politically relevant theories and analytic approaches like actor–network theory are likely to be especially useful here. These approaches seek to explain rather than find explanation in the various socio-technical arrangements and configurations that constitute the *natural* landscapes of classrooms.

Recognizing the *political* form of the work involved is an appropriate way to end this book. It reminds us – if we needed reminding – that successful transformative practice is not an individual endeavour, even if at specific moments we are thinking and acting literally on our own. An important part of the work to be done involves actively seeking out the company of compatible minds and bodies – whether face to face or in mediated ways – and lending our efforts to theirs, and drawing on theirs in turn. This, after all, is how socio-technical forms and patterns, manifested as gender and gender relations, literacy practices, learning and technological activity of whatever kind, are constituted in the first place.

As a final point, let us say that while we are sensitive to the sheer hard work associated with gender reform, we are equally aware of the energy, excitement and pleasure that this work can produce. The journey of a nomadic subject may not be clear cut, and the direction may change regularly, but there is intense pleasure to be had from moving beyond traditional boundaries, from trying new pathways, from *going*. This, indeed, is our final point. Those who are committed to the transformation of gender, literacy and technology may find themselves in strange, unfamiliar and seemingly dangerous territories: but there is pleasure to be found in the strange *and* the known; and there is possibility and hope to be found in those less regulated spaces between the new and the old, the foreign and the familiar, the risky and the safe. It is towards those spaces and the future they promise that we direct our own energies, and in which we invest our own hope.

Bibliography

AAUW (American Association of University Women) (1998) *Gender Gaps: Where Schools Still Fail Our Children – Executive Summary.* Washington, DC: American Association of University Women Educational Foundation. http://www.aauw.org/2000/GGES.pdf (accessed 28 May 2000).

AAUW (2000a) *Tech-Savvy: Educating Girls in the New Computer Age. Executive Summary.* Washington, DC: American Association of University Women Educational Foundation. http://www.aauw.org/2000/techsexecsum.html (accessed 20 June).

AAUW (2000b) *Tech-Savvy: Educating Girls in the New Computer Age.* http://www.aauw.org/2000/techsavvybd.html (accessed 20 June).

ABC Radio (2000) *Dietary Habits and the Incidence of Asthma.* 23 August. Rockhampton, Queensland: ABC Local Radio.

ABS (Australian Bureau of Statistics) (1997) *Aspects of Literacy: Assessed Skill Levels Australia.* Canberra: Commonwealth of Australia.

ACER (Australian Council for Educational Research) (1997) *Mapping Literacy Achievement. Results of the 1996 National School English Literacy Survey.* Camberwell: ACER.

Adams, P. (2000) Secret parents' business, *The Weekend Australian: Review,* 15–16 July, 32.

Agoglia, J. (1999) The lost generation? *Sporting Goods Business,* 32(11): 34–5.

Aidman, A. (1999) Disney's *Pocahontas:* conversations with Native American and Euro-American girls, in S. Mazzarella and N. Odom Pecora (eds) *Growing up Girls: Popular Culture and the Construction of Identity.* New York: Peter Lang.

Ainley, J. (1999) Outcomes and funding in the Commonwealth Literacy and Numeracy Programme. Camberwell: Australian Council For Educational Research. http://www.detya.gov.au/literacyweek/ (accessed 28 April 2000).

Albion, P. (1998) Challenging the unquestioning rush towards adopting laptop programs in schools. Paper presented at QSITE conference, Sunshine Coast University, 14–15 August. http://www.qsite.edu.au/conference/qsite98/albion/albion.html (accessed 18 July 2000).

Allard, A., Copper, M., Hildebrand, G. and Wealands, E. (1995) *Stages: Steps towards Addressing Gender in Educational Settings*. Melbourne: Curriculum Corporation.

Alloway, N. (1995) *Foundation Stones: The Construction of Gender in Early Childhood*. Carlton: Curriculum Corporation.

Alloway, N. (2000) Boys and Literacy, Conference presentation, 2010: A Springboard to the Future. Central Queensland University, Rockhampton.

Alloway, N. and Gilbert, P. (1996) Boys and literacy: meeting the challenge, in N. Alloway, B. Davies, P. Gilbert, R. Gilbert and D. King (eds) *Boys and Literacy: Meeting the Challenge. Book 1*. Canberra: Commonwealth Department of Employment, Education, Training and Youth Affairs.

Alloway, N. and Gilbert, P. (1997) Introduction, in N. Alloway and P. Gilbert (eds) *Boys and Literacy: Professional Development Units*. Carlton, Victoria: Curriculum Corporation.

Alloway, N. and Gilbert, P. (1998) Video game culture: playing with masculinity, violence and pleasure, in S. Howard (ed.) *Wired-up: Young People and the Electronic Media*. London: Taylor & Francis.

Alloway, N., Davies, B., Gilbert, P., Gilbert, R. and King, D. (1996) *Boys and Literacy: Meeting the Challenge*. Canberra: Australian Government Publishing Service.

Alvermann, D. and Hagood, M. (2000) Fandom and critical media literacy, *Journal of Adolescent and Adult Literacy*, 43(5): 436–47.

American Association of University Women (1992) *How Schools Shortchange Girls: A Study of Major Findings on Girls and Education*. Washington, DC: AAUW Educational Foundation, The Wellesley College Center for Research on Women.

American Library Association (1989) *American Library Association Presidential Committee on Information Literacy. Final Report*. Chicago: American Library Association.

Anderson, N. (2000) Inclusion: can teachers and technology meet the challenge? Unpublished PhD thesis, Queensland University of Technology, Brisbane.

Anstey, M. (1998) Being explicit about literacy instruction, *Australian Journal of Language and Literacy*, 206(1): electronic version.

Asch, K. (1999) Girls overtake boys in school performance, *Insight on the News*, 15(7): 39.

Ashdown, C. (1999) Presenting the right role model, *Education Review: The Journal of Australia Education*. http://edreview.camrev.com.au/boys.html (accessed 22 October 2000).

Australian Education Council (1991) *Listening to Girls: A Report of the Consultancy Undertaken for the Review of the National Policy for the Education of Girls in Australian Schools*. Carlton: Curriculum Corporation.

Bantick, C. (2000) The trouble with boys, *The Sunday Mail*, 6 August, 79.

Baudrillard, J. (1983) *Simulations*. New York: Semiotext(e).

Beato, G. (1997) Girl Games. *Wired*. 5.04. Online version. http://www.wired.com/wired/archive//5.04/es_girlgames.html (accessed 30 June 2000).

Beavis, C. (1999) Literacy, English and computer games. Paper presented at the International Federation for the Teaching of English Conference, University of Warwick, 7–10 July. http://www.nyu.edu/education/teachlearn/ifte/beavis1.htm (accessed 30 June 2000).

Bennahum, D. (1998) *Extralife*. New York: Basic Books.

Biddulph, S. (1995a) Foreword, in R. Browne and R. Fletcher (eds) *Boys in Schools: Addressing the Real Issues*. Lane Cove, NSW: Finch Publishing.

Biddulph, S. (1995b) *The Cotswold Experiment*. Lane Cove: Finch Publishing.

Biddulph, S. (1997) *Raising Boys: Why Boys Are Different – And How to Help Them Become Happy and Well-balanced Men*. Melbourne: Celestial Arts.

Bigum, C. (1990) Computers and the curriculum: the Australian experience, *Journal of Curriculum Studies*, 22(1): 63–7.

Bigum, C. (2001) *Beyond the Cyber-tooth Curriculum: New Technologies, New Literacies and the Futures of Schooling*. New York: Peter Lang.

Bigum, C. and Green, B. (1992a) Technologizing literacy: the dark side of the dreaming, *Discourse*, 12(2): 4–28.

Bigum, C. and Green, B. (1992b) *Understanding New Information Technologies in Education*. Geelong: Centre for Studies in Information Technologies and Education, Deakin University.

Blair, T. (1999) Foreword. *Open for Learning, Open for Business*. The Government's National Grid for Learning Challenge. London: DfEE. http://www.dfee.gov.uk/grid/challenge/foreword.htm (accessed 3 May 2000).

Blanchot, M. (1986) *The Writing of Disaster*. Lincoln: University of Nebraska Press.

Bloome, D., Sheridan, D. and Street, B. (1993) *Reading Mass-observation Writing: Theoretical and Methodological Issues in Researching the Mass-observation Archive*. Mass-observation Archive Occasional Paper No. 1. Brighton: University of Sussex.

Blunkett, D. (1999a) Empowering people and communities for a better future. 30th Anniversary Lecture, National Centre for Social Research, London, 16 June. http://www.dfee.gov.uk/empowering/index.htm (accessed 22 October 2000).

Blunkett, D. (1999b) Excellence for the many not just the few: raising standards and extending opportunities in our schools. CBI President's Reception Address, 19 July. http://www.dfee.gov.uk/excellenceformany/ (accessed 22 October 2000).

Bocchino, T. (1999) *Emotional Literacy: A Different Kind of Smart*. Port Chester, NY: National Professional Resources.

Boler, M. (1999) *Feeling Power: Emotions and Education*. London: Routledge.

Bondy, E. (1984) Thinking about thinking: encouraging children's use of metacognitive processes, *Childhood Education*, 60(4): 234–8.

Bordo, S. (1990) Feminism, postmodernism, and gender-scepticism, in L. Nicholson (ed.) *Feminism/Postmodernism*. New York: Routledge.

Bowers, C. A. (1988) *The Cultural Dimensions of Educational Computing: Understanding the Non-neutrality of Technology*. New York: Teachers College Press.

Bowers, C. (2000) Environmental education, in D. Gabbard (ed.) *Knowledge and Power in the Global Economy: Politics and the Rhetoric of School Reform*. Mahwah, NJ: Lawrence Erlbaum.

Braidotti, R. (1994a) *Nomadic Subjects: Embodiment and Sexual Difference in Contemporary Feminist Theory*. New York: Columbia University Press.

Braidotti, R. (1994b) Toward a new nomadism: feminist Deleuzian tracks, or, meta physics and metabolism, in C. V. Boundas and D. Olkowski (eds) *Gilles Deleuze and the Theatre of Philosophy*. New York: Routledge.

Brandon, S. (1998) Workers as thinkers in new times: critical literacy development in the restructured workplace. MEd dissertation. Education, QUT, Brisbane.

Brown, A. and Palincsar, A. (1982) Inducing strategic learning from texts by means of informed, self-control training. *Topics in Learning and Learning Disabilities*, April, 1–17.

Brown, J. (2000a) Bulging brains – and breasts. *Salon*, 7 July. http://www.salon.com/tech/log/2000/07/07/brains_beauty/index.html (accessed 8 July).

Brown, J. (2000b) Women proto-programmers get their just reward, *WiredNews*, 8 May.

Brown, J. and Duguid, P. (2000) *The Social Life of Information*. Boston: Harvard Business Press.

Browne, R. (1995) Schools and the construction of masculinity, in R. Browne and R. Fletcher (eds) *Boys in Schools: Addressing the Real Issues*. Lane Cove: Finch Publishing.

Buchanan, E. (2000) Strangers in the 'Myst' of video gaming: ethics and representation, *The CSPR Newsletter*, 18(1). http://www.cpsr.org/publications/newsletters/issues/200/Winter2000/buchanan.html (accessed 13 July).

Buckingham, D. (2000) *After the Death of Childhood: Growing up in the Age of Electronic Media*. Cambridge: Polity Press.

Buckingham, D. and Sefton-Green, J. (1994) *Cultural Studies Goes to School: Reading and Teaching Popular Media*. London: Taylor and Francis.

Buckingham, J. (1999) *The Puzzle of Boys' Educational Decline: A Review of the Evidence*. Canberra: Centre for Independent Studies. www.cis.org.au (accessed 3 May).

Buckingham, J. (2000) *Boy Trouble: Understanding Rising Suicide, Rising Crime and Educational Failure*. St Leonards, NSW: The Centre for Independent Studies.

Burbules, N. (1997a) Rhetorics of the web: hyperreading and critical literacy, in I. Snyder (ed.) *From Page to Screen*. Sydney: Allen and Unwin.

Burbules, N. (1997b) Misinformation, malinformation, messed-up information, and mostly useless information: how to avoid getting tangled up in the 'Net, in C. Lankshear, C. Bigum *et al.* (investigators) *Digital Rhetorics: Literacies and Technologies in Education – Current Practices and Future Directions, Vol. 3*. Project Report. Children's Literacy National Projects. Brisbane: QUT/DEETYA.

Burbules, N. and Callister, T. (1996) Knowledge at the crossroads: alternative futures of hypertext environments for learning, *Educational Theory*, 46(1): 23–50.

Butler, J. (1990) *Gender Trouble: Feminism and the Subversion of Identity*. New York: Routledge.

Buttrose, I. (2000) Turning boys into sissies, *The Australian Women's Weekly*, September, 78.

Casey, J. (1992) Counseling using technology with at-risk youth. ERIC Digest. ERIC Clearinghouse on Counseling and Personnel Services. MI: Ann Arbor.

Castells, M. (1996) *The Rise of the Network Society*. Oxford: Blackwell.

Chaika, M. (2000) Computer game marketing bias. *Crossroads*, February. http://www.acm.org/crossroads/xrds3-2/girlgame.html (accessed 30 June).

Christian-Smith, L. (1993a) Voices of resistance: young women readers of romance fiction, in L. Weis and M. Fine (eds) *Beyond Silenced Voices*. Albany: State University of New York Press.

Christian-Smith, L. (ed.) (1993b) *Texts of Desire: Essays on Fiction, Femininity and Schooling*. London: Falmer Press.

Clark, M. (1976) *Young Fluent Readers*. Oxford: Heinemann Educational.

Clinton, W. (1994) *Goals 2000: Educate America Act*. Washington, DC: Department of Education. http://www.ed.gov/legislation/GOALS2000/TheAct/

Clinton, W. (1999) Educational Excellence for All Children Act of 1999. http://www.ed.gov/offices/OESE/ESEA/legislation/index.html (accessed 4 May 2000).

Cole, B. (1986) *Princess Smartypants*. London: Hamish Hamilton.

Collins, C., Batten, M., Ainley, J. and Getty, C. (1996) *Gender and School Education: A Project Funded by the Commonwealth Department of Employment, Education, Training and Youth Affairs*. Canberra: Australian Government Publishing Service.

Collins, C., Kenway, J. and McLeod, J. (2000) *Factors Influencing the Educational Performance of Males and Females in School and Their Initial Destinations after Leaving School*. Canberra: Commonwealth Department of Education, Training and Youth Affairs.

Comber, B. and Green, B. (1999) *More Than Just Literacy? Vol. 1*. Information Technology, Literacy and Disadvantage Research Development Project. Adelaide: Department of Education, Training and Employment of South Australia.

Comber, B. and Simpson, A. (1995) Reading cereal boxes: analysing everyday texts, in P. Adams and H. Campagna-Wildash (comps.) *Texts: The Heart of the English Curriculum*. No. 1. Adelaide: Department of Childhood Services.

Connell, B. (1998) Foreword, in C. Hickey, L. Fitzclarence and R. Matthews (eds) *Where the Boys Are: Masculinity, Sport and Education*. Geelong: Deakin University Centre for Education and Change.

Connell, R. W. (1987) *Gender and Power: Society, the Person and Sexual Politics*. Stanford, CA: Stanford University Press.

Connell, R. W. (1995) *Masculinities*. St Leonards, NSW: Allen and Unwin.

Connell, R. W. (1996) Teaching the boys: new research on masculinity, and gender strategies for schools, *Teachers College Record*, 93(2): 206–35.

Cooper, R. and Groves, M. (1999) Report finds students' writing skills sorely lacking. *Los Angeles Times/Tribune News*, 29 September. http://www.thetribunenews.com/stories/0999/6335029.htm (accessed 29 April 2000).

Corboy, D. (2000) Telly tubbies: is television making our kids tubby? *Screen Education*, 20/21: 30–4.

Cordukes, L. (1997) Parents and early literacy: is gender an issue?, in N. Alloway and P. Gilbert (eds) *Boys and Literacy: Teaching Units*. Carlton, Victoria: Curriculum Corporation.

Coupland, D. (1995) *Microserfs*. New York: HarperCollins.

Cowley, G. (2000) Generation XXL, *Newsweek*, 3 July, 40–4.

Cox, E. (1995) Girls and boys and the cost of gendered behaviour. *Proceedings of the Promoting Gender Equity Conference*, Canberra, pp. 303–11.

Creenaune, T. and Rowles, L. (1996) *What's Your Purpose? Reading Strategies for Non-fiction Texts*. New Town, NSW: Primary English Teaching Association.

Cuban, L. (1986) *Teachers and Machines: The Classroom Use of Technology Since 1920*. New York: Teachers College Press.

Cue, K. (2000) Boys just can't be boys, *Herald Sun*, 15 August, 18.

Cummins, J. and Sayers, D. (1995) *Brave New Schools: Challenging Cultural Illiteracy through Global Learning Networks*. New York: St Martins Press.

Curriculum Corporation of Australia (1997) *Boys and Literacy: Professional Development Units and Teaching Units*. Melbourne: Curriculum Corp.

Davidson, M. J. and Burke, R. J. (eds) (1994) *Women in Management: Current Research Issues*. London: Paul Chapman Publishing.

Davies, B. (1992) Women's subjectivity and feminist stories, in C. Ellis and M. G. Flaherty (eds) *Investigating Subjectivity: Research on Lived Experience*. London: Sage Publications.

Davies, B. (1993) *Shards of Glass: Children Reading and Writing Beyond Gendered Identities*. St Leonards, NSW: Allen and Unwin.

Davies, B. (1994) *Poststructuralist Theory and Classroom Practice*. Geelong, Victoria: Deakin University.

Davies, B. (1996) *Power, Knowledge, Desire: Changing School Organisation and Management Practices*. Canberra: Department of Employment, Education, Training and Youth Affairs.

Dearing, R. (1997) *Higher Education in the Learning Society*. Executive summary. National Committee for Inquiry into Higher Education, United Kingdom. http://www.leeds.ac.uk/educol/ncihe/ (accessed 18 July 2000).

de Beauvoir, S. (1973) *The Second Sex*. New York: Vintage (originally published as *Le deuxième sexe*, 1949).

de Certeau, M. (1988) *The Practice of Everyday Life*. Berkeley: University of California Press.

DEET (Department of Education, Employment and Training, Australia) (1991a) *Australia's Language: The Policy Paper*. Canberra: Australian Government Publishing Service.

DEET (1991b) *Australia's Language: Companion Volume to the Policy Paper*. Canberra: Australian Government Publishing Service.

DEETYA (Department of Employment, Education, Training and Youth Affairs, Australia) (1995) *Gender Equity: A Framework for Australian Schools*. Canberra: AGPS.

DEETYA (1998) *Literacy for All: The Challenge for Australian Schools*. Canberra: AGPS.

Deleuze, G. and Guattari, F. A. (1987) *A Thousand Plateaus: Capitalism and Schizophrenia*. Minneapolis: University of Minnesota Press.

Delgado-Gaitan, C. (1991) *Literacy for Empowerment: The Role of Parents in Children's Education*. London: Falmer Press.

DENI (Department of Education, Northern Ireland) (1999) *Learning for Tomorrow's World: Towards a New Strategic Plan for Education Services in Northern Ireland. 2000–2006*. Belfast: DENI.

Department for Education, UK (1993) *Boys and English*. London: DfE.

Department for Education, UK (1999) *National Curriculum Assessments of 7, 11 and 14 Year Olds by Local Education Authority*. Table 5: Key Stage 1 test results for 1999, analysed by Government Office, Local Education Authority and gender. http://www.dfee.gov.uk/statistics/DB/SFR/s0088/tab005.html (accessed 28 April 2000).

Department for Education, UK (2000) *Classroom Issues: Is Single Sex Teaching the Way to Boost Results?* London: DfE. http://www.dfee.gov.uk/teacher teachmag0200/data/issues/data/s_sex06.htm (accessed 28 April).

Department for Education and Employment, UK (1996) *General Requirements for*

English: Key Stages 1–4. London: DfEE. http://www.dfee.gov.uk/nc/enggener. html (accessed 1 May 2000).

Department for Education and Employment, UK (1999a) *National Curriculum Assessments of 7, 11 and 14 Year Olds by Local Education Authority 1999*. London: DfEE.

Department for Education and Employment, UK (1999b) *National Learning Grid: Open for Learning, Open for Business*. London: DfEE. http://www.dfee.gov.uk/grid/challenge/index.htm (accessed 22 October 2000).

Department of Education, USA (1998) *Voluntary National Tests*. http://www.ed.gov/nationaltests/ (accessed 28 April 2000).

DETYA (1999a) *Literacy Standards in Australia*. Canberra: DETYA. http://www.detya.gov.au/schools/literacy/summary.htm#Overview (accessed 27 April 2000).

DETYA (1999b) *Literacy Standards in Australia – Students Performance Charts: Summary of Performance*. Canberra: DETYA. http://www.detya.gov.au/schools/literacy/performa.htm#Chart 6 (accessed 27 April 2000).

Doneman, M. (1997) Multimediating, in C. Lankshear, C. Bigum *et al.* (investigators) *Digital Rhetorics: Literacies and Technologies in Education – Current Practices and Future Directions, Vol. 3*. Project Report. Children's Literacy National Projects. Brisbane: QUT/DEETYA.

Dorman, S. (1997) Video and computer games: effect on children and implications for health education, *Journal of School Health*, 67(4): 133–8.

Dorman, S. (1998) Technology and the gender gap, *Journal of School Health*, 68(4): 165–6.

Duncombe, S. (1997) *Notes from Underground: Zines and the Politics of Alternative Culture*. London: Verso.

Economist (1996) Tomorrow's second sex, *The Economist*, 28 September, 23–8.

Education Queensland (2000) *Partnerships for Success*. Brisbane: Education Queensland.

Educom Review Staff (1998) *Technology, Silver Bullets and Big Lies: Musings on the Information Age with Author Michael Schrage*, Educom Review volume 33, number 1. http://www.educause.edu/pub/er/review/reviewArticles/33/32.html (accessed 26 January 2000).

Edwards, A. and Magarey, S. (1995) *Women in a Restructuring Australia: Work and Welfare*. St Leonards, NSW: Allen and Unwin.

ERO (Education Review Office, New Zealand) (1999) *The Achievement of Boys*. No. 3. Winter. http://www.ero.govt.nz/Publications/eers1999/Boys/boys1.htm#Contents (accessed 27 April 2000).

EU (European Union) (1996) *Teaching and Learning: Towards the Learning Society*. White Paper on Education and Training. http://europa.eu.int/comm/education/lb-en.pdf (accessed 3 May 2000).

Faludi, S. (1999) *Stiffed: The Betrayal of the Modern Man*. London: Chatto and Windus.

Fitzclarence, L. and Hickey, C. (1998) Learning to rationalise abusive behaviour through football, in C. Hickey, L. Fitzclarence and R. Matthews (eds) *Where the Boys Are: Masculinity, Sport and Education*. Geelong: Deakin University Centre for Education and Change.

Flynn, J. M. (1994) Prevalence of reading failure in boys compared with girls, *Psychology in the Schools*, 31(1): 66–71.

Foster, M. (2000) A black perspective, in K. Myers (ed.) *Whatever Happened to Equal Opportunities in Schools? Gender Equality Initiatives in Education*. Buckingham: Open University Press.

Frater, G. (1997) *Improving Boys' Literacy*. London: The Basic Skills Agency.

Frazer, E. (1987) Teenage girls reading Jackie, *Media, Culture, and Society*, 9(4): 407–25.

Freebody, P. and Welch, A. (1993) Individualization and domestication in current literacy debates in Australia, in P. Freebody and A. Welch (eds) *Knowledge, Culture and Power: International Perspectives on Literacy as Policy and Practice*. London: Falmer Press.

Funk, J. B. and Buchman, D. D. (1996) Children's perceptions of gender differences in social approval for playing electronic games, *Sex Roles: A Journal of Research*, 35(3/4): 219–32.

Gardner, H. (1983) *Frames of Mind: The Theory of Multiple Intelligences*. New York: Basic Books.

Gardner, H. (1989) Zero-based arts education: an introduction to Arts PROPEL, *Studies in Art Education: A Journal of Issues and Research*, 30: 71–83.

Gardner, H. (1994) Intelligence in theory and practice: a response to Elliot W. Eisner, Robert J. Sternberg, and Henry M. Levin, *Teachers College Record*, 95: 576–83.

Gee, J. (1992) *Social Mind*. New York: Bergin and Garvey.

Gee, J. (1996) *Social Linguistics and Literacies: Ideology in Discourses*, 2nd edn. London: Taylor and Francis.

Gee, J. (2000) Teenagers in new times: a new literacy studies perspective, *Journal of Adolescent and Adult Literacy*, 43(5): 412–23.

Gee, J., Hull, G. and Lankshear, C. (1996) The *New Work Order: Behind the Language of the New Capitalism*. Boulder, CO: Westview Press.

Ghosh, N. (2000) India's slum kids latch onto IT. *The Straits Times*, 13 June. http://chora.virtualave.net/india-kids-it.htm (accessed 22 October).

Gilbert, P. (1989) *Gender, Literacy and the Classroom*. Carlton, Victoria: Australian Reading Association.

Gilbert, P. (1993) (Sub)versions: using sexist language practices to explore critical literacy, *Australian Journal of Language and Literacy*, 16(4): 323–32.

Gilbert, P. (1994) *Divided by a Common Language? Gender and the English Curriculum*. Carlton, Victoria: Curriculum Corporation.

Gilbert, P. (1997) Discourses on gender and literacy: changing the stories, in S. Muspratt, A. Luke and P. Freebody (eds) *Constructing Critical Literacies: Teaching and Learning Textual Practice*. Cresskill, NJ: Hampton Press.

Gilbert, P. and Rowe, K. (1989) *Gender, Literacy and the Classroom*. Sydney: Australian Reading Association.

Gilbert, P. and Taylor, S. (1991) *Fashioning the Feminine: Girls, Popular Culture and Schooling*. St Leonards, NSW: Allen and Unwin.

Gilbert, R. and Gilbert, P. (1998) *Masculinity Goes to School*. St Leonards, NSW: Allen and Unwin.

Giroux, H. (1997) *Channel Surfing: Race Talk and the Destruction of Today's Youth*. New York: St Martin's Press.

Goleman (1995) *Emotional Intelligence*. New York: Bantam.

Green, B. (1988) Subject-specific literacy and school learning: a focus on writing, *Australian Journal of Education*, 32(2): 156–79.

Green, B. (1997a) Literacy, information and the learning society. Keynote address at the Joint Conference of the Australian Association for the Teaching of English, the Australian Literacy Educators' Association, and the Australian School Library Association, 8–11 July, Darwin High School, Darwin, Australia.

Green, B. (1997b) Literacies and school learning in new times. Keynote address at the 'Literacies in Practice: Progress and Possibilities' Conference, 1 May, South Australian Department of Education and Children's Services and the Catholic Education Office, Adelaide, Australia.

Green, B. and Bigum, C. (1993) Aliens in the classroom, *Australian Journal of Education*, 37(2): 119–41.

Greene, J. (1998) Microsoft plays with the big boys in computer-games business. *Seattle Times*, 20 December. http://seattletimes.nwsource.com/news/technology/html98/game_122098.html (accessed 13 July 2000).

Grosz, E. (1989) *Sexual Subversions: Three French Feminists*. St Leonards, NSW: Allen and Unwin.

Grosz, E. (1995) *Space, Time, and Perversion: Essays on the Politics of Bodies*. New York: Routledge.

Haraway, D. (1985) A manifesto for cyborgs: science, technology and socialist feminism in the 1980s, *Socialist Review*, 80: 65–107.

Haraway, D. (1991) *Simians, Cyborgs, and Women. The Reinvention of Nature*. New York: Routledge.

Harris, L. (1997) *The Metropolitan Life Survey of the American Teacher 1997: Examining Gender Issues in Public Schools*. New York: Louis Harris and Associates.

Hayes, D. (2000) Genealogical tales about educational provision in Australia since colonisation: tracing the descent of discourses of gender equity, *Australian Educational Researcher*, 27(1): 47–69.

Heath, S. (1982) What no bedtime story means: narrative skills at home and school, *Language and Society*, 11: 49–76.

Heath, S. (1983) *Ways with Words: Language, Life and Work in Community and Classrooms*. Cambridge: Cambridge University Press.

Heath, S. and Langman, J. (1994) Shared thinking and the register of coaching, in D. Biber and E. Finegan (eds) *Sociolinguistic Perspectives on Register*. New York: Oxford University Press.

Hekman, S. (1999) *The Future of Differences: Truth and Method in Feminist Theory*. Cambridge: Polity Press.

Helbers, D. (2000) Reading and culture. Unpublished paper.

Hellman, H. (1996) A toy for the boys only? Reconsidering the gender effects of video technology, *European Journal of Communication*, 11(1): 52–82.

Hills, E. (1998a) The action heroine as feminist figuration: mapping the transgressive potential of Hollywood's post-Woman women. PhD dissertation, Central Queensland University.

Hills, E. (1998b) The 'Ripley' effect: action heroines and the transformation of feminist film theory, in L. Rowan and M. Brennan (eds) *Cultural Transformation: Essays in Culture and Change*. Rockhampton: Central Queensland University Press.

Hirst, P. (1974) *Knowledge and the Curriculum*. London: Routledge and Kegan Paul.

Holland, J., Ramazanoglu, C. and Sharpe, S. (1993) *Wimp or Gladiator: Contraditions in Acquiring Masculine Sexuality.* London: Tufnell Press.

Homer, D. (1999) Botanic High, in B. Comber and B. Green (eds) *Information Technology, Literacy and Educational Disadvantage Research and Development Project. Vol. 2, Site Studies.* Adelaide: Department of Education, Training and Employment of South Australia.

hooks, b. (1990) Talking back, in R. Ferguson, M. Gever, Trinh T. Minh-ha and C. West (eds) *Out There: Marginalization and Contemporary Cultures.* New York: The New Museum of Contemporary Art.

Hopkins, P. (2000) Gender treachery: homophobia, masculinity and threatened identities, in E. Ashton-Jones, G. A. Olson and M. G. Perry (eds) *The Gender Reader*, 2nd edn. Needham Heights, MA: Allyn and Bacon.

Horton, M. and Freire, P. (1990) *We Make the Road by Walking: Conversations on Education and Social Change.* Philadelphia: Temple University Press.

Hutchinson, S. (2000) Wasting Away. *The Weekend Australian*, 28–29 October, 1–2.

Jackman, C. (2000) War on boys? *The Sunday Mail*, 9 July, 40.

Jackson, D. (1998) Breaking out of the binary trap: boys' underachievement, schooling and gender relations, in D. Epstein, J. Elwood, V. Hey and J. Maw (eds) *Failing Boys? Issues in Gender and Achievement.* Buckingham: Open University Press.

Janks, H. (1993) *Language, Identity and Power.* Johannesburg and Randburg: Witswaterland University Press and Hodder and Stoughton Educational.

Jennings, C. (1999) Girls make music: polyphony and identity in teenage rock bands, in S. Mazzarella and N. Odom Pecora (eds) *Growing up Girls: Popular Culture and the Construction of Identity.* New York: Peter Lang.

Johnson, C. (2000) *'Framing Youth: Media War Against Kids' Book Review.* http://www.sightings.com/health3/agkids.htm (accessed 7 September).

Johnson, S. (1997*) Interface Culture: How New Technology Transform the Way We Create and Communicate.* San Francisco: HarperEdge.

Jones, D. (1996) Critical thinking in an online world. University of California, Santa Barbara Library. http://www.library.ucsb.edu/untangle/jones.html (accessed 29 April 2000).

Jones, K. (1990) Citizenship in a woman-friendly polity, *Signs*, 15(4): 75–88.

Kellner, D. (1995) *Media Culture: Cultural Studies, Identity and Politics between the Modern and the Postmodern.* London: Routledge.

Kemp, D. (1997) *Literacy Standards in Australia.* Canberra: DETYA. http://www.detya.gov.au/lsia/index.htm (accessed 27 April 2000).

Kendall, L. (1999) 'The nerd within': mass media and the negotiation of identity among computer-using men, *The Journal of Men's Studies*, 7(3): 353–69.

Kenway, J. (1995) Masculinities in schools: under siege, on the defensive and under reconstruction? *Discourse: Studies in the Cultural Politics of Education*, 16(1): 59–79.

Kenway, J. (1998) Masculinity studies, sport and feminism: fair play or foul?, in C. Hickey, L. Fitzclarence and R. Matthews (eds) *Where the Boys Are: Masculinity, Sport and Education.* Geelong: Deakin University Centre for Education and Change.

Kenway, J., Willis, S., with Blackmore, J. and Rennie, L. (1997) *Answering Back: Girls, Boys and Feminism in Schools.* St Leonards, NSW: Allen and Unwin.

Kindlon, D. and Thompson, M. (2000) *Raising Cain: Protecting the Emotional Life of Boys*. San Francisco: Ballantine Books.

Kleinfeld, J. (1998) The myth that schools shortchange girls: social science in the service of deception. Paper prepared for The Women's Freedom Network. http://www.uaf.edu/northern/schools/myth.html (accessed 3 May 2000).

Kling, R. (ed.) (1996) *Computerization and Controversy: Value Conflicts and Social Choices* (2nd edn). San Diego: Academic Press.

Knobel, M. (1999) *Everyday Literacies: Students, Discourse and Social Practice*. New York: Peter Lang.

Koch, M. (1994) No girls allowed! *TECHNOS Quarterly*, 3(3). http://www.technos. net/journal/volume3/2Koch.html (accessed 13 July 2000).

Koerner, B. (1999) Where the boys aren't. *US News and World Report Online*. http://www.usnews.com/usnews/edu/college/coboys.htm (accessed February 2000).

Kostanski, M. and Gullone, E. (1998) Adolescent body image dissatisfaction: relationships with self-esteem, anxiety, and depression controlling for body mass, *Journal of Child Psychology and Psychiatry and Allied Disciplines*, 39(2): 255–62.

Kress, G. and van Leeuwen, T. (1995) *Reading Images: The Grammar of Visual Design*. London: Routledge.

Ladd, D. (1999) Technology helps close the educational – and gender – gaps. *Colorado Springs Independent*. 7 October. http://www.csindy.com/csindy/1999-10-07/siliconlounge.html (accessed 8 October 2000).

Lake, M. (2000) Tips for new arrivals. *PC World*, 18(3). http://www.pcworld.com/resource/article.asp?aid=14875 (accessed 2 June 2000).

Lankshear, C. (1991) Getting it right is hard: redressing the politics of literacy in the 1990s, in P. Cormack (ed.) *Selected Papers from the 16th Australian Reading Association National Conference*. Adelaide: ARA.

Lankshear, C. (1994) *Critical Literacy*. Belconnen, ACT: Australian Curriculum Studies Association.

Lankshear, C. (1997) *Changing Literacies*. Buckingham: Open University Press.

Lankshear, C. (1998) Literacy and critical reflection, in M. Knobel and A. Healy (eds) *Critical Literacies in the Primary Classroom*. Newtown, NSW: Primary English Teaching Association.

Lankshear, C. and Bigum, C. (1999) Literacies and new technologies in school settings, *Curriculum Studies*, 7: 445–65.

Lankshear, C., Bigum, C., Durrant, C. *et al.* (1997) *Digital Rhetorics: Literacies and Technologies in Education – Current Practices and Future Directions*, 3 vols. Project Report. Children's Literacy National Projects. Brisbane: QUT/DEETYA.

Lankshear, C. and Knobel, M. (1997a) Literacies, texts and difference in the electronic age, in *Changing Literacies*. Buckingham: Open University Press.

Lankshear, C. and Knobel, M. (1997b) Different worlds? Technology-mediated classroom learning and students' social practices with new technologies in home and community settings, in *Changing Literacies*. Buckingham: Open University Press.

Lankshear, C. and Knobel, M. (2001a) What *is* 'Digital Epistemologies'?, in M. Ylä-Kotola, J. Suoranta and M. Kangas (eds) *The Integrated Media Machine, Vol. 2*. Hämeenlinna: Edita.

Lankshear, C. and Knobel, M. (2001b) Mapping postmodern literacies: A preliminary chart, in M. Ylä-Kotola, J. Suoranta, and M. Kangas (eds) *The Integrated Media Machine, Vol. 2.* Hämeenlinna: Edita.

Lankshear, C. and McLaren, P. (eds) (1993) *Critical Literacy: Politics, Praxis, and the Postmodern.* Albany: State University of New York Press.

Lankshear, C., Peters, M. and Knobel, M. (1996) Critical pedagogy and cyberspace, in H. Giroux, C. Lankshear, P. McLaren and M. Peters (eds) *Counternarratives: Cultural Studies and Critical Pedagogies in Postmodern Spaces.* New York: Routledge.

Lankshear, C. and Snyder, I. (2000) *Teachers and Technoliteracy: Managing Literacy, Technology and Learning in Schools.* St Leonards, NSW: Allen and Unwin.

Lather, P. (1991) *Getting Smart: Feminist Research and Pedagogy With/in the Postmodern.* New York: Routledge.

Latour, B. (1996) *Aramis or The Love of Technology,* trans. Catherine Porter. Cambridge, MA: Harvard University Press.

LaTrobe, K. and Havener, W. M. (1998) Teaching information literacy in a CMC environment: the school library media specialists as a collaborative partner, in Z. Berge and M. Collins (eds) *Wired Together: The Online Classroom in K-12. Vol. 2, Case Studies.* Cresskill, NJ: Hampton Press.

Laurel, B. (1995) *How Gender Differences Affect Play Behavior of Girls and Boys, Ages 7–12.* Palo Alto: Interval Research Corp.

Laurel, B. (1999) Making better media for kids. Keynote address at the Interactive Frictions Conference, UCLA, June. http://www.tauzero.com/Brenda_Laurel/Recent_Talks/MakingBetterMediaForKids.html (accessed 30 June 2000).

LeCompte, M. and de Marrais, K. (1992) The disempowering of empowerment: From social revolution to classroom rhetoric, *Educational Foundations,* 6(3): 5–33.

Lemke, J. (1995) *Textual Politics: Discourse and Social Dynamics.* London: Taylor and Francis.

Lindsey, L. (1994) *Gender Roles: A Sociological Perspective,* 2nd edn. Englewood Cliffs, NJ: Prentice Hall.

Lingard, B. and Douglas, P. (1999) *Men Engaging Feminisms: Pro-feminism, Backlashes and Schooling.* Milton Keynes: Open University Press.

Livingstone, J. (1997) Metacognition: an overview. http://www.gse.buffalo.edu/fas/shuell/cep564/Metacog.htm (accessed 2 May 2000).

Lorde, A. (1984) The master's tools will never dismantle the master's house, in A. Lorde (ed.) *Sister Outsider: Essays and Speeches.* Freedom, CA: The Crossing Press.

Lorde, A. (1990) Age, race, class and sex: women redefining difference, in R. Ferguson, M. Gever, Trinh T. Minh-ha and C. West (eds) *Out There: Marginalization and Contemporary Cultures.* New York: New Museum of Contemporary Art.

Luchetta, T. (2000) Gender and computers: toolbox or toystore? Gender differences and similarities among children, youth, and college students concerning computer attitudes and use. Paper presented at the Spring 1000 Wisconsin Association of Academic Librarians Conference, 12 April. http://www.uwgb.edu/luchettt/waaltalk_outline.htm (accessed 19 October).

Luke, A. (1993) The social construction of literacy in the primary school, in L. Unsworth (ed.) *Literacy Learning and Teaching.* Sydney: Macmillan.

Luke, A. (2000) Critical literacy in Australia: a matter of context and standpoint, *Journal of Adolescent and Adult Literacy*, 43(5): 448–61.

Luke, C. (1996) ekstasis@cyberia, *Discourse*, 17(2): 187–208.

Luke, C. (1997) Media literacy and cultural studies, in S. Muspratt, A. Luke and P. Freebody (eds) *Constructing Critical Literacies: Teaching and Learning Textual Practice.* Cresskill, NJ: Hampton Press.

Luke, C. (2000) New literacies in teacher education, *Journal of Adolescent and Adult Literacy*, 43(5): 424–35.

Luke, C. and Roe, K. (1993) Editorial, *Australian Journal of Education*, 37(2): 118.

Lyotard, J.-F. (1984) *The Postmodern Condition: A Report on Knowledge.* Minneapolis: University of Minnesota.

Mac an Ghaill, M. (1994) *The Making of Men: Masculinities, Sexualities and Schooling.* Buckingham: Open University Press.

McCarthy, S. (2000) Home-school connections: a review of the literature, *Journal of Educational Research*, 93(3): 145–55.

Macedo, D. (1993) *Literacies of Power: What Americans Are Not Allowed to Know.* Boulder, CO: Westview Press.

Macedo, D. (2000) Cultural literacy, in D. Gabbard (ed.) *Knowledge and Power in the Global Economy: Politics and the Rhetoric of School Reform.* Mahwah, NJ: Lawrence Erlbaum.

McGuiness, C. (1999) *From Thinking Skills to Thinking Classrooms.* Nottingham: Department for Education and Employment Publications.

Mclean, C. (1997) Engaging with boys' experiences of masculinity: implications for gender reform in schools, *Curriculum Perspectives*, 17(1): 61–4.

McManaman, D. (2000) Introduction to philosophy. *A Catholic Philosophy and Theology Page.* http://www.tcdsb.on.ca/external/schools/ (accessed 9 January 2001).

MacNaughton, G. (2000) *Rethinking Gender in Early Childhood Education.* St Leonards, NSW: Allen and Unwin.

Macpherson, J. (1983) *The Feral Classroom: High School Students' Constructions of Reality.* Melbourne: Routledge and Kegan Paul.

McRobbie, A. (1991) *Feminism and Youth Culture: From Jackie to Just Seventeen.* London: Macmillan.

McRobbie, A. (1994) *Postmodernism and Popular Culture.* London: Routledge.

Madison Avenue (2000) Don't call me baby. *Polyester Embassy CD.* Richmond, Victoria: Vicious Grooves.

Mahiri, J. (1997) Street scripts: African American youth writing about crime and violence, *Social Justice*, 24(4): 56–76.

Mahiri, J. (1998) *Shooting for Excellence: African American Youth Culture in New Century Schools.* New York: National Council of Teachers of English.

Mahiri, J. (ed.) (2001) *What They Don't Learn in School: Literacy in the Lives of Urban Youth.* New York: Peter Lang.

Mahiri, J. and Sablo, S. (1996) Writing for their lives: the non-school literacy of California's Urban African American Youth, *The Journal of Negro Education*, 65(2): 164–80.

Mahiri, J., Van Rheenen, D., Smith, A. *et al.* (2001) *Stepping Out-of-bounds: When Scholarship Athletes Become Academic Scholars.* New York: Teachers College Press.

Mahony, P. (1998) Girls will be girls and boys will be first, in D. Epstein, J. Elwood,

V. Hey and J. Maw (eds) *Failing Boys? Issues in Gender and Underachievement.* Buckingham: Open University Press.

Martino, W. (1995) Gendered learning practices: exploring the costs of hegemonic masculinity for girls and boys in schools, in Ministerial Council for Education, Training and Youth Affairs, *Proceedings of the Promoting Gender Equity Conference.* Canberra: ACT Department of Education and Training.

Martino, W. (1998) 'When you only have girls as friends, you got some serious problems': Interrogating masculinities in the literacy classroom, in M. Knobel and A. Healy (eds) *Critical Literacies in Primary Classrooms.* Sydney: Primary English Teaching Association.

Martino, W. (2000) Policing masculinities: investigating the role of homophobia and heteronormativity in the lives of adolescent school boys, *The Journal of Men's Studies*, 8(2): 213–36.

Marvin, C. (1988) *When Old Technologies Were New: Thinking About Communications in the Late Nineteenth Century.* New York: Oxford University Press.

Mattel Media (1996) Barbie Fashion Designer. http://www.mattelmedia.com/barbie/fashiondesigner/ (accessed 9 October 2000).

Mattel Media (1999) Barbie PC. http://www.barbiepc.com (accessed 9 October 2000).

Maxson, J. and Hair, B. (1990) *Managing Diversity: A Key to Building a Quality Workforce.* Columbus, OH: National Alliance of Community and Technical Colleges.

Mercer, P. (1998) A mandate to force computer expertise. *New York Times on the Web*, 29 April. http://www.leeds.ac.uk/educol/ncihe/ (accessed 18 July 2000).

Merskin, D. (1999) What every girl should know: an analysis of feminine hygiene advertising, in S. Mazzarella and N. Odom Pecora (eds) *Growing up Girls: Popular Culture and the Construction of Identity.* New York: Peter Lang.

Metropolitan Life Foundation (1997) *Metropolitan Life Survey of the American Teacher: Examining Gender Issues in Public Schools.* New York: MetLife.

Meyers, C. (2000) Talking 'bout my Generation, *Successful Meetings Magazine*, 1–5.

Millard, E. (1997) *Differently Literate: Boys, Girls and the Schooling of Literacy.* London: Falmer Press.

Mills, M. and Lingard, B. (1997a) Masculinity politics: myths and boys' schooling: a review essay, *British Journal of Educational Studies*, 45(3): 276–92.

Mills, M. and Lingard, B. (1997b) Reclaiming the 'what about the boys?' discourse for gender justice in schools and society, *Social Alternatives*, 16(3): 51–4.

Ministry of Education, New Zealand (1998) *Literacy and Numeracy Strategy.* Wellington: Ministry of Education.

Misson, R. (1998) Theory and spice, and things not nice: popular culture in the primary classroom, in M. Knobel and A. Healy (eds) *Critical Literacies in the Primary Classroom.* Newtown, NSW: Primary English Teaching Association.

Moody, F. (1995) *I Sing the Body Electric: A Year with Microsoft on the Multimedia Frontier.* New York: Penguin.

Moore, C. (1998) Guest editorial: Australian masculinities, *Journal of Australian Studies*, 56: 1–16.

Moore, T. (2000) Negotiating skills? A feminist poststructural analysis of five academic women's negotiation of communication technologies and technological discourses in a rural university. PhD in progress, Central Queensland University.

Morris, H. and Veen, A. (2000) Virtual sexpots: no end in sight. *Wired News*, 14 July. http://www.wired.com/news/culture/0,1284,37416,00.html (accessed 15 July).

Munsch, R. N. (1989) *The Paper Bag Princess*. Sydney: Ashton Scholastic.

Murray, M. and Kliman, M. (1999) Beyond point and click: the search for gender equity in computer games. *Focus: A Magazine for Teachers*. http://www.enc.org/focus/documents/0,1341,FOC-000697-index,00.shtm (accessed 13 July 2000).

Muspratt, S., Luke, A. and Freebody, P. (Eds.) (1997) *Constructing Critical Literacies: Teaching and Learning Textual Practice*. Cresskill, NJ: Hampton Press.

MWK (2000) Social-cultural animation. http://www.mwk16.com/pageSAC.html (accessed 9 October).

National Institute for Literacy (1999) Fast facts on literacy. http://www.nifl.gov/newworld/FASTFACT.HTM

National Literacy Trust (1998) The government's response to boys' underachievement. http://www.literacytrust.org.uk (accessed 17 February 2000).

National Science Foundation (1997) *US teens and technology. Gallup Poll Executive Summary*. http://www.nsf.gov/od/lpa/nstw/teenov.htm (accessed 13 July 2000).

NCEE (National Commission on Excellence in Education) (1983) *A Nation at Risk: The Imperative for Educational Reform*. Washington, DC: US Department of Education.

NCPA (National Centre on Policy Analysis) (1999) *Australian Boys' Declining School Performance*. Dallas: NCPA.

Newell, W. R. (1998) The crisis of manliness. *Weekly Standard*, 3 August, cover story.

New London Group (1996) A pedagogy of multiliteracies: designing social futures, *Harvard Educational Review*, 66(1): 60–92.

New South Wales Government (1994) *Inquiry into Boys' Education (The O'Dougherty Report)*. Sydney: New South Wales Government.

Newsweek (1997) Teenagers and Technology. *Newsweek*, 28 April, 86.

Nintendo 64 (2000) Perfect dark. http://www.nintendo.com/n64/perfectdark/ (accessed 6 September).

Nixon, H. (1997) Researching multimedia multiliteracies. Paper presented at the Australian Association for Research in Education Annual Conference, 30 November to 4 December, Brisbane.

Noble, D. D. (1991) *The Classroom Arsenal: Military Research, Information Technology and Public Education*. London: Falmer.

O'Brien, J. (1994) Critical literacy in an early childhood classroom: a progress report, *Australian Journal of Language and Literacy*, 17(1): 36–44.

O'Connor, D.-M. (1992) *'Boys Will Be . . .' A Report on the Survey of Year 9 Males and Their Attitudes to Forced Sex*. Brisbane: Domestic Violence Resource Centre.

OECD (Organisation for Economic Cooperation and Development) (1998a) *Technology, Productivity and Job Creation: Best Policy Practices. The OECD Jobs Strategy*. Paris: OECD.

OECD (1998b) *Information Technology and the Future of Post-secondary Education*. Paris: OECD.

OFSTED (Office for Standards in Education, UK) (1993) *Boys and English*. London: The Office for Standards in Education.

OFSTED (1998) *The National Literacy Project*. London: The Office for Standards in Education.

Orr, D. (1992) *Ecological Literacy: Education and the Transition to a Postmodern World*. Albany: State University of New York Press.

Outlook (1996) Closing the gender gap on PSATs. *US News and World Report*. 14 October, 121.

Pease, A. and Pease, B. (1998) *Why Men Don't Listen and Women Can't Read Maps*. Mona Vale, NSW: Pease Training International.

Peters, M. and Lankshear, C. (1996) Postmodern counternarratives, in H. Giroux, C. Lankshear, P. McLaren and M. Peters (eds) *Counternarratives: Cultural Studies and Critical Pedagogies in Postmodern Spaces*. New York: Routledge.

Pollack, W. (1998) *Real Boys. Rescuing Our Sons from the Myths of Boyhood*. New York: Henry Holt.

Postman, N. (1994) *The Disappearance of Childhood*. New York: Vintage Books.

Prior, M., Smart, D., Sanson, A. and Oberklaid, F. (1999) Relationship between learning difficulties and psychological problems in preadolescent children from a longitudinal sample, *Journal of the American Academy of Child and Adolescent Psychiatry*, 38(4): 429–37.

Provenzo, E. F. (1991) *Video Kids: Making Sense of Nintendo*. Cambridge, MA: Harvard University Press.

Purple Moon (2000) Research Highlights. Summary of National Research: Process and Results. http://www.purple-moon.com/cb/laslink/pm?stat+corp+research_highlights (accessed 27 June).

QCA (Qualifications and Curriculum Authority, UK) (1998) QCA publishes guidance to schools on raising boys' achievement in English. Press release, 10 February. http://www.qca.org.uk/press-rels/ (accessed 27 April 2000).

Quesada, A. and Summers, A. (1998) Literacy in the cyberage: teaching kids to be media savvy, *Technology and Learning*, 18(5): 30–7.

Rare (1999) *Perfect Dark*. Nr. Twycross: Rare Ltd.

Rawstorne, T. (2000) Girls are just born to chatter. *The Courier Mail*, 27 July, 14.

Reich, R. (1992) *The Work of Nations*. New York: Vintage Books.

Rogoff, B. (1995) Observing sociocultural activity on three planes: Participatory appropriation, guided participation, apprenticeship, in J. V. Wertsch, P. del Rio and A. Alvarez (eds) *Sociocultural Studies of Mind*. Cambridge: Cambridge University Press.

Rogoff, B. (1996) Developing understanding of the idea of communities of learners, *Mind, Culture, and Activity*, 1: 209–29.

Roper Starch Worldwide (1998) *Roper Youth Report*. Princeton, NJ: Roper Starch Worldwide.

Rowan, L. (1998) Cabbages grow on the tundra yet the moose feeds by night: feminism, universities and other cultural mysteries, in L. Rowan and M. Brennan (eds) *Cultural Transformation: Essays in Culture and Change*. Rockhampton: CQU Press.

Rowan, L. (2000) 'Human' resource management, 'flexible' learning and difference: a feminist exploration, in V. Jakupec and J. Garrick (eds) *Flexible Learning, Human Resource and Organisational Development: Putting Theory to Work*. London: Routledge.

Rowan, L. and Bigum, C. (1999) Episode IV. A new hope: Jedi Knights, Cyborgs and other educational fantasies, *Teaching Education*, 10(1): 55–64.

Rowan, L. O. and Bigum, C. J. (2001) Of heaven and hell, in D. Murphy, R. Walker and G. Webb (eds) *Online Learning and Teaching With Technology: Case Studies, Experience and Practice*. London: Kogan Page.

Rowan, L., Knobel, M., Lankshear, C., Bigum, C. and Doneman, M. (2000) *Confronting Disadvantage in Literacy Education: New Technologies, Classroom Pedagogy, and Networks of Practice*. Rockhampton: Central Queensland University.

Rushkoff, D. (1996) *Playing the Future: How Kids' Culture Can Teach Us to Thrive in an Age of Chaos*. New York: HarperCollins.

Rushkoff, D. (1997) *Children of Chaos: Surviving the End of the World as We Know It*. London: Flamingo.

Ryan, J. (1998) Boys to men. *San Francisco Chronicle*, 16 March, 1–5.

Ryan, L. (1999) Are you emotionally literate enough? EM. 118. http://www.informinc.co.uk/LM/LM118/LM118_Emotional.html (accessed 13 May 2000).

Schrage, M. (2000) *Serious Play: How the World's Best Companies Simulate to Innovate*. Boston: Harvard Business School.

Searle, C. (1998) Words and life: critical literacy and cultural action, in M. Knobel and A. Healy (eds) *Critical Literacies in the Primary Classroom*. Newtown, NSW: PETA.

Shepard, R., Fasko, D. and Osbourne, F. (1999) Intrapersonal intelligence: affective factors in thinking, *Education*, 119(4): 633–4.

Shor, I. (1992) *Empowering Education: Critical Teaching for Social Change*. Chicago: University of Chicago Press.

Shores, D. (1995) Boys and relationships, in R. Browne and R. Fletcher (eds) *Boys in Schools: Addressing the Real Issues*. Lane Cove: Finch Publishing.

Shropshire County Council (1998) *Raising Achievement of Boys in English*. Shrewsbury: Shropshire County Council.

Slattery, L. (1998) The snag for 1990s men: misogynist predator or feminist victim. *The Weekend Australian*, 4–5 April, 5.

Snyder, H. N. and Sickmund, M. (1999) *Juvenile Offenders and Victims: 1999 National Report*. Washington, DC: National Center for Juvenile Justice.

Sofia, Z. (1996) The mythic machine: gendered irrationalities and computer culture, in H. Bromley and M. Apple (eds) *Education/Technology/Power*. Albany: State University of New York Press.

Spivak, G. C. (1985) Criticism, feminism and the institution, *Thesis Eleven*, 10/11: 175–89.

Sproull, L. and Kiesler, S. (1991) *Connections: New Ways of Working in the Networked Organization*. Cambridge, MA: The MIT Press.

Steinberg, S. (1997) The bitch who has everything, in S. Steinberg and J. Kincheloe (eds) *Kinderculture: The Corporate Construction of Childhood*. Boulder, CO: Westview Press.

Stone, A. (1996) *War of Desire and Technology at the Close of the Mechanical Age*. Cambridge, MA: MIT Press.

Strassmann, P. A. (1997) *The Squandered Computer: Evaluating the Business Alignment of Information Technologies*. New Canaan, CT: Information Economics Press.

Street, B. (1984) *Literacy in Theory and Practice*. Cambridge: Cambridge University Press.

Suchman, L. A. (1987) *Plans and Situated Actions: The Problematic of Human/Machine Communication.* Cambridge: Cambridge University Press.

Sommers, C. H. (2000a) *The War on Boys: How Misguided Feminism is Harming Our Young Men.* Simon & Schuster: New York.

Sommers, C. H. (2000b) The war on boys, *The Atlantic Monthly: Digital Edition,* May.

Taylor, H. and Larsen A. (1999) Social and emotional learning in middle school, *The Clearing House,* 72(6): 331–6.

Teese, R., Davies, M., Charlton, M. and Polesel, J. (1995) *Who Wins at School? Boys and Girls in Australian Secondary Education.* Canberra: DEETYA, AGPS.

Teeside Probation Office (1999) *Criminal Lives: Facts and Figures about Criminal Justice.* Middlesbrough: Teeside Probation Office.

Theis, F., Bautier, P. and Simes, A. (2000) *Community Labour Force Survey,* 16 May, no. 56/2000. Luxembourg: Eurostat Press Office.

Thompson, T. (2000) PE and the 'normal' American child. *The Clearing House,* 73(4), 189.

Toch, T. (1991) *In the Name of Excellence.* New York: Oxford University Press.

Townsend, K. and McLennan, W. (1995) *Australian Women's Year Book.* Canberra: Australian Government Publishing Service.

Trinh T. Minh-ha (1990) Cotton and iron, in R. Ferguson, M. Gever, Trinh T. Minh-ha and C. West (eds) *Out There: Marginalization and Contemporary Culture.* New York: The New Museum of Contemporary Art.

Truth, S. (1851) Ain't I a Woman?, in E. Ashton-Jones, G. A. Olson and M. G. Perry (eds) *The Gender Reader,* 2nd edn. Boston: Allyn and Bacon.

Tunbridge, N. (1995) The cyberspace cowboy, *Australian Personal Computer,* September, 2–4.

Turkle, S. (1995) *Life on the Screen: Identity in the Age of the Internet.* London: Phoenix.

Turner, A. (1992) *Patterns of Thinking: Top-level Structure in the Classroom.* Newtown, NSW: Primary English Teaching Association.

Ullman, E. (1997) *Close to the Machine: Technophilia and Its Discontents.* San Francisco: City Lights Books.

Universal (1995) *Babe. The Motion Picture.* New Zealand: Universal.

US Department of Education (1997) Strategic Plan, 1998–2000. The US Department of Education's Seven Priorities. http://www.ed.gov/pubs/StratPln/priority.html (accessed 4 May 2000).

US Department of Education (1998) Voluntary National Tests: 4th Grade Reading; 8th Grade Maths. Washington, DC: US Department of Education. http://www.ed.gov/nationaltests/ (accessed 22 October 2000).

Wagner, C. (2000) Threats to children's health, *The Futurist,* 34(3): 6–7.

Walker, J. (1988) *Louts and Legends: Male Youth Culture in an Inner-city School.* Sydney: Allen and Unwin.

Walkerdine, V. (1990) *Schoolgirl Fictions.* London: Verso.

Wallace, C. (1992) *Reading.* Oxford: Oxford University Press.

Walsh-Sarnecki, P. (1998) *Girls Trail Boys in Technology Training.* Detroit Free Press. http://www.nabe.org/press/reprints/981014c.htm (accessed 1 June 2000).

Wearing, B. (1996) *Gender: The Pain and Pleasure of Difference.* Melbourne: Longman.

Webb, G. and Singh, M. (1998) '. . . and what about the boys?' Re-reading signs of masculinities, *Australian Journal of Language and Literacy*, 21(2): 135–46.

Weizenbaum, J. (1984) *Computer Power and Human Reason: From Judgement to Calculation*. Harmondsworth: Penguin.

Wells, D. (1999) Teachers challenged on boys and literacy. Press release, Queensland Government, Brisbane.

Wertheim, M. (1997) *Pythagorus' Trousers: God, Physics and the Gender Wars*. London: Fourth Estate.

West, P. (1999) Class struggle epitomises the male identity crisis. *Education Review: The Journal of Australian Education* (electronic version). http://edreview.camrev.com.au/boys.html

Willis, R. (1999) Boys will be boys, *The Age*, 29 March, 1–2.

Wilson, J. (1999) Unequal opportunity employer: creating worlds for adventure/role-playing games, *Computer Gaming World*, January: 228.

Wilson, N., Quigley, R. and Mansoor, O. (1999) Food ads on TV: a health hazard for children? *Australian and New Zealand Journal of Public Health*, 23(6): 647–50.

Winner, L. (1997) Technologies as forms of life, in Shrader-Frechette and L. Westra (eds) *Technology and Values*. Boulder, CO: Rowman and Littlefield.

Winters, K. (1996) *America's Technology Literacy Challenge*. Washington, DC: US Department of Education, Office of the Undersecretary. acw-l@unicorn.acs.ttu.edu

Wired News (2000) The web: it's a women's thing. *Wired News*, 9 August. http://www.wired.com/news/culture/0,1284,38126,00.html

Yelland, N. (1998) Making sense of gender issues in mathematics and technology, in N. Yelland (ed.) *Gender in Early Childhood*. London: Routledge.

Young, J. P. (2000) Boy talk: critical literacy and masculinities, *Reading Research Quarterly*, 35(3): 312–37.

Yucht, A. (1999) New literacy skills needed, *Teacher Librarian*, 27(2): 29–30.

Zohrab, P. (1999) *What About Us? Boys in Schools and Men in Society*. The New Zealand Equal Rights for Men Association. http://www.zohrab.org/boysnws1. html

Index

Adams, P., 165–6, 167
Agoglia, J., 168, 169
Allard, A., 39
Alloway, N., 23, 37, 62, 24, 35, 122
American Association of University
    Women (AAUW), 134–5
anti-essentialist perspectives, 8, 29,
    35–46, 92, 148, 185, 198–211
    see also essentialist perspectives
Aristotle, 63–4
Arnot, M., 11
Australian Aboriginal students, 23, 193
autonomy, 154

Bantick, C., 13, 15
Barbie, 130–1
    Barbie PC, 125, 131
Barlow, J. P., 171–2
Baudrillard, J., 18
Beato, G., 136
Biddulph, S., 13, 15, 66
Bigum, C., 80, 85, 92, 142, 164, 175
biological determinism, 101, 102
    see also essentialist perspectives
Blair, T., 86
Blanchot, M., 18
Boler, M., 85
Bordo, S., 23
'boys as victim' discourse, 180
Braidotti, R., 7, 71
Brown, J., 130

Browne, R., 59
Buckingham, D., 23, 84, 165, 166
Buckingham, J., 170
bullying, 108
Butler, J., 72
Buttrose, I., 13, 179

childhood, 166, 167
    nostalgia for, 166, 167, 186
    'normal', 170
    loss of, 170–1
    new figurations, 171
coach-like talk, 152
Collins, C., 18, 21, 22, 23
Comber, B., 91
computer-based technologies
    attitudes towards, 128
    fragility of, 140
    games, 130, 136–7
    gendered, 125–37, 142, 149, 160,
        187
    girls' interests, 130–2
    as literacies, 140
    non-neutrality of, 127–37
    patterns of use, 126–7
    programming, 133–4, 145, 152, 157
    school uses, 141–2
    students-as-experts, 157
    and teenagers, 132–3
computer literacy, 135
    see also literacy education; literacies

Connell, B., 11, 33, 43, 48, 51, 52, 59, 60
counternarratives, 49, 72–3, 74, 75, 97, 190
Coupland, D., 133
Cox, E., 23
crime, *see* juvenile crime
crisis
  discourse, 17, 18, 27
  gender, 10, 100
  literacy, 79, 100
  rhetoric, 13, 16, 70
critical literacy, *see* literacy education
critical thinking, 81, 87
Cuban, L., 140
Cue, K., 30–1
cultural apprenticeship, 151
cultural resources, 66
culture of defeat, 13, 103
cyberspace, 172

Davies, B., 61, 68, 74
de Beauvoir, S., 44
de Certeau, M., 17
Deleuze, G., 73, 122
digital technologies, *see* computer-based technologies
Digitarts, 93–4
dimensions of literacy, *see* literacies
disability issues, 120
disadvantage discourse, 54
  hegemonic, 68
  reproduction of, 71
discourse analysis, 96–7
discourse theory, 54
'display masculinity', 153
Doneman, M. and L., 146
Douglas, P., 11, 15, 22, 24, 100

education achievement
  girls outperforming boys, 13, 19–22, 40–1
  see also literacy test outcomes
English, school subject, 114, 149–50, 157, 192
  boys only, 104, 115
  remedial, 142
  see also literacy education; literacies

entertainment technologies, 167, 189
  see also computer-based technologies
'equalists', 181
essentialist perspectives, 8, 29–35, 48, 69, 77, 100, 101, 102–9, 127, 185, 198
  see also anti-essentialist perspectives; strategic essentialism; biological determinism
ethnicity, *see* literacy education; literacies

failing at school, 13, 18, 21, 22, 23, 115, 151
failure, *see* failing at school; literacy failure
fairytales, non-traditional, 190
Faludi, S., 16
femininity, 55, 64–5, 75, 101
  dominant versions of, 47, 52, 162, 175
  new figurations, 185
feminist poststructuralism, 46–55, 67, 95, 99
feminization of school, 103
feminization of subject English, 26, 62, 41, 84, 162
feminization of the world, 31
figurations, 71, 185
Fitzclarence, L., 105–6
football culture, 105–6
Funk, J., 187

Gardner, H., 83
Gee, J. P., 91
gender, 180
  backlash, 2, 3, 103
  competition, 14
  complementarian approaches to, 30–6, 103
  crisis, *see* crisis
  as cultural group, 101
  discourses of, 52, 58, 65–6, 69, 110
  discrimination, 182
  equity, 12, 16, 50–1, 94, 179
  fictions, 96
  identity, 47, 49, 52, 60–3

reform, 26, 27–9, 54, 55, 57, 94, 99, 103–4, 112–13, 114, 122, 162, 178, 181, 210
relations, 47, 103, 113, 120, 178, 196
as a social construction, 12, 44, 50, 123
university subject, 1–2, 180
see also education achievement; femininity; girls; masculinity; masculine knowledge; transformative mindsets
gender-inclusive language, 113
gendered knowledge, 34, 41
gendered nature of work, 25, 103
gendered patterns of behaviour, 38, 41, 53, 100, 101, 203
generational differences, 164, 172–3, 188, 196
generational framework, 163, 173, 176–8
Gilbert, P., 23, 34, 38, 62, 91, 111, 122
Gilbert, R., 34, 58, 111
'girl power', 181
girls, 12, 27–56, 120
as complementary to boys, 38–9
school experiences, 10, 24–6, 115
see also education achievement
Green, B., 85, 164, 173
Grosz, E., 33, 100, 101
Guattari, F., 122

harrassment, 25, 108
Haraway, D., 71
Hayes, D., 61
health issues, 168–9
Heath, S. B., 156
Hekman, S., 101
Hickey, C., 105–6
Holland, J., 59
homophobia, 120
Hopkins, P., 68–9
Horton, M., 203
Hot Wheels PC, 125, 131

identity, see gender, identity
Innis, H., 166
intellectual nomads, 7

Internet use and gender, 131
see also computer-based technologies; literacy education; literacies

Jackson, D., 52
juvenile crime, 170
Little Criminals, 169–70
see also violence

Kenway, J., 12, 20, 23
Knobel, M., 80, 82, 92, 136, 142
knowledge
boys', 43
kid, 188, 195
masculine, 41, 44
school, 191
Koch, M., 142

Lankshear, C., 72–3, 80–1, 92, 140, 174
Lather, P., 147
Laurel, B., 131–2, 160
Learning Grid, see National Grid for Learning
Lindsey, L., 25
Lingard, B., 11, 15, 22, 24, 25, 100
literacies
'computer literacy', 85
'kid literacy', 184, 187
out-of-school, 123, 140–1, 136–7, 164, 177–8
three dimensions of, 89–90, 99
see also computer-based technologies; literacy education; mindsets; transformative literacy practice
literacy education, 62, 105, 159, 170, 174
critical literacy, 88–91, 95–7, 106, 171
elite, 82–3
emotional, 83–5
and ethnicity, 23–4, 43, 47, 107
excellence in, 86
genderization of, 66
'new basics', 80–92, 123
'old basics', 78–80, 123

remedial, 79, 151
technological, 85–8, 115, 125–61
see also literacy failure; literacy test
  outcomes; literacies; computer-
  based technologies; mindsets
literacy failure, 19–20, 79, 102–3, 107
literacy test outcomes, 19–20, 106
  see also test outcomes
literacy reform, gender-based, 67
literate performances, 9
'lost generation', 169
Lourde, A., 115
Lovelace, Lady Ada Byron, 134
Luchetta, T., 125, 128
Luke, C., 127, 175

Mac an Ghaill, M., 59–60
Macedo, D., 156
McLean, C., 108
McLuhan, M., 166
McNaughton, G., 38, 49, 67
Mahiri, J., 80, 92, 152, 156
Mahoney, P., 49, 50
Males, M., 188
Martino, W., 41, 62, 84, 91
masculinities, 12, 16, 32, 33, 50, 64–5,
  75, 101, 104, 161, 199
  boys' sense of, 48, 107
  classifications of, 60
  dominant versions of, 32, 47, 57,
    103, 107, 108, 110, 153, 162–3,
    175
  hegemonic, 43, 46, 58, 61, 101, 108,
    162
  literate performances of, 70
  new figurations of, 185
  normative, 43, 62
  and pop psychology of, 52
  subordinate, 101
  see also essentialist perspective;
    display masculinity; protest
    masculinity; transformative
    framework
Mattel, 125, 131
mens' movement, 32–3
Meyers, C., 185
Millard, E., 11, 40–1
Mills, M., 25, 32

mindsets, 8, 28, 27–56, 108, 195
  anti-literacy, 102, 114
  discourse of, 43
  equal opportunity, 36
  generational, 163
  literacy, 77–98
  sociocultural, 88
  transformative, 46–55, 77, 94
Minh-ha, T., 72
Misson, R., 174, 178, 192
Moody, F., 133
Moore, T., 115
multiple subjectivities, *see* subjectivity

National Coalition of Girls' Schools, 135
National Grid for Learning, 86
national literacy goals, 78–9
natural selection processes, *see*
  biological determinism
new literacy studies, 91–4, 97–8, 147,
  177
new literacies, 92–4, 97–8, 99, 146, 177
  see also literacies
new losers, 11, 13
new morbidities, 168
new times, 81, 92
New Zealand Education Review
  Office, 23–4
nomads, intellectual, *see* intellectual
  nomads

obesity, *see* health issues
O'Brien, J., 91
O'Connor, D., 25
out-of-school literacies, *see* literacies

Pease, A. and B., 33
Perfect Dark, 130
performance at school, *see* failing at
  school; literacy education; literacy
  test outcomes
Peters, M., 72–3
phallocentrism, 33, 121
politics of rhetoric, 18–19
popular culture, 91, 96, 162–97
post-feminism, 181
Postman, N., 165, 166, 170
post-school experiences, 22, 24–5, 27

poststructuralism, *see* feminist
   poststructuralism
'protest masculinity', 31–2
Potter, H., 104, 109
pro-feminist positions, 15
Provenzo, G., 167
Purple Moon, 131
Pythagorus, 63

Queer, *see* masculinities

rhizomatic structures, 73–4, 99,
   101–2, 108, 121, 127, 161, 162,
   163, 177, 184, 194, 196
rhizomes, *see* rhizomatic structures
Rogoff, B., 150
Rowan, L., 25, 92, 122, 140, 142, 172
Rushkoff, D., 165, 172–3
Ryan, L., 84

self-esteem, 114
sexed identity, 100
sex role therapy, 45
school failure, *see* failing at school
school retention rates, 24
school 'self', 58
school subjects, 65, 112, 133
   boys only, 104, 113
Schrage, M., 138, 208
Shores, M., 91
Simpsons, The, 169
Singh, M., 91
Slattery, I., 15
socio-cultural analysis, 97
socialization frameworks, 44–5, 61,
   64, 67
Spivak, G., 100, 101
Starr, P., 202
status
   social, 59
   socioeconomic, 23, 24, 43, 47, 107,
      110
Stone, A., 83, 128–9, 201
strategic essentialism, 100
subject English, *see* English, school
   subject
subjectivity, 67–70, 71, 74, 113, 121,
   162, 181, 196

multiple subjectivities, 115, 120,
   176, 193
Suchman, L., 197
suicide rates, 22
Summers, C. H., 13, 14, 32

Taylor, H., 84
television, 166–7, 181–3
test outcomes, 19–20, 22
   see also literacy test outcomes
Thompson, T., 168
Torres Strait Islander students, 23
transformative framework, 5–7, 57–76,
   122, 123, 191, 202
transformative literacy practices, 8,
   158, 180, 208
transformative mindset, 7, 158
transformative pedagogy, 207
transformative schooling practices, 5,
   158, 180, 208
transformative strategies, 203–4
troublemakers, 111, 114, 122, 142,
   149, 151, 153, 157
Truth, S., 42
Turkle, S., 133, 201–2, 206

Ullman, E., 83, 134

violence, 119, 128, 170
   see also juvenile crime

Walkerdine, V., 47, 80
Wallace, C., 98
war against boys discourse, 10–26,
   179
Warrior Princess, *see* Xena
Wearing, 67, 68
Weedon, C., 55
Wertheim, M., 95, 133
'wild child', 169
Winters, K., 85

Xena, 181–2

Young, J. P., 43
Yunupingu, 23

Zena, *see* Xena

CONSUMING CHILDREN
EDUCATION-ENTERTAINMENT-ADVERTISING

Jane Kenway and Elizabeth Bullen

Consuming Children is an important, exciting, funny and tragic book, addressing key issues for education in the twenty-first century. It dramatically charts the corporatizing of education and the corporatizing of the child. It is a book that demands to be read by teachers and policy-makers – before it is too late.

Stephen J. Ball, Karl Mannheim Professor of Sociology of Education, Institute of Education, University of London

Accessible, insightful and boldly argued, *Consuming Children* makes a refreshing contribution to current discussions of young people, schooling and the culture industry. Jane Kenway and Elizabeth Bullen draw on a strong base of research and scholarship to advance powerful critiques and interesting and workable pedagogical responses to corporate culturalism.

Colin Lankshear, National Autonomous University of Mexico

Consuming Children offers a challenging perspective on one of the most pressing educational issues of our time – the changing relationships between childhood, schooling and consumer culture. Combining incisive commentary on established debates with new insights from empirical research, it should be read by all those concerned with the future of learning.

Professor David Buckingham,
Institute of Education, University of London

- Who are today's young people and how are they constructed in media-consumer culture and in relation to adult cultures in particular?
- How are the issues of pleasure, power and agency to be understood in the corporatized global community?
- How are teachers to educate young people? What new practices are required?

Consuming Children argues that we are entering another stage in the construction of the young as the demarcations between education, entertainment and advertising collapse and as the lines between the generations both blur and harden. Drawing from the voices of students and from contemporary cultural theory this book provokes us to ponder the role of the school in the 'age of desire'.

Contents
Introduction – Devouring theory – Inventing the young consumer – Polarizing pleasures: the allure of the grotesque – Promiscuous corporations: desiring schoolchildren – Designer schools, packaged students – Popular and profane pedagogies – Pedagogies that bite/byte back – Bibliography – Index.

224pp   0 335 20299 3 (Paperback)   0 335 20300 0 (Hardback)

CHANGING LITERACIES

Colin Lankshear (ed.)

'undeterred by sociological pessimism, Colin Lankshear hacks away at the underbush, clearing a path for a new critical-liberatory discourse'.
James Paul Gee, Clark University, Worcester, Massachusetts

This book explores everyday social practices and how they influence who people are, what they become, the quality of their lives, the opportunities and possibilities open to them, and those they are denied. It focuses especially on language and literacy components of social practices, asking:

- How are language and literacy framed within different social practices?
- How are social practices in turn shaped and framed by language and literacy?
- What are the consequences for the lives and identities of individuals and groups?
- How can we understand these relationships, and build on this understanding to develop critical forms of literacy and language awareness that enhance human dignity, freedom and social justice?

In addressing these questions the book draws on social practices from diverse settings: from classrooms using conventional texts to so-called 'enchanted workplaces'; from a Third World peasant cooperative enterprise to modern technologically-equipped homes and classrooms. The result is a rich socio-cultural account of language and literacy, which challenges narrow psychological and skills-based approaches, and provides an excellent theory base for informing the practice of literacy educators.

It will be compelling reading for academics, teachers and students of language and literacy education, critical literacy, discourse studies and cultural studies.

Contents
Introduction – Part 1: Critical and cultural perspectives on literacy – Language and cultural process – Critical social literacy for the classroom – Literacy and empowerment – Part 2: Literacy and social justice – Language, literacy and the new work order – Appendix: a sample of fast capitalist books – Literacy, work and futures – Part 3: Literacy, new technologies and old patterns – Literacies, texts and difference in the electronic age – Appendix: glossary of technical terms – Different worlds? Technology-mediated classroom learning and students' social practices with new technologies in home and community settings – Conclusion – Afterword – References – Index.

The Contributors
James Paul Gee, Michele Knobel, Chris Searle.

240pp   0 335 19636 5 (Paperback)   0 335 19637 3 (Hardback)

MEN ENGAGING FEMINISMS
PRO-FEMINISM, BACKLASHES AND SCHOOLING

Bob Lingard and Peter Douglas

For readers concerned with the current debates about boys' education and gender justice, this is the best guide available. Bob Lingard and Peter Douglas have written a book that is judicious, very well informed, carefully argued and creative. It combines a commitment to equity with a practical concern for good schooling.

R. W. Connell, University of Sydney, Australia

Lingard and Douglas have produced a brilliant contribution to the tradition of men's pro-feminist theory and politics. This is that rare treat: a theoretically sophisticated and politically balanced intervention into an important and contentious public issue. Especially useful for teachers and educational theorists is their account of how men's negotiations with various conflicting feminist theoretical agendas play out for issues about educational policies and practices.

Sandra Harding, University of California, Los Angeles

Men Engaging Feminisms is a most engaging book, challenging both men and women to consider afresh their political commitments and practices. It argues against those who would resist such considerations about changing gender politics and it openly commits to a pro-feminist stance which is robustly argued. It is a must for all interested in issues of social justice and is particularly important for those concerned with issues of gender equity in schools.

Miriam David, Institute of Education, London University

Men Engaging Feminisms is about men's responses to feminist reforms in schooling. These have become closely intertwined with the 'what about the boys?' backlash. This and other forms of backlash are deconstructed. Written by two men from a pro-feminist perspective, *Men Engaging Feminisms* seeks to open up a dialogue about schooling and changing gender relations and changing gender order while also desiring to contribute to a more equal gender order in the future.

Contents

Men engaging in feminisms in education – Contemporary masculinity politics – The structural backlash and emergent emotional economy in education – Deconstructing the 'What about the boys?' backlash – Programmes for boys in schools – Towards a pro-feminist politics of alliance – Bibliography – Index.

208pp   0 335 19817 1 (Paperback)   0 335 19818 X (Hardback)

·openup

ideas and understanding
in social science

www.**openup**.co.uk

Browse, search and order online

Download detailed title information and sample chapters*

*for selected titles

www.**openup**.co.uk